Varieties of Happiness

Varieties of Happiness

Eudaimonism and Greek Ethical Theory

IAKOVOS VASILIOU

OXFORD
UNIVERSITY PRESS

Oxford University Press is a department of the University of Oxford.
It furthers the University's objective of excellence in research, scholarship,
and education by publishing worldwide. Oxford is a registered trade mark of
Oxford University Press in the UK and in certain other countries.

Published in the United States of America by Oxford University Press
198 Madison Avenue, New York, NY 10016, United States of America.

© Oxford University Press 2025

All rights reserved. No part of this publication may be reproduced, stored in a retrieval system,
transmitted, used for text and data mining, or used for training artificial intelligence, in any form or
by any means, without the prior permission in writing of Oxford University Press, or as expressly
permitted by law, by license or under terms agreed with the appropriate reprographics rights
organization. Inquiries concerning reproduction outside the scope of the above should be sent to the
Rights Department, Oxford University Press, at the address above.

You must not circulate this work in any other form and
you must impose this same condition on any acquirer

CIP data is on file at the Library of Congress

ISBN 9780197645062

DOI: 10.1093/9780197645093.001.0001

Printed by Marquis Book Printing, Canada

for Nancy

Contents

Acknowledgments   ix

Introduction: Eudaimonism and Greek Ethical Theory   1
  1. Eudaimonism and Ethical Theory   1
  2. The Roles of Eudaimonia in Eudaimonism   7
  3. Eudaimonia as a Practical Principle   9
  4. Historical Note: The Importance of Cicero   13
  5. Chapter Synopses   14
  6. A Note on and for the Intended Audience   16

1. Rethinking Eudaimonism   18
  1. Eudaimonia and Virtue in Greek Philosophy   18
  2. The Eudaimonist Project: Julia Annas   21
  3. Virtue and the Highest Good   27
  4. Sarah Broadie on the *Summum Bonum*   30
  5. The Third Role of Eudaimonia: As Motivation   34
  6. Irwin's Eudaimonism   37
  7. Plato and Kant: Two Eudaimonists?   41
  8. Conclusion   45

2. Socrates and Eudaimonism   46
  1. Introduction: Ethics and Deliberation in the *Apology* and *Crito*   46
  2. The Eudaimonist Approach and Its Discontents   48
  3. Virtue, Wisdom, and the Eudaimonist Hope   50
  4. *Euthydemus*   55
  5. *Meno*   60
  6. The *Protagoras*'s Hedonist Argument: The Exception that Proves the Rule   63
  7. *Lysis*   72
  8. *Gorgias*   73

3. Plato and Eudaimonism   81
  1. Introduction   81
  2. The Just Person Is Happier than the Unjust   82
  3. Eudaimonia in the *Republic*   85
  4. Eudaimonia in the *Symposium*   91

4. Aristotle and His Interpreters on Eudaimonia   98
  1. Scholars on Aristotle on Eudaimonia   99

2. Aristotle on Eudaimonia as a Practical Principle	102
3. McDowell on Aristotle on Eudaimonia	105
4. McDowell's Account and the Problem of External Goods	112

5. Aristotle on Happiness, Being Happy, and External Goods — 118

1. The *Eudaimōn/Eudaimonia* Distinction (EED)	120
2. EED in I.7–13 and VII.13: Happiness and External Goods	122
3. EED in IX.9: Friendship	129
4. Eudaimonia and the Completeness of Activities: The Case of Pleasure	131
5. EED in X.7–8: Two Kinds of Eudaimonia	132
6. Eudaimonia as Contemplation	134
7. Conclusion	140

6. Epicurus, Pleasure, and Happiness — 142

1. Epicurus	143
2. Eudaimonia as a Practical Principle in Epicurus	146
3. The Evidence of the *Principle Doctrines*	149
4. The *Letter to Menoeceus*	154
5. Pleasure and Living Blessedly	162
6. Epicurus on Virtue and Happiness	164

7. Virtue and Happiness in Early Stoicism — 168

1. Introduction	168
2. Stoics on Indifferents: An Overview	170
3. The Iconoclast Aristo	175
4. Stoics on Moral Luck	182
5. Appropriate Actions: A Hypothesis	183
6. Appropriate Actions versus Mistakes	189
7. Intermediate Appropriate Actions	192
8. Objections to Intermediate Appropriate Actions	197
9. The Perfection of the Sage	201
10. The Stoics on Suicide	205

Epilogue: Reassessing Eudaimonism — 209

1. Overview	209
2. Coda: Cicero and the Eudaimonist Framework	214

Bibliography	219
Index Locorum	229
General Index	233

Acknowledgments

I am very grateful to many people over many years for their comments, criticisms, and contributions to this project. I single out Cinzia Arruzza, Rachel Barney, George Boys-Stones, Tad Brennan, Charles Brittain, Sarah Broadie, Eric Brown, Amber Carpenter, David Charles, Miranda Fricker, Erik Gunderson, Rachana Kamtekar, Mitzi Lee, Hendrik Lorenz, Susan Sauvé Meyer, Jessica Moss, Pietro Pucci, Paul Schollmeier, Adriana Renero, Thomas Slabon, Rosemary Twomey, Katja Vogt, Matt Walker, and Victoria Wohl. I am particularly grateful to Denise Vigani for extensive and extremely valuable discussion as well as helpful written comments, especially about theoretical issues early in the project.

I offer special thanks to Brad Inwood, who read and commented thoroughly on the entire first draft, with the conscientiousness and attention to detail familiar to all who know him. In addition, I have greatly benefitted from his encouragement and support not only for this book but over my entire career. I owe a unique debt to Matt Evans, who has listened to me talk about aspects of this project for well over a decade—in seminars, formal talks, and over drinks—while offering insightful and deep criticisms all the while. In the eleventh hour, he kindly offered some final comments, which greatly helped the present version, but which I will still be trying to address for a long time to come. Jennifer Whiting, my PhD thesis advisor, has been supportive of (and appropriately skeptical about!) various aspects of the book as we have discussed it over the past bunch of years. Finally, Phillip Mitsis, whom I have known since he was my undergraduate advisor in Classics, offered crucial assistance with the chapters on Epicurus and the Stoics as well as with issues concerning how best to frame the project. His interventions have been invaluable.

I am grateful as well to audiences at The Graduate Center, CUNY, the New York University Workshop on Ancient Philosophy, the New York University Ancient Philosophy WIP group, the APA Central Division Meetings 2012 and 2016, the University of Thessaloniki 2400 Year Aristotle Anniversary Conference, La Sapienza University of Rome, the University of Queensland (Brisbane), Yale-NUS College (Singapore), the University of Texas, Austin, the University of Nevada, Las Vegas, Yale University, Queen's University, Kingston, and the University of Toronto.

I also thank Peter Ohlin for his support of the project, the two anonymous reviewers from the press, and Katherine Caldwell and Andre Dobronic Parola for their work on the indices. Thank you to the Estate of Jake Berthot for permission to use his painting, *For the Rose*, on the cover.

On a more personal note, while working on this book my father-in-law, Nathaniel Worman, and mother-in-law, Eugenia Worman, died. They were unfailingly interested in hearing about my work in general and intrigued by this topic in particular. I owe my deepest gratitude to my parents, Bill and Irene Vasiliou. Unfortunately, my father, who was my first and longest-standing philosophical interlocutor, died in March 2021. I had discussed many aspects of this project with him; I regret most of all that he will not see the finished product.

Finally, I dedicate this book to my wife, Nancy Worman, for her support and love through all my endeavors, personal and professional. She has been a brilliant example for me of how to combine the activities of *theōria* and *eudaimonia* into a beautifully lived life.

Introduction
Eudaimonism and Greek Ethical Theory

1. Eudaimonism and Ethical Theory

This book challenges the almost universal belief that Greek ethics is a distinctive type of ethical theory labeled "eudaimonist." While philosophers still debate the relevance and value of history of philosophy for philosophy's contemporary practice,[1] over the last fifty years the history of philosophy has claimed no more significant contribution to contemporary Anglo-American philosophy than its contribution to the emergence and development of virtue ethics, including philosophical reflection about human happiness and well-being. Ancient Greek philosophy, while not the only historical period of relevance, is clearly the most important, with Aristotle as its star.[2] Ancient ethics is supposed to be radically different in both approach and doctrine from the moral or ethical philosophy of the modern era. Whereas the latter focuses on how to determine which actions are morally obligatory, permissible, or forbidden, the former eschews focus on action in exchange for a focus on character or virtue. Modern moral philosophy asks, "what is our duty?" and "what is right and wrong and how do we know?"; the ancients ask, "what sort of life ought I to lead?" and "what sort of person ought I to be?" The alleged split in practical rationality between reasoning about one's own good, and the actions conducive to it, and reasoning about morality and one's duty, as discussed by Henry Sidgwick, is thought to be at the heart of the difference. The ancients, on this view, focused only on "self-love" or the happiness of the individual, and lacked even a conception of morality.[3]

---

[1] See, as a sample, Rorty, Schneewind, and Skinner (1984), Sorell and Rogers (2005), and Laërke, Smith, and Schliesser (2013).

[2] While there is no doubt that study of ancient ethical philosophy has led to a prodigious amount of new work in contemporary ethics, there is plenty of dispute about the value of "virtue ethics," with objections and rebuttals on both empirical and philosophical grounds. Even some who think that the modern era has mistakenly left consideration of virtue and happiness behind for an overly narrow focus on the nature of morality nevertheless argue that a broadly Greek or Aristotelian approach to virtue is mistaken; see, e.g., Swanton (2003).

[3] Adkins (1960) is the most-cited example of a work that denies that the Greeks had, or perhaps even could have had, any conception of morality and associated concepts, such as duty and obligation. See too a memorable quote from De Quincey's "The Last Days of Immanuel Kant"

Varieties of Happiness. Iakovos Vasiliou, Oxford University Press. © Oxford University Press 2025.
DOI: 10.1093/9780197645093.003.0001

As a historian of philosophy, I am reluctant to push back against what is arguably history's greatest recent contribution to contemporary philosophy. I am also hesitant to precipitously assume that a similar set of problems besets "The Greeks" and moral philosophers 2,000–2,500 years later, with all the distance in philosophical and historical context that entails. Nevertheless, I am skeptical that there is any substantive, common "eudaimonist framework," as traditionally understood, to which all (or almost all) ancient theories adhere such that it importantly distinguishes their approach to ethics and morality.

By contrast, almost all scholars of ancient philosophy as well as those interested in using the ancients to develop contemporary ethical positions share the assumption that all Greek ethical philosophers, beginning with Socrates,[4] theorize within the "eudaimonist framework."[5] "Eudaimonism" is a term derived from its central concept eudaimonia, traditionally translated "happiness" or "human flourishing."[6] It is even typically taken as an a priori assumption that Greek ethics *must be* eudaimonist.[7] Discussions of eudaimonism in ancient philosophy are thus already deeply influenced (or, perhaps, skewed) by *philosophical* views both about the nature of eudaimonism and about Greek ethics itself that are not as solidly grounded in the historical texts as one might think.

Consider a well-known example of this in Gregory Vlastos's discussion of eudaimonism and Socrates from his book, *Socrates: Ironist and Moral Philosopher*:[8] "I shall now introduce the principle I shall call 'the Eudaemonist Axiom,' which, once staked out by Socrates, becomes foundational for virtually all subsequent moralists of classical antiquity. This is that happiness is desired by all human beings as the ultimate end (*telos*) of all their rational acts."

(1827/1871), which according to the *OED* contains the first English use of "eudaemonism": "[Kantian] Ethics, braced up into stoical vigour by renouncing all effeminate dallyings with Eudaemonism, would [were it better known] indirectly have cooperated with the sublime ideals of Christianity."

[4] Throughout, unless explicitly stated otherwise, by "Socrates" I refer to the character in Plato's dialogues, not the historical figure.
[5] The Cyrenaics are the oft-cited exception: see Irwin (1991) and Annas (1993), but even they have their defenders: see especially Tsouna-McKirahan (2002) and Tsouna (2020b), O'Keefe (2022). Tad Brennan (unpublished) brought to my attention the little-known "Elpistikoi" as another possible exception. Since this book argues that even Socrates, Plato, Aristotle, Epicurus, and the Stoics fail to adopt certain features typically taken to be central to eudaimonism, the eudaimonist status of the Cyrenaics or the "Elpistikoi" one way or the other becomes relatively unimportant.
[6] Oxford English Dictionary, s.v. "eudemonism": "That system of ethics which finds the foundation of moral obligation in the tendency of actions to produce happiness."
[7] Nicholas White (2002), (2006) is a rare voice of dissent.
[8] Vlastos (1991), ch. 8, "Happiness and Virtue in Socrates' Moral Theory," 203.

INTRODUCTION 3

Later in the same chapter, Vlastos argues that, while Socrates believes that virtue is both necessary and sufficient for happiness, he does not believe that they are identical. Vlastos's argument depends, crucially, on the demands of eudaimonism:

> It follows that if Identity were the true relation of virtue to happiness, *we would have no rational ground for preference between alternatives which were equally consistent with virtue* [his italics]—hence no rational ground for preference between states of affairs differentiated only by their non-moral values. **And if this were true, it would knock out the bottom from eudaemonism as a theory of rational choice.** [my emphasis.] For many of the choices we have to make in our day-to-day life have to be made between just such states of affairs, where moral considerations are not in the picture at all. Shall I walk to my destination or ride the bus? Shall I have my hair cut today or next week? [...] the grounds on which we have to make them [such choices] are clearly non-moral: hedonic, economic, hygienic, aesthetic, sentimental, or whatever. **If the Identity Thesis were true it would bankrupt the power of eudaemonism to give a rational explanation of all our deliberate actions by citing happiness as our final reason for them.** [my emphasis.] On that theory, if happiness were identical with virtue, our final reason for choosing anything at all would have to be only concern for our virtue; so the multitude of choices that have nothing to do with that concern would be left unexplained.[9]

The a priori basis of this argument is plain: eudaimonism is a theory whose aim is to explain the rationality of all of an agent's (deliberate and non-acratic) actions; Socrates is a eudaimonist; so Socrates must reject the Identity Thesis, since otherwise he would fail to explain the rationality of all of an agent's deliberate actions. It is clear as well that eudaimonia functions for Vlastos as the ultimate end of all deliberate, non-acratic actions.[10] The crucial assumption, however, is that Socrates *is* a eudaimonist in Vlastos's sense. But what is the textual evidence for this? Vlastos's attention to the texts focuses on whether there is justification for Socrates's believing that happiness and virtue are identical; he does not look for textual evidence, however, that supports his attribution of eudaimonism in his sense to Socrates

---

[9] Vlastos (1991), 225.
[10] What I shall describe below as a "Comprehensive Practical Principle."

in the first place.[11] In the quotation above, Vlastos's "Eudaemonist Axiom" is presented some twenty pages earlier in the essay, as a foundational statement "staked out by Socrates [. . .] for virtually all subsequent moralists of classical antiquity."[12] As we shall see, Socrates certainly on occasion makes remarks about what makes for a happy life or happy person, but I shall argue that these are not sufficient to attribute to him Vlastos's eudaimonism, which seemed so obvious that it could be stated not as the conclusion of the essay, but as one of its first principles.[13]

This book thus focuses on theoretical questions about the structure of ancient ethical theory. Overall, it seeks primarily to explain how the concept of eudaimonia functions in, for example, Plato's ethical theory rather than to settle debates about what Plato's understanding of eudaimonia itself *is*—for example, whether he thinks virtue is sufficient for happiness. I shall examine the *role* of concepts like virtue, happiness, and the happy life in ancient ethics to see how and whether they play a radically different role than they do in modern views. It will come as no surprise to the reader that this issue depends on what precisely is meant by eudaimonism. It should also come as little surprise that I will not try to establish definitively what eudaimonism is, for example by supplying necessary and sufficient conditions for a theory to be eudaimonist. Of course, we can and should decide for ourselves what we want a eudaimonist theory to be, just as we may decide what we want other concepts to be. So, the book will not simplistically conclude that the Greeks are or are not eudaimonists. Rather, it seeks to be more conceptually precise about the different roles that eudaimonia is being asked to play in different accounts of Greek

---

[11] Brickhouse and Smith (2000), 128, attempt to explain this absence: "Not only does the principle [of eudaimonism] seem to Socrates obviously true, but it seems obviously true to others when he brings it up. As a result, nowhere do we find him arguing for the *Principle of Eudaimonism*." In my view, the only thing that Socrates takes to be "obviously true" is the idea that everyone wants to do well, to be happy; but this is a far cry from the much more contentious idea that Socrates brings up the *Principle of Eudaimonism* and that *this* is taken to be obviously true. See Chapter 2.

[12] Irwin (1995) and (2007) is more circumspect. He makes no such sweeping theoretical claim, but rather indicates that Socrates makes certain claims about happiness, and its relationship to virtue, that raise questions, many of which are only partly or inadequately addressed in the dialogues. Irwin avoids attributing anything as formal as a "eudaimonist axiom" or even formal statement of "eudaimonism" as a philosophical position to Socrates or Plato; this waits for Aristotle. See below, and Chapters 1 and 4.

[13] In fact, Socrates's remarks on happiness are far less frequent and less systematic than one might expect from a philosopher who allegedly adheres to the Principle of Eudaimonism; see Vasiliou (2008), White (1999), and Chapter 2 below.

eudaimonism. It will turn out that although I do not offer definitive criteria for a theory's being eudaimonist, I do argue that certain features are clearly *necessary* for a theory to be eudaimonist, while others are clearly *insufficient* to make a theory eudaimonist.

I shall outline these roles and features in some detail below, but what has been said so far needs further explication so that the position defended here will not seem to be a complete non-starter. No one can reasonably doubt that Greek philosophers and schools offer a variety of accounts of eudaimonia. Furthermore, the question "what sort of life should I lead?" is manifestly an ethical question and, as its ancient and modern proponents emphasize, one of central importance. Given this, we might straightforwardly conclude that to provide a theory of human happiness is clearly to provide an *ethical theory*, since the topic of human happiness is an ethical topic. Is it not obvious and completely uncontroversial, then, to call such theories "eudaimonist," since they are theories about eudaimonia? I answer this negatively because I doubt that a "eudaimonist ethical theory," in the limited sense just described, could be a substantive *rival* to some other type of ethical (or moral) theory, such as deontology, consequentialism, or intuitionism, as opposed to a mere *supplement* to it.

Recall that the standard way of describing Greek ethics is as engaging in a *distinctive type of ethical theorizing* captured by the phrase "the eudaimonist framework." One claim made by those who argue for the distinctiveness of Greek ethics is that "modern" ethics has neglected the topic of human happiness or well-being, focusing exclusively on right and wrong action (morality or ethics, in a narrower sense). We can accept that the resurgence of interest in happiness and well-being in the last couple of decades is due in large part to reflection on Greek ethical thinking and that it has resulted in broadening our notion of ethics to include questions about the structure and content of a good human life. If all that is meant by an ethical theory's being "eudaimonist," then, is that it *offers an account* of human happiness, there is no question that Greek ethical theories are eudaimonist. Indeed, even eminent scholars say something like, "Of course Socrates is a eudaimonist, for he asks whether everyone wishes to do well and live well (i.e., to be happy and live happily)!" I claim, by contrast, that the mere statement that everyone wants to be happy or even more substantive accounts of what happiness consists in are *by themselves insufficient* for eudaimonism. At a minimum, a stand must be taken on how eudaimonia is supposed to guide action; and even then we shall see that we may not have a position usefully labeled "eudaimonist." An initial, critically important point, then, is that *merely giving an account of eudaimonia*—that is, giving an account of what human happiness consists in—is *not sufficient* for an ethical theory to be eudaimonist.[14]

But, of course, there is typically more involved in calling a theory "eudaimonist" than simply the fact that it includes an account of human happiness. Rather, the Greek account of happiness is thought to play some significant, distinctive role or roles in addressing the more traditional questions of ethical (and moral) philosophy, concerning which token actions (or action-types) are right and wrong, how we tell, and why we should engage in moral/ethical action rather than the contrary.[15] This stronger sense of ethical or moral theory depends, rather, on how the account of human happiness relates to moral or ethical virtue or excellence, how it relates to moral or ethical action. For one could have one account of the good life and what it consists in and a second, entirely distinct, account of what ethical or moral action consists in (say, following the Categorical Imperative or obeying Rule Utilitarianism). It is only when a theory explains how right action is subsumed under or connected in some way to the concept of human happiness that we have a candidate for a genuinely "eudaimonist ethical theory," a theory that explicitly claims a distinctive relationship between the human good and the morally right or virtuous action. As most readers already know, this concerns the ancient topic of the relationship of happiness to virtue. So far, however, I hope only to have established that offering, and even philosophically defending, an account of the human good is insufficient for making a theory a eudaimonist one in the stronger sense that might make it a rival to other types of ethical theory. It is the stronger sense that has been claimed for Greek eudaimonism, and that is the focus of this study.

---

[14] One claim that has been made regarding the Cyrenaics (though disputed, see footnote 5 above) is that they do not offer *any* account of eudaimonia, advocating only the pursuit of pleasure in the moment. If this is correct, it would indeed rule them out as eudaimonists, for having an account of eudaimonia is certainly a necessary condition for being a eudaimonist. But this reasoning may have led some to suppose that so long as one *does* provide an account of eudaimonia that is *sufficient* for one to be a eudaimonist; and this is the claim I reject.

[15] Unless I say otherwise, I shall understand virtuous action, moral action, and ethical action as synonymous expressions. So, "moral actions" and "moral requirements" do not refer to morality in some more narrow, specific sense, such as is discussed and criticized by Williams (1985), ch. 10. See too more recently Doyle (2018).

2. The Roles of Eudaimonia in Eudaimonism

In the chapters that follow, I shall examine philosophical texts related to eudaimonia and eudaimonism with a view to distinguishing three roles that a conception of eudaimonia might be asked to play: (1) as a practical principle, (2) as supplying the content of the conception of virtue (what I label "the Eudaimonist Hope"), and (3) as motivating one's commitment to virtue. Briefly, the first involves how and what sort of role a conception of eudaimonia plays and ought to play with respect to guiding our decisions and actions.[16] The second concerns whether it is the conception of happiness that provides the content of our conception of virtue or right action; that is, having determined what the human good is, virtuous action is then what is either an instrumental means to or constitutive of it. The third role considers how eudaimonia might provide motivation to be committed to virtue; so, for some agents, appeal to eudaimonia would explain in what sense one is "better off" or "happier" acting virtuously.

If one adheres to the Eudaimonist Hope (the second role above), so that the content of eudaimonia establishes the content of virtue, one would most plausibly also hold that eudaimonia provides the ground, justification, and motivation for being virtuous and acting virtuously as well. But one could reject the Eudaimonist Hope and believe that virtue has an independent, objective nature of its own, but still think that the conception of happiness, cashed out, for example, in an account of naturalistic human flourishing, is what provides the metaethical or metaphysical ground for commitment to an independent conception of virtue.[17] I should note that I do not discuss ancient naturalism in this book and whether it plays a metaethical role in ultimately grounding virtue and virtuous action. Even those who are most sanguine about the extent to which the Greeks thought that virtue and virtuous action could be grounded in human nature rarely

---

[16] When I speak of a "conception of eudaimonia," I mean some substantive account of it, such as eudaimonia as pleasure, or virtue, or virtuous activity. I deny that a formal account of eudaimonia, say, as the "highest good" or "living well" or "doing well," is something that can function as a practical principle in the sense I intend.

[17] Terence Irwin's *Development of Ethics* (2007-9) defends Aristotle's naturalism quite generally, including against contemporary critics such as Bernard Williams and Alaisdair MacIntyre (see volume 3, §§1396-1399). He summarizes his account at §1399, (882): " ... we may recollect Aristotle's position schematically: (1) Human nature consists in rational agency, that is, in exercising the capacity to guide behavior by practical reason. (2) The human good consists in the full actualization of this capacity in fulfilling our other capacities. (3) The virtues are the different ways of actualizing this capacity." Irwin repeatedly refers to these Aristotelian claims as supplying a "basis for morality" or "foundation of morality". See Darwall (2011) for some critical discussion of Irwin's position.

8   VARIETIES OF HAPPINESS

argue that the justification of a token action's being, say, just, consists in something about our nature; more often, the thought is that the ultimate ground of why we ought to be virtuous consists in something about the sort of beings we are. If the reader believes that Aristotle, for example, grounds his substantive conception of virtue and what it is to act "for the sake of the *kalon*" simply in what it is to be a human being by nature (via some sort of argument beginning in the Function Argument), I do not offer explicit arguments against such a reading. I hope, however, that the interpretations I offer will not incline people to read Aristotle or the other ancients I discuss in such a way.[18]

I will state up front that I view ancient ethics as proceeding the other way round: it does not start with a prior and independent conception of eudaimonia (established in turn by a more prior and independent conception of human nature) and then seek to show that only living virtuously in a substantive sense will satisfy it. Rather, it starts—as is clearly, if extravagantly, brought out in Plato's "Theory of Forms"—with a prior conception of virtue with its own independent nature and then argues that part of what makes virtuous agents virtuous is that they appreciate that acting virtuously is essential to eudaimonia as properly understood.[19] The specific accounts I offer of figures and schools support such an interpretation.

As I just mentioned, I do discuss whether there is evidence that ancient figures maintain the Eudaimonist Hope—the claim that the conception of eudaimonia (however established) can supply specifically the content of virtue and virtuous action. I think this is true, partly, only in the case of Epicurus. So, even if there is a more elaborate grounding of eudaimonia in nature, it would fall short of justifying the specific decisions and actions that are essential to our living well according to Socrates, Plato, Aristotle and the Stoics. Throughout I am focused on the relationship between eudaimonia and virtue—being virtuous, but also and especially, acting virtuously in specific instances.

In the third role outlined above, I allow especially for the possibility that the conception of eudaimonia may not supply either the metaphysical ground or the epistemological justification for a particular conception

---

[18] I have argued against such a reading of Aristotle in Vasiliou (1996), though of course much more would need to be said at this point. For present purposes, I suspend judgment on what it means for the ancients to think that "there is a naturalistic foundation for ethics" and how (and whether) such a project differs from how we think of such projects in contemporary ethics.

[19] See Beaton and Whiting (2013), 1764, who describe this approach; they cite McDowell (1980/1998b) as defending this sort of reading of Aristotle.

of virtue, but it may still provide an agent, or at least an agent of a certain sort, with rational motivation for being committed to that conception of virtue.

While the texts themselves may not keep discussion of each of these issues distinct, the hypothesis of this book is that we ought to do so in order to avoid implicitly shifting among them, and so missing significant similarities and differences among Greek ethical philosophies both with one another and with modern theories. I will describe these roles in greater detail in the chapters that follow, but it will be worthwhile to explicate eudaimonia as a practical principle a bit further here in the Introduction, since it is arguably the most significant role that eudaimonia has been taken to play and the one that I believe has been most misunderstood.

3. Eudaimonia as a Practical Principle

By a "practical principle" I refer to a statement about what one's ultimate aim in acting is. Any view that merits the label eudaimonism must *at least* include an explicit stand on what the practical role of eudaimonia is. To say that something is one's ultimate aim or highest good, however, is susceptible to at least three different interpretations, appreciation of which will be critical for understanding eudaimonia's practical role. The most minimal role a conception of eudaimonia could plausibly play as a practical principle is what I will call a "Prudential Practical Principle"; this is simply the idea that a conception of eudaimonia, assuming one has it, provides a principle about what one's good consists in and thus recommends actions that constitute or lead to that good as, at least, prudent. If one is rational and a human being and it is true that X is the human good, then one has been given a strong reason to pursue X. I say "a strong reason" because, as we shall see in greater detail in the following chapter, it clearly remains possible that one has an even stronger reason in some circumstance to pursue something else—most relevantly, perhaps one has a moral obligation that impedes or conflicts with the pursuit of one's own happiness.

Almost universally, however, Greek conceptions of eudaimonia are interpreted as what I call "Comprehensive Practical Principles." Briefly, if eudaimonia is a Comprehensive Practical Principle, then it embraces all of our deliberate, non-acratic actions under it. Everything that one does is, ultimately, for the sake of eudaimonia; it is the *only* thing I do only for its own sake and not for the sake of anything further.[20] There are, I think, two primary explanations for thinking that this is the obvious way to understand the practical role of eudaimonia. First, there is an idiomatic line, repeated by Plato, Aristotle, Epicurus, and the Stoics, that happiness, the highest good, is, roughly "that for the sake of which we all do everything we do."[21] Scholars have interpreted the universals in the statement "we all" and "everything" rather literally and in some cases extremely strictly as universal quantifiers.[22] The only actions that are excluded are either mere behaviors (such as moving one's hands while talking), which do not rise to the level of a deliberate action, or else acratic actions, which, by definition, are deliberate actions that run counter to the agent's good. To plant a seed of doubt about an interpretation that may strike many readers as obvious, let me say that, first, the line itself may be read as "we all make every effort" and not, more literally, as we all do *everything*. Second, by itself such a phrase, even translated as "we all do everything," is in Greek as in English governed by some pragmatics. When one says to a particularly talented graduate student, "I will do everything in my power to get you an academic position," it of course does not mean *everything*, such as eliminating potential rivals from contention. In the case of the human good as well, I may be doing everything (making every effort) to achieve it and make it my own, as it were, but there may well be limits on what I will do. I am not arguing that this phrase *cannot* be understood as a Comprehensive Practical Principle, but only that it is not *mandatory* to interpret it in that way. Scholars, in line with Vlastos as quoted above, almost all believe that eudaimonia operates as a Comprehensive Practical Principle throughout all of Greek ethical philosophy. It will be one of the primary aims of this book to argue that in fact until the writing of Cicero there

---

[20] This is typically taken to be the import of Aristotle's remarks in *NE* I.7 (1097b), when he describes happiness as something that is most complete (*teleiotaton*). I read the passage differently. Aristotle contrasts eudaimonia as an end with "honor, pleasure, understanding, and every virtue." While we choose each of the latter for its own sake, we also choose it for the sake of eudaimonia, "thinking that through them we shall be happy." Happiness, by contrast, we do not choose for the sake of anything further. The list, "honor...," however, is not a random list of all things that are desirable in themselves, but a list of specific and plausible candidates for the highest good (cf. I.4–5, where each of these reputable beliefs, that eudaimonia is honor, and so on, is canvassed.) So, this does not preclude the possibility that a person might seek other things, for example harmless pleasures or recreation of some sort, merely for their own sakes without also thinking that by, say, playing ping pong, one was contributing to one's eudaimonia. This is another way of saying that this passage by itself is not sufficient grounds for thinking that Aristotle believes that eudaimonia must be a "comprehensive" practical principle. See Chapters 4 and 5.

[21] As we shall see in the chapters to follow, the exact formulation varies slightly, but the differences are unimportant.

[22] We have already seen this explicitly in the account of Gregory Vlastos above, but we shall see that Julia Annas, Terence Irwin, and many others understand eudaimonia as playing this practical role.

is no clear textual evidence that eudaimonia operates as a Comprehensive Practical Principle and much evidence that it does not; in particular, the major figures in Classical Greek and Hellenistic philosophy—Socrates, Plato, Aristotle, the early Stoics, and Epicurus—do not hold that eudaimonia operates as Comprehensive Practical Principle, thereby embracing all rational reasons for acting. The argument for this will not be complete until the end of the book.

A second reason for assuming that eudaimonia is a Comprehensive Practical Principle is because as the "highest good" it should be understood as always operative in a person's life. So, while we pursue many small, local ends in our everyday life, they are all, without exception, ultimately related to eudaimonia. This idea, that eudaimonia is operative always everywhere—there are no (or at least no substantive) occasions where it does not (or ought not to) ultimately apply and govern one's action—I call the idea of "ubiquity." I think that this captures something important about the concept of eudaimonia (and, as we shall see, about the concept of virtue), but that it too, like the idiom we considered above, does not require that one interpret eudaimonia as a Comprehensive Practical Principle.

There is a third kind of practical principle that also has a way of capturing ubiquity, which I call a "Superseding Practical Principle." A Superseding Practical Principle is a principle that states an end that ought to supersede or trump any other end one has in acting.[23] In Plato's dialogues, Socrates champions a practical principle that I label the "Supremacy of Virtue": doing the virtuous action ought to trump any other end one might have in acting.[24] For Socrates virtue is a Superseding Practical Principle, which means that doing the virtuous action or (much more frequently in life) not doing anything contrary to virtue supersedes any other end one might have in acting. In dictating that one should never do anything contrary to virtue, the Supremacy of Virtue is acting as a "limiting condition" on one's actions rather than as an explicit aim.[25] So, in choosing which shirt to wear (under ordinary

---

[23] I shall treat the verbs "trump," "supersede," and "supplant" as synonymous. The notion I want them to convey is the idea that a certain end of action wins out over and should replace any competing end.

[24] See Vasiliou (2008) and below Chapters 2 and 3 for argument about the importance of the Supremacy of Virtue, understood as a Superseding Practical Principle, for the interpretation of Socratic and Platonic ethics. In Vasiliou (2008) I used the label "Supreme Practical Principle" for the same idea that I here label "Superseding Practical Principle."

[25] "Limiting condition" is used in the same way by Barbara Herman (1993), 17, in explaining what it means for the motive of duty to be "ubiquitous"; Kant himself uses the term at, for example, *Groundwork* 4:431. Socrates advocates commitment to the Supremacy of Virtue in the same way: as

circumstances), one is not, for example, explicitly aiming at virtue, but one is still subject to the Superseding Practical Principle that is the Supremacy of Virtue as a limiting condition insofar as *if*, in some particular circumstance, wearing a particular shirt *were* contrary to virtue, then that shirt must not be worn. Thus, a Superseding Practical Principle is in a sense always operative in one's life and in all one's actions, at least in its role as a limiting condition.

We will explore the substantial differences among these types of practical principles in the chapters that follow, but we might just note here that they are not in any straightforward way classifiable as weaker or stronger than one another. A Prudential Practical Principle tells one what one's ultimate good is but leaves it open that it may well be rational or ethically best to act in a way contrary to that end. By contrast, a Superseding Practical Principle provides an end or aim of action that supersedes any other, but itself provides no practical guidance when that end or aim is not at issue, except as a limiting condition. So, if a given choice is neutral as far as virtue is concerned—chocolate or vanilla?—the Supremacy of Virtue says nothing about how one should or may decide. More importantly, it is not even *attempting* to say anything about the rationality of *all* of our actions. A Comprehensive Practical Principle, however, seeks, as we saw Vlastos say above,[26] to explain the rationality of all of our actions, claiming that all of our deliberate, non-acratic actions are aimed at one end. It does not, however, supply any account of how to organize or hierarchize lower-level ends: Does virtue supersede pleasure as an end of action? Does career trump health? Indeed, there is little conceptual room for one ultimate end to supersede another since belief in a Comprehensive Practical Principle holds that there is really only *one* (rational) end of all action; one end superseding another could, at best, take place among lower-level ends. If an end is comprehensive, then it is the *only* end we act (or ought to act) for the sake of; we do (or ought to do) everything for the sake of it, which *already rules out* the idea that any other end could supersede it.[27] So, a Comprehensive Practical Principle is not simply stronger,

---

a superseding end of action and as a limiting condition; see Vasiliou (2008), Introduction and ch.1, and Chapter Two below.

[26] Vlastos (1991), 225.

[27] The distinction here indicated in parentheses is marked sometimes by a distinction between psychological eudaimonism and rational or ethical eudaimonism; the former describes how humans do behave, the latter how they ought to behave. I will say a little more about this distinction in later chapters, but ultimately I am focused on rational eudaimonism. It is clear that many ancient philosophers believe we have what might be called a natural desire for the good; but they believe that love of genuine virtue takes proper upbringing.

in any straightforward sense, than a Superseding Practical Principle. Finally, to avoid confusion, let me also note that a philosopher may hold a *comprehensive account of eudaimonia*, that is, the philosopher's account of happiness may include all or most (types of) goods within it so that, in some sense, nothing could be added to it to make it a *happier* life, without that necessitating that eudaimonia *itself* operates as a Comprehensive Practical Principle.

4. Historical Note: The Importance of Cicero

While it is the philosophical argument about the theoretical structure of eudaimonism, as briefly outlined in this Introduction, that drives this study, there is also a hypothesis about the history of philosophy that develops over the course of the book. I suspect that Cicero, in his historical and critical survey of ethics, *De Finibus Bonorum et Malorum* (*On Moral Ends*[28]), may be directly or indirectly responsible for the widespread view since the modern period of Graeco-Roman ethical philosophy as eudaimonist.[29] In the coda of the Epilogue, I call attention to the fact that a full-fledged version of the eudaimonist framework flowers in Cicero's work, stemming in some way from the Academy of the late second century. The famous Academic Carneades, who wrote nothing himself, is understood to be behind what is known as the "Carneadean Division (*Carneadea Divisio*)." In Cicero at least it purports to be a way of classifying all the disparate ethical theories that had been developed from Cicero's time back to the Classical Greek era. Details aside, the method and its assumptions are strikingly similar to assumptions that characterize scholarship today: Greek ethical theory shares a eudaimonist framework, and so the way to compare and contrast theories is by plugging in the particular conception of happiness into the framework and then attacking or defending the resulting account.

The historical hypothesis, then, is that the eudaimonist framework that was, according to Vlastos, "staked out by Socrates," was in fact staked out sometime in the late second century by Carneades and the Academics and then adopted and perhaps transformed by Cicero. This book will argue that the use of this framework—not only as a way of classifying, but also, in the

---

[28] As it is translated by Raphael Woolf in the Cambridge edition (Annas [2001]).
[29] I cannot pursue the detailed historical work that would be required to defend such a thesis here.

modern period, as a way of grasping what is distinctive about ancient ethical theory from Socrates through the early Stoics—turns out to be significantly misleading and inaccurate in several respects.

5. Chapter Synopses

The progression of the chapters is mostly straightforward, following the chronological order of the figures and schools. Nevertheless, perhaps it will be worthwhile as a guide to the reader to highlight some particularly notable elements of the interpretation and to indicate where they appear.

Chapter 1 is anomalous in that it contains a general discussion of the way in which the concept of eudaimonia has been deployed by prominent contemporary philosophers and scholars, such as Julia Annas, Sarah Broadie, and Terence Irwin. In particular, I consider the various roles eudaimonia has been seen to play in eudaimonism and how well they fit with one another and with certain basic elements of Greek philosophy, such as we find in Plato and Aristotle. Overall, the chapter seeks to establish one claim: that the mere fact that one is *better off* or "happier" by being virtuous and acting virtuously (or morally) is insufficient for a theory to be considered eudaimonist. The chapter also provides an overview of larger theoretical issues that will arise in the detailed treatments of authors and texts to follow in Chapters 2 to 7.

In Chapter 2 I look in detail at evidence for eudaimonism in the "Socratic" dialogues. While Socrates seems to hold that commitment to the Supremacy of Virtue is at least necessary for happiness, there is no evidence that happiness is operating as a Comprehensive Practical Principle; rather Socrates consistently urges that one act according to the Supremacy of Virtue understood as a Superseding Practical Principle. Through detailed discussions of the *Euthydemus*, *Meno*, *Lysis*, *Protagoras*, and *Gorgias*, I argue that Socrates does not hold any form of the Eudaimonist Hope; the one exception, examined in detail, is the Hedonist Argument in the *Protagoras*. Finally, while it is universally agreed that Socrates believes that one is always better off (and so happier) acting virtuously than contrary to virtue, Chapter 1 has already shown that this alone does not suffice for his position to be eudaimonist.

Chapter 3 elaborates these themes in Plato's "middle" dialogues, examining the roles of eudaimonia in the *Republic* and *Symposium*. I argue that the conception of eudaimonia is already familiar from the remarks in the Socratic dialogues; like them, it also requires that a happy person be virtuous (or at least be committed to the Supremacy of Virtue). As far as its practical role is concerned, eudaimonia does not operate in Plato as either a Superseding Practical Principle or a Comprehensive Practical Principle, but rather as a Prudential Practical Principle.

Chapters 4 and 5 turn to Aristotle, the alleged paradigmatic eudaimonist. Chapter 4 examines bigger-picture questions concerning competing interpretations of the role of eudaimonia in Aristotle's ethics. I focus on what I argue are important but neglected elements of John McDowell's interpretation where, in our language, he offers an account that disputes that Aristotle conceives of eudaimonia as a Comprehensive Practical Principle; I support and defend this interpretation. I also, however, highlight certain serious tensions in McDowell's position when it comes to understanding Aristotle's views on external goods (in Chapter 4) and the role of contemplation (in Chapter 5). Chapter 5 analyzes the concept of happiness in the *Nicomachean Ethics* in detail and argues that Aristotle himself distinguishes between eudaimonia (as an activity) and being a happy person or having a happy life (being *eudaimōn*). Recognizing this distinction allows us to reconcile conflicts between "comprehensivist" or "inclusivist" and "exclusivist" or "monistic" interpretations of happiness. Moreover, I argue that, together with the rejection of the idea that eudaimonia operates as a Comprehensive Practical Principle, it enables a simple solution to the alleged conflict between eudaimonia as engaging in morally virtuous activity versus the conception of eudaimonia as contemplation that emerges in X.7–8.

Chapter 6 turns to Epicurus's account of living blessedly. I argue that Epicurus's distinction between "katastematic" pleasure (the state of being without physical or mental pain) and "kinetic" pleasure (the enjoyment of, say, drinking cool water when thirsty) is central to his account and that we cannot properly understand his account of pleasure without understanding its role in helping to eliminate the fear of death. Furthermore, I claim that katastematic pleasure operates as a Superseding Practical Principle. When it comes to virtue, however, Epicurus does agree with the Eudaimonist Hope, although given the nature of katastematic pleasure, the actions dictated will largely be in line with the conventional virtues; this marks another crucial distinction between Epicurean hedonism and the monistic calculating hedonism we saw operative in Plato's *Protagoras* in Chapter 2.

Chapter 7 turns to the Stoics and argues for two claims that cut against traditional scholarship. The first is that the Stoic category of "intermediate appropriate action" is an important category that covers actions that are not required by virtue but that pursue promoted value. The second is that the perfection of the Sage consists in the Sage's being a perfect Socratic and perfectly adhering to the Supremacy of Virtue understood as a Superseding Practical Principle. What this means is that a Sage never does wrong, but, contrary to almost all interpretations, it does not mean that every token action a Sage performs need be understood as virtuous.

I wish to emphasize that each chapter includes independent, mostly self-contained arguments about how to interpret ancient (and in Chapter 1, contemporary) figures on happiness and virtue. I hope that there are many particular arguments and interpretations of texts that will be persuasive and have value for readers, even in cases where they may be more skeptical about the overall claims about Greek ethics. In fact, I understand much of the value, such as it is, of the book to consist in those detailed readings, even though the overall claims about the mistaken attribution of the eudaimonist framework to central Greek ethical theories may be more provocative. So, for example, one may be persuaded by my arguments about how to understand the role of katastematic pleasure in Epicurus or how to reconcile the apparently competing conceptions of eudaimonia in Aristotle's *Nicomachean Ethics*, even if one maintains that either or both should still be labeled "eudaimonist" theories for other reasons. Indeed, as I have said, my aim is not to deny aspects of ancient theories that might merit the label eudaimonism, but to engage more critically with the eudaimonist framework itself and to examine in greater detail just how it fits or fails to fit what we find in the texts—especially when we do not assume a priori that it will be operating there. I am more concerned with arguing that eudaimonia in Aristotle is not functioning as a Comprehensive Practical Principle than with whether that claim (if one agrees with it) makes or does not make Aristotle a eudaimonist.

6. A Note on and for the Intended Audience

In a certain respect this book runs the risk of satisfying neither an ethical philosopher nor a historian of philosophy. Some scholars of ancient philosophy eschew (and even criticize) any philosophical distinctions not made in specifically ancient terms (such as "Superseding Practical Principle" above) as alien conceptual importations that at best are irrelevant to and at worst distort what should be the scholar's primary aim: interpreting the ancient texts as carefully, accurately, and holistically as possible. On the other hand, contemporary philosophers are often impatient with detailed textual exegesis: the point is the argument and its worth, not which text or author supports which interpretation. This book, however, engages in both extensive theoretical discussion about the understanding of eudaimonism and the roles of crucial concepts in that understanding (especially in Chapter 1), while the subsequent chapters also engage in detailed textual exegesis on the ancient figures. I wish to emphasize that the conceptual distinctions I label and employ are not inventions of mine out of whole cloth; rather, I argue that they are critical for properly understanding the philosophical issues at hand. I do not impose them "top down" (even if, for example in this Introduction, that is the order of exposition) but argue that they emerge from the ancient texts or else from the work of contemporary scholars interpreting those texts.

Another source of potential confusion concerns the aim and purpose of the sort of discussion that dominates Chapter 1 in particular. The ancient scholar may be frustrated that the close analysis of texts does not begin until Chapter 2.[30] But given that a critical appraisal of eudaimonism as an interpretation of Greek ethical theory is one of the aims of the book, what is often deemed "secondary literature" becomes of more central importance and a subject of examination in its own right. For, as I said above, although I argue against substantive interpretations of this or that text or concept in a particular ancient philosopher or school, I am also arguing against the way in which ancient ethical philosophy has been theorized in the English-speaking tradition.

I thus add a final note here that the vast majority of secondary literature and scholars whom I discuss are in the Anglophone tradition. There are increasingly insurmountable difficulties given the sheer amount of scholarship—especially for a book like this that covers so many major figures and schools—to be sure that one treats all of the "relevant" literature; and no doubt I have fallen short. It should be noted, however, that the issue of eudaimonism (unlike, of course, discussion of particular philosophers and schools) has been a focus primarily of those writing in English about ancient ethical theory over the last half-century, which at least partly explains and, I hope, justifies what may appear to some readers to be a partial and more arbitrary selection.

---

[30] As an anonymous reader from OUP objected.

1
Rethinking Eudaimonism

1. Eudaimonia and Virtue in Greek Philosophy

Greek philosophy, and indeed Greek culture more generally as reflected in poetry (epic, lyric, and tragic), oratory, and history, is clearly interested in what the good or best life for a human being is. Is Achilles's short but extraordinarily glorious life to be preferred over Odysseus's long life of continuous wandering? Achilles's underworld lament in *Odyssey* 11 seems to say "no." These texts also discuss *aretē*, typically translated as virtue or excellence. One of the invaluable upshots of scholarship on Greek ethics over the last half century is that Greek philosophers' conception of virtue and virtuous action frequently overlaps with much of what we consider essential to morality and moral action, namely, carrying about others for their own sakes.[1] It is true that virtue in ancient philosophy is a broader concept than our concept of morality, including virtues such as temperance. Nevertheless, when Socrates says that one should not act contrary to virtue, he clearly understands this to be equivalent to acting wrongly, where that means ethically or morally wrongly. There is now strong scholarly consensus that the Greeks recognize and value other-regarding action undertaken for its own sake; in fact, the texts are so clear on this point it can be difficult to see how readers could have thought otherwise. So, while Greek ethics remains "formally egoistic," in the sense that acting for the sake of others for their own sakes is also, in some sense, beneficial for me, it does not adhere to a "selfish egoism," according to which I aim only at my own good or benefit in every rational action. Rather, caring about others for others' sakes will be part of my own happiness. Some contemporary defenders of virtue ethics emphasize the manifest examples of others' happiness being part of one's own, such as the relationship of a child's happiness to that of their parents'. The upshot

---

[1] Annas (1993) and Irwin (1988), (1995), and especially (2007–2009) are particularly prominent examples of this work. Consideration of the fact that ancient ethics frequently focuses on the agent's own happiness had led philosophers and scholars in the modern period to conclude that the ancients have no concept of morality, since morality concerns duties to others; a *locus classicus* for this view is Adkins (1960).

Varieties of Happiness. Iakovos Vasiliou, Oxford University Press. © Oxford University Press 2025.
DOI: 10.1093/9780197645093.003.0002

here is the claim that genuine concern for others can be accommodated within a eudaimonist structure.[2]

In opposition to the emergence of contemporary virtue-ethics and its association with eudaimonism, philosophical common sense has said for at least a couple of centuries that human happiness or well-being and morality or virtue are crucially distinct; deliberation about self-interest is one thing, deliberation about virtue another. This verdict does not arise simply because a popular, contemporary view of happiness, especially outside of philosophy, tends to be subjectivist, concerning people's own reports about how they feel about themselves and their lives.[3] Even when one agrees that our own contemporary conception of happiness contains objective as well as subjective elements, as may be brought out particularly when one thinks about wishing a child or, say, a high-school graduate a happy life, this is not yet obviously to recognize a role for moral or virtuous action.[4] In fact, ethical action probably plays a relatively small part in many people's descriptions of a good life, as perhaps at most one component among many.[5] For example, some people might say that in addition to health, pleasure, some wealth, satisfying and worthwhile work, and good personal relationships, a good life should include working for justice, aiding those "less fortunate," or some such; I am thinking of cases in which moral or virtuous activity counts for the person as a *part* or *component* of a good, happy life. But the demands of virtue or morality also (or alternatively) enter discussions of the good life in the role of *limitations* or *intrusions* upon it; many would say that people should pursue their own happiness, but in a way constrained by morality.[6] For example,

---

[2] See the essays collected in Whiting (2023).

[3] See, e.g., the "World Happiness Report" and discussions of happiness in psychology, economics, and the social sciences. In some recent discussions "eudaimonia" refers to well-being, while "happiness" is reserved for a psychological state of feeling satisfied, which is typically thought to be *part* of well-being but not the whole of it. For objections regarding the subjectivist nature of accounts of happiness depending on feeling, desire-satisfaction, or even overall life-satisfaction, see Annas (2011), esp. 131–140, and Badhwar (2014), ch. 3. I will use "happiness" as a translation of εὐδαιμονία and not as a term to contrast with "well-being."

[4] Unless I say otherwise, I shall understand virtuous action, moral action, and ethical action as synonymous expressions.

[5] Experimental philosophers can head off to the labs to test this. Obviously, I am not making a claim about what all (or even most) human beings would say; I am making a claim about the attitudes of people who might read this book. This book is a critical discussion of the beginning of Western ethics, where, apparently, a central ethical notion is the happiness of an individual. Of course, many peoples and traditions may not begin from such assumptions or take "what sort of life should I lead?" as a basic, intuitive starting point for ethical reflection.

[6] Describing a position similar to the one I am outlining, Annas (2008), 216, writes: "Moreover, we are used to the idea that happiness might be a local aim in my life, so that I can do my duty and neglect my happiness, whereas the conception of happiness as my final end demands that it be complete, not just one local aim among others for my deliberations." It will be of primary concern in this

morality or virtue may plausibly be thought to intrude on one's projects and activities: "Duty calls!" so I must, for example, set aside (the pursuit of) my own happiness for now in order to help someone.[7]

A great hook for eudaimonist theories is their universally desired aim: *everyone* wants to live well and do well; *no one* wants to live poorly and do poorly.[8] Plainly, however, the universal desire to live a good life—what is the starting point for eudaimonist reflection—is missing for the case of acting virtuously; we do not all simply desire from the start to do the morally right thing and so have only to figure out what that is.[9] So far, then, two differences have emerged between eudaimonia and acting virtuously: the former but not the latter is the object of a plausibly universal desire; the latter but not the former is most naturally taken as a practical end that supersedes any other.

Prima facie, such a view at least sounds as though it fits easily with all non-skeptical moral theories: the moral or virtuous action trumps any other ends one might pursue, including even one's own happiness. Of course, as those well-versed in the study of ancient ethics know, the superficial similarity

---

book to look at just what such a notion of completeness entails; here, it is contrasted with a "local aim." But as I am sketching the position above, it would be inaccurate to say that happiness counts as a merely "local" aim. Rather the conception of happiness above is a large-scale, overall aim, including what the agent conceives of as their life's work, their personal relationships, their health, and so on; indeed, it includes *everything* they most value as ends in their life. Even with such a comprehensive scope, however, it seems at least *prima facie* clear that duty can intrude and demand that they interrupt the pursuit of their own happiness. Of course, on the version of virtue ethics Annas and many others defend and attribute to the Greeks, virtue and virtuous action will be at least partly constitutive of happiness and so not something that could intrude "from outside," as it were. The idea of happiness being "complete" in Annas' description must therefore be *extremely* comprehensive: will there be *any* significant, deliberate actions that are not supposed to be caught by it? We will see that most, but not all, contemporary scholars think that the answer to this is "no," as we saw in the Introduction on Vlastos' account.

[7] This invites the question, "why should it?" What is this "duty" or "virtue" that trumps the pursuit of my own happiness? Of course, most moralists—defenders of virtue and morality—will have some account of why one *ought* to act according to the dictates of morality/virtue, as opposed to saying, "you just should." Prichard (1968[1912]) may constitute an exception. We might note as well, with an eye to subsequent discussion of Plato's and Aristotle's accounts, that this duty may be a political one, so that in a sufficiently unjust political situation one might be required to spend time and energy on resistance or on defense from an external threat, or perhaps take an onerous turn at ruling rather than focusing on the activities and ends that one would prefer to pursue and that one understands to be constitutive of one's happiness. See Chapters 3 and 5.

[8] For present purposes, I ignore potential counterexamples, such as the suicidal, the self-hating, or perhaps Satanists under some description.

[9] This contrast is manifest in Plato and Aristotle when they take the desire to live well and do well to be universal and obvious, a starting-point for reflection and argument (e.g., *Euthydemus* 278e3–c9; *Symposium* 205a; *Nicomachean Ethics* I.2, I.4), but then understand the love of virtue and the noble (*to kalon*) as generated through habituation and a carefully controlled education, by no means something universally desired or achieved (see, e.g., *Republic* II–IV; *Nicomachean Ethics* I.4, 1095b4–14, and II.1–4).

between the contemporary and the Socratic view is thought to end very quickly. According to almost all scholars, it would be deeply misleading to say that Socrates believes that virtuous action supersedes *any* other end one might have in acting, including the end of one's own happiness. For the fact that Socrates, like all other Greek ethicists, is a eudaimonist must mean that acting virtuously is somehow *also* acting for the sake of one's happiness, either constitutively or at least as an instrumental means. One of the central aims of this book is to examine the extent to which this traditional interpretation is accurate. In the Introduction, it was argued that merely offering an account of eudaimonia is insufficient for an ethical theory to be eudaimonist. Via an examination of contemporary scholarship, this chapter aims to establish an additional, more controversial thesis: the mere claim that one is *better off* or *happier* acting according to virtue is also insufficient for being a eudaimonist ethical theory. For most theories that advocate any set of values (even an "immoralist" one like Nietzsche's) argues that one is, in some sense, "better off" by pursuing it. The bar for a theory to be eudaimonist ought to be set higher.

2. The Eudaimonist Project: Julia Annas

Julia Annas is one of the foremost interpreters of Greek eudaimonism and one of its strongest advocates as a plausible theory within contemporary ethics. I shall therefore begin with her description of eudaimonia and eudaimonism, which she has articulated in many places.[10] Annas repeatedly calls reflection on what sort of life we ought to lead "the entry point for ethical reflection."[11] The idea is that if we begin to reflect on our lives and what we do in them, we will notice a couple of things. First, that we do some things for the sake of others and that in our actions and activities we pursue goals. We also quickly recognize that some goals are more general, or "higher" than others. My particular goal at this moment might be completing twenty-five

---

[10] While details of the positions she holds in Annas (1993) on different ethical theories are certainly controversial and the topic of scholarly dispute, how she is thinking about eudaimonism and the eudaimonist framework is, I think, part of the common background for almost all discussions of Greek eudaimonism and of particular theories, such as Plato's or the Stoics'. It is these background assumptions and the motivations for them that I am most interested in here; I shall turn to the details in subsequent chapters.

[11] Annas (2011), 121; see also Annas (1993), passim, and her introduction to the translation of Cicero's *De Finibus* (2001), xviii.

sit-ups, but my higher goal, for the sake of which I do the sit-ups, is to acquire strength, which I take, in turn, to be one component of my physical health; and, of course, one may engage in many different activity tokens and types that aim at the over-arching goal of health. A little further thought shows that we have several of these higher goals, such as, perhaps, significant and satisfying personal relationships, physical health, valuable and satisfying work, and so on. Reflection on my life is supposed to get me to "look at my life critically, ask whether my life currently embodies the right goals and priorities, and work out better ways of living. Ethical theory analyses, clarifies, and refines my thoughts about my life as a whole and overall aims."[12] So, the single aim of living a life well—happiness—ends up as the final end of all the subordinate ends, like work, health, and so on, that we pursue. This reveals what Annas calls "the basic structure of [ancient] ethical thinking," which Plato already takes for granted and which includes "everyone's thought that we all seek a single final end in everything do, that this must be 'complete' in including everything we need for the good life, and that this is what we all mean by seeking happiness, although people have radically different ideas as to what it takes to achieve happiness."[13]

Annas's view, then, includes a more substantial understanding of eudaimonia than merely living well or doing well; it is not just the idea of the good or best life, but the idea of the final end of that life, albeit an often still quite indeterminate one. "Eudaimonist thinking" does not begin with the concept of eudaimonia, but works its way up to it (so to speak) via "the entry point for ethical reflection," which is a question about how my life is and ought to be going.[14] What am I doing each day and why? How do concrete daily actions, such as going running or working at a job, relate to certain aims I have? Reflecting in this way we begin to think about how we ought to organize and structure our life: are my goals achievable given constraints ("time, money, energy"),[15] and are they mutually achievable? Further reflection then leads us to think of an overall, unifying goal—a final end—that provides structure to all of the subordinate goals. This is the concept of happiness or eudaimonia. According to Annas, except for "a very few people, usually those who from an early age have a vocation for art, or politics, or spirituality,"[16] most of us have a vague, muddled, and indeterminate idea of

---

[12] Annas (2001), xvii–xviii; (2011), 120–121.
[13] Annas (2001), xviii. See too Russell (2012).
[14] Annas (2011), 120ff.
[15] Annas (2011), 122.
[16] Annas (2011), 123; I return to this point below.

what our final end is, expressing it vaguely as "a good life" or "a life lived well." The role of ethical thinking is to get us to think more determinately about this initially indeterminate end. Happiness is a useful concept because it has more content than simply a formally defined final end, but is still indeterminate enough to allow for and even to require debate about what it consists in and how to get it. All ancient theories agree with common sense on happiness as the starting point for ethical *theory* (i.e., not ethical reflection, which is "how should my life go?"), and so Aristotle, Epicurus, the Stoics, and others offer "competing hypotheses of what happiness is when you think carefully and rigorously about it [...] In eudaimonist thinking we are seeking happiness whether or not we explicitly think to ourselves that we are, because we are all implicitly working out *how to adjust our goals*, as we live the one life we have."[17] As far as I can tell, Annas takes this conception of ethical theory not only to be necessary for a thinker to be a eudaimonist (and adhere to eudaimonism) but also to be sufficient.

Annas is certainly right that reflection on one's life and how it ought to go, and what kind of person one ought to be, are *ethical* questions, questions about our central values and what we consider good and worthwhile. Perhaps they are also questions that modern philosophy, as compared with ancient philosophy, has until recently largely ignored. But, as I queried in the Introduction, is this merely to *add* questions and positions to our philosophical repertoire, or does this sort of inquiry in a substantive sense displace or replace more standard questions in moral philosophy, such as: Which actions are right and wrong and how do we identify them? What *makes* certain actions right or wrong? And *why* should we do what is right and avoid what is wrong, particularly in cases where it seems obvious that adhering to the demands of morality or virtue will leave us worse off?

Clearly, to engage in eudaimonist reflection or even to have a fairly determinate conception of eudaimonia as so far described is *not yet* to have an ethical or moral theory in the sense that we have answers to what we should do and when, what is right and wrong, and what makes an action right or wrong. In the quotation above from Annas, she mentions rare individuals who from an early age have a vocation for "arts, politics or spirituality." The point of mentioning this, I presume, is to indicate the possibility of relatively rare individuals who, unlike most of us, have a quite determinate conception of their eudaimonia. So, for example, consider

---

[17] Ibid., 125, my emphasis.

a young piano prodigy who knows (or thinks they know) that they will devote their life to playing piano.[18] This is certainly, we might say, an *ethical* decision: they have made a value judgment about the activity around which they will organize their life. But, we should note two things, which I shall come back to at several points. First, such a person is not plausibly setting up the final end of their life, piano-playing, as something to which absolutely *all* of their deliberate, non-acratic actions are aimed; so, the role their conception of eudaimonia plays as a practical principle is not, as Annas describes eudaimonia above, an *all-encompassing* or *comprehensive* one. While their life, as we are supposing, is organized around playing the piano as their final end, they nevertheless plausibly engage in other activities, even activities pursued for their own sakes, such as perhaps recreation and friendships, which are not aimed at eudaimonia as they conceive it. This will be the case even though these non-piano-playing activities may well be affected by their "ultimate end," insofar as presumably they carefully limit themselves to engaging in activities not incompatible with piano-playing, such as ones that would put the condition of their hands at substantial risk of injury or that are so demanding that they could not practice the many hours a day they need and want to. Second, what is not mentioned here at all is what the pianist's relationship is to virtue or morality: What if the demands of morality and the demands of piano playing come into conflict? What are they to do and how are they to decide? This remains open, in two key respects. First, when the demands of piano playing and virtue conflict, which trumps? Second, despite their engagement in eudaimonist thinking and reflection in Annas's sense, *and* their possession of a substantive account of their final end, that is, what constitutes eudaimonia for them (namely, piano-playing excellence), when it comes to moral or ethical action they could well be a Kantian, Utilitarian, Nietzschean, Constrained Maximizer, or whatever. So, prima facie, there is nothing about their *eudaimonist thinking as such* that conflicts with any particular theory or approach to moral philosophy or moral values.

The only hint in Annas's account that my elaboration of the pianist's situation might be inaccurate is in the idea that happiness is something *complete*: that for the sake of which we do everything we do. In the context of *Intelligent Virtue*, at least, Annas does not particularly emphasize the term

---

[18] This is my example; Annas herself does not elaborate.

"everything" as being meant in some technical, literal sense.[19] If we use the term loosely, as a description of actions I take toward the ultimate ends around which I organize my life, then it need not and would not naturally mean literally *every* non-acratic, deliberate action. As I have indicated, we could use this term loosely as a part of stating what we take our happiness to consist in, just as our rather single-minded pianist does.

A much stronger (and prima facie implausible) comprehensive claim regarding happiness—according to which every deliberate, non-acratic action is aimed at it (in this case, piano-playing excellence)—would need significant argument in order to be accepted in its own right, and, with respect to the history of philosophy, we would need excellent textual evidence to ascribe such a view to a particular thinker. Of course, I am not claiming that a eudaimonist could not have the resources to build the idea of ethical obligation *into* a conception of happiness. Presumably the ancients frequently do: as we shall see, some figures and schools make virtuous activity (including actions we would call ethical or moral actions) constitutive of or at least part of happiness. My point here is simply that *until this is done*, we do not have an ethical theory that even begins to treat the "traditional" questions of moral theory. And, insofar as we think those questions pressing, even if not the *only* questions that a broader ethical theory ought to consider, we will have not gone far toward answering them just by inquiring into what sort of life we would, on reflection, like to lead—that is, inquiring into what our final end is, even if we appreciate that a conception of eudaimonia should operate for us as a "final end."

So far, then, there has been nothing in Annas's description of eudaimonism, eudaimonist thinking, and eudaimonist theory that would count against the traditional, modern understanding of a split between practical reasoning about the good and practical reasoning about the right. These two kinds of practical reasoning will only be fused if a person somehow subsumes the account of right conduct within the scope of her conception of eudaimonia, either at least as a necessary means to it or as a component part of it. For this, as the reader no doubt already grasps, we will need to consider the relationship between virtue and happiness more closely.

---

[19] In fact, I think Annas does mean every deliberate, non-acratic action; see the frequent repetition of the phrase "in everything we do" in Annas (2011), 126–127. Also, in Annas (1993), 332, summing up the eudaimonism of the Greeks, she writes: "Happiness comes in, in the first place, as something that we obviously all go for. Once we see the need for a final end, *an end we pursue in some way in every action*, there is no better specification than happiness that we can come up with for it" (my emphasis). As we saw in the Introduction, Vlastos (1991) makes it explicit that "everything" means every deliberate, non-acratic action.

We might step back first, however, and ask what the difference is between a person who has a conception of happiness that she pursues in everything she does (having engaged in the sort of reflection Annas recommends) *except* on the occasions when the demands of virtue or morality intrude, and a person who includes moral and virtuous action as at least partly constitutive of their conception of eudaimonia. Now the eudaimonist holds that we can retain the value of moral activity and still bring it under the umbrella of eudaimonia and eudaimonist thinking. Indeed, this is what Plato, Aristotle, and others actually *do*, according to Annas and others: virtuous activity is at least necessary and may be also sufficient for eudaimonia.

But adding the demands of virtue and morality to one's conception of eudaimonia is a complicated matter and comes with significant theoretical costs. Even if we have a plausible, inclusivist conception of eudaimonia (let's keep it simple: family/social life, great pianist, virtuous/moral activity), we are faced with a problem about how these ends are mutually achievable and what to do in cases of conflict. This is a way of putting a point that will be central to this study: a complete, workable eudaimonism must have an account of how eudaimonia is supposed to operate *as a practical principle of action*.[20] There are strong constraints here. If we are going to get the treatment of moral action correct, then it is going to have to supersede other practical ends; so, if eudaimonia is some sort of Superseding Practical Principle, it will have to include virtuous action as a trumping component. The only other option is to develop a theory (along the lines, on some interpretations, of the Epicureans),[21] where the rightness or virtue of actions is determined by their being conducive to my achievement of eudaimonia, which is conceived of *independently of* moral virtue. This is not a position that a defender of the supreme importance of ethical virtue, like Socrates, Plato, or Aristotle, would endorse.[22]

We might think we could improve matters by avoiding the narrow concept of "the moral" and replacing it with the more expansive concept, "virtue." We would then no longer have to worry about finding higher-order principles to adjudicate among family actions, piano-playing actions, and moral actions; we can simply include them all under "virtuous actions." Saving a drowning child counts as virtuous activity, but, exploiting the idea of *aretē*

---

[20] See discussion in the Introduction.
[21] See Chapter 6.
[22] One might wonder, in Plato's and Aristotle's cases, about intellectual virtue (theoretical contemplation); see Chapters 3 and 5.

as excellence, so does having genuine friends and, arguably, even artistic activity. This does not help much, however, since although we now have one activity that constitutes eudaimonia, virtuous activity, that type of activity is so broad that we need ways of adjudicating among its species: surely saving a child's life supersedes my efforts to play a beautiful arpeggio. If this is the case, how does the conception of eudaimonia that contains the trumping actions that constitute virtuous/moral actions differ from a conception of eudaimonia that sees these demands as intruding from outside? From the perspective of a practical principle of action, they do not seem to differ. But perhaps they do from the perspective of answering the moral skeptic of the "why should I?" variety.[23]

Thus, I preliminarily conclude that there needs to be more to a eudaimonist theory, one that is going to merit the label *eudaimonism*, than an organized and reflectively endorsed conception of the good life, even if we add finality of a sort as a criterion. The sort of account Annas has given is insufficient for describing a eudaimonism that is to count as a moral or ethical theory of a sort that can be a rival to, say, Kantianism or Utilitarianism.

3. Virtue and the Highest Good

A reader may object that I have so far attributed much too little significance to the obvious fact that most ancient ethical theories, and in particular Socrates', Plato's, Aristotle's, and the Stoics', make virtue and virtuous activity a, if not *the*, central component of happiness. And, of course, Julia Annas is well aware of this.[24] Most generally, as we have seen, virtue (*aretē*)

---

[23] As opposed to a different sort of skeptic who accepts that one should act morally but thinks we cannot ever know what the moral action is.

[24] Indeed, Annas (1993), ch. 15, argues that the ancients typically hold the concept of virtue fixed and bend the concept of happiness to fit. For contemporary accounts see, e.g., Badhwar (2014), who holds that virtue is necessary for well-being, and Rossi and Tappolet (2016). Hursthouse (1999), ch. 8, argues that virtue is a generally reliable bet for well-being, although in particular cases it may be neither necessary nor sufficient; see below. Becker (1999) argues for a Stoic thesis that virtue is both necessary and sufficient for happiness. If we take virtue or virtuous activity as roughly equivalent to right conduct (see next section), then Parry and Thorsrud's (2021) formulation of eudaimonia builds the connection between eudaimonia and virtue *into* the definition of eudaimonism: "[the] position that links happiness and virtue is called eudaimonism—a word based on the principal Greek word for happiness, *eudaimonia*. By eudaimonism, we will mean one of several theses: (a) virtue, together with its active exercise, is identical with happiness; (b) virtue, together with its activities, is the most important and dominant constituent of happiness; (c) virtue is the only means to happiness." Thus Parry and Thorsrud take eudaimonism to *be* a thesis about the relationship between happiness and virtue; they are, of course, explicitly discussing *ancient ethical theory* and so perhaps not what might theoretically count as eudaimonism more generally. But the point is that their description makes

is simply the idea of excellence; a virtuous x is an excellent example of an x. As is well known, the Greeks might speak of an excellent horse or even an excellent knife. If we think of excellence in a formal way, without a substantive conception of what excellence is, then the question of whether a person wants to be excellent could be as trivial as the question of whether a person wants to do and live well. Of course, everyone wants to be an excellent person, not a shameful, terrible one.[25] As used by Socrates, Plato, and Aristotle, however, the virtues (as states of character) and the virtuous actions that stem from agents who possess the virtues, such as courageous actions, just actions, temperate actions, and so on, have significant substantive content. A merely formal notion of excellence could be filled in, for example, in the way that Callicles appears to advocate in Plato's *Gorgias*: an excellent person is one who has large and numerous appetites and the power to satisfy them. The figure we might call, by contrast, the "morally virtuous person," defended by Socrates, refrains from engaging in the sorts of actions lauded by Thrasymachus in his aptly named "immoralist speech" in Book 1 of the *Republic* or the actions of the shepherd who finds the Ring of Gyges in Book 2, such as theft, rape, or murder. Thus, the central question of the *Republic* is often described in textbooks as "why be moral?" because this accurately captures the challenge of the *Republic*, which is to explain the motivation an agent might have to engage in just actions that appear to benefit others rather than themselves.

As I mentioned, an upshot of scholarship on ancient ethics in the last few decades has been an acknowledgment that genuinely other-regarding actions done for their own sakes are part of Greek ethics, albeit still under the conceptual framework of eudaimonism. In this way Greek ethics has a place for what we would call moral thinking. A focus of this book is to consider how moral virtue, the virtue advocated by Socrates, is supposed to function within the eudaimonist framework. Of course, if we employ only the "formal" notion of excellence, then the connection with eudaimonia may be simple; indeed, one might think that in such a case our conception of eudaimonia will supply the content of our conception of virtue—what I labeled "the Eudaimonist Hope" in the Introduction.[26] So, the virtues or

taking a stand on the relationship between eudaimonia and virtue a necessary condition of a view's counting as eudaimonism in the first place.

[25] Again, setting aside remote counterexamples: the self-hating, possibly the Satanic, and so on.
[26] In Chapter 2 I consider some formulations of eudaimonism, for example by Christopher Bobonich (2010), that make this idea central to what eudaimonism is.

excellences would be *whatever* states of character either constitute or lead to eudaimonia.

Nevertheless, a proper appreciation of the relationship between virtue and happiness can take the virtues (in the ordinary, good-person sense, not the Calliclean one) as very plausibly constituting at least part of the happy life. For, as Hursthouse and Annas argue,[27] surely one wants one's children to be honest, loyal, and just, and not dishonest, disloyal, and unjust. Furthermore, we should agree that a plausible conception of eudaimonia includes possession of these virtues. A happy person will plausibly be kind, loyal, honest, just, and so on, and not their opposites. But this point concerns what the best life appears to be or to include. It importantly leaves aside the issue, which is central to Annas's earlier description of eudaimonia in the same book (126–127), that happiness is the end of *everything* we do. Hursthouse's account, crucially, claims that the virtues are merely a *reliable bet* for living well and living happily, under ordinary circumstances. But she maintains that they are *neither* necessary *nor* sufficient. The evil might "flourish like the bay tree" and the virtuous might end up miserable.[28] That said, it is explicit on Hursthouse's account that when it comes to a practical principle of action, the virtuous action supersedes any other. So, for Hursthouse, while acquiring the virtues is a good *bet* for living happily, when push comes to shove in action, one ought (as every moralist thinks) to do what is right—ignoring the effect on one's happiness. What this means is that according to Hursthouse when you think about the role of eudaimonia *as a practical principle*, it is neither Comprehensive as Annas seems to hold (and Vlastos certainly does) *nor* does it trump, as it would as a Superseding Practical Principle. Rather, it is a Prudential Practical Principle, offering practical principles with respect to the restricted domain of the good.[29] So, the fact that a person wants to be excellent, formally speaking, or even that, more substantively, the canonical virtues are a reliable bet for achieving a happy life, is not yet to have a position that merits the label *eudaimonism*; rather, Hursthouse adheres to a division between an account of the good life and an account of right action and, correspondingly, to the division between reasoning about the good life and reasoning about what is right.

---

[27] Hursthouse (1999); Annas (2008), 217–218 and (2011), ch. 9, 146–147.
[28] See Hursthouse (1999), ch. 8, 172–174; see also Foot (2001), ch. 6.
[29] Like the *summum bonum* on Sarah Broadie's account, as we shall see in the following section.

4. Sarah Broadie on the *Summum Bonum*

Sarah Broadie argues that the concept of the *summum bonum* from ancient philosophy has been fundamentally misunderstood in the modern period.[30] The mistake has been to treat the highest good as though it were supposed to provide "a standard of right and wrong." This is what enables Mill in the opening lines of *Utilitarianism* to locate his own project as one that began at "the dawn of philosophy," namely the search for the *summum bonum* or, "what is the same thing," "the foundation of morality." Broadie argues that while Mill himself clearly does seem to be putting forward a standard of right and wrong, and so concerning himself with the foundation of morality, he is making a significant error in identifying this project with the ancient project of seeking the highest good. Broadie importantly considers two very different roles one might think that the highest good might play, which speaks directly to the concerns I have raised in the previous sections. According to her, the ancient way of conceiving of the highest good has it play a practical role only for those actions that are aimed at pursuing either the highest good itself or subordinate goods. But the highest good is manifestly *not* comprehensive in scope; rather, it concerns only a subset of all of one's actions:

> For example, if hedonism is the theory that says that pleasure is the highest good, then a hedonist according to the 'ancient' fashion may coherently and with perfect intellectual clarity decide that something is wrong without ever considering whether doing it will bring anyone less pleasure and more pain. One might ask: but what is it to hold that pleasure is the highest good if not to treat it as the general standard of right and wrong? The answer would go: this kind of hedonist holds (a) that a lot of actions are to be done or refrained from simply because they conform or fail to conform to some familiar principle such as that one has a duty to keep promises or to show gratitude to benefactors, and not because they lead towards or away from a greater good of some kind; and (b) that **such principles are self-sustaining, not grounded on anything else;** *however*, when it is a question of bringing about some good G, considered as good, this hedonist is bound to consider (c) whether G will add to the pleasantness of the life of whoever it is supposed to benefit, since if it does not, the highest good has been missed, which would mean that pursuing G as a good was not after

---

[30] Broadie (2005), esp. 42–43.

all worthwhile. [. . .] Consequently, there are two forms of hedonism: R-hedonism and G-hedonism [. . .] **The R-form says that all actions are right or practices justified in so far as they conduce to pleasure (whether one's own or another's), while the G-one says that pleasure is what should be principally kept in view in just the sub-set of actions specifically directed at bringing about good things.**[31]

This is a significantly alternative way of thinking about the highest good and its role as a practical principle. Unlike on Vlastos's and Annas's accounts, there is explicitly no "completeness" or comprehensiveness involved in the scope of the highest good's control over actions. If Broadie is correct about this being the "'ancient' fashion," then we have precisely the split I described above, with the example of the pianist. Their conception of piano-playing excellence as the highest good means that piano playing functions as a constraint on their pursuit of any other good. But it says nothing, *nor is it meant to say anything*, about how they are to decide cases of what is virtuous or right and whether and when to pursue it, in particular in cases of conflict with their own good. The highest good, on Broadie's account, refers only to "the sub-set of actions specifically directed at bringing about good things." Thus, she clearly rejects the idea that the highest good functions as a Comprehensive Practical Principle.

Later in the paper, Broadie returns to the issue of the relationship of a theory of the good to recognition of right and wrong.

I have been assuming that our agent who operates as if *V* [an open variable] is the highest good is, in practice at any rate, a G-style *V*-ist. That is to say, **his or her adherence to *V* [e.g., pleasure as the highest good] affects only those commitments for which the reason or justification consists in the pursuit of good things as such. Otherwise this agent recognizes all the usual duties and claims, and (I am assuming) gives them the weightings a decent person would give.**[32]

Here Broadie repeats the split I have in mind. The hedonist, for example, makes all their judgments about good and bad, and their practical decisions about what to pursue and avoid as good or bad, by reference to pleasure and

---

[31] Broadie (2005), 46–47 (my bold).
[32] Broadie (2005), 56 (my emphasis).

pain. Decisions about what we would call moral virtue or duty (helping someone in need, abiding by a pledge, and so on), however, are not assessable in terms of their hedonism. How they make these decisions and what justifies their being made as they do, including decisions in situations where their good conflicts with what they take to be their moral duties, depends on whether they are a "decent person." Thus hedonism, for a G-type hedonist (i.e., one who does not understand hedonism as supplying the standard for right action), does not tell us what to do *tout court*. Such a hedonist faces serious practical questions. First, what are they to do when their hedonism conflicts with what they take to be right or required by virtue? Broadie's response is that they will adhere to "all the usual duties and claims, and (I am assuming) gives them the weightings a decent person would give." In our language, they will adhere to the Supremacy of Virtue, which is of course a Superseding Practical Principle. Insofar as the hedonist thinks that fulfilling some duty (doing some virtuous action) is what is required in some circumstance (because of their adherence to SV), since their hedonism clearly gives them no guide whatsoever on how to determine what the virtuous action is, they must determine that in some other way, and Broadie does not discuss how the determination of what the virtuous or right course of action is to be determined.[33]

Thus, Broadie rejects that the highest good functions as a Comprehensive Practical Principle, embracing all reasons for action; rather the highest good is a Prudential Practical Principle, telling the agent in what their good consists and therefore what they have a reason to pursue as good. Secondly, she rejects the Eudaimonist Hope in that the good does not provide "the standard of right and wrong." And, finally, Broadie is explicit that ancient style theories of the *summum bonum* are not in the business of justifying one's virtuous or right actions: "such principles are self-sustaining, not grounded on anything else." If Broadie believes that this is indeed the ancient way, then, it seems that she rejects all three roles eudaimonia might play in a eudaimonist theory as I outlined them in the Introduction. Thus she should seriously question as well whether the ancients are eudaimonists as Vlastos, Annas, and, as we shall see below, Irwin understand eudaimonism.

---

[33] I do not intend this as a criticism of Broadie: she is clearly assuming that a "decent person" would do decent things, as all of us decent people appreciate. What is important to me is that the reasons for action that adherence to SV gives the decent person are not captured in her conception of the highest good. That is, to repeat, according to Broadie, it is not the role of the highest good to provide "a standard of right and wrong."

There is a further complexity, however, that Broadie touches on but leaves at the end of her article. What if we adopt Broadie's distinction between G-type and R-type understandings of the highest good, but consider the case where the highest good is deemed to *be* virtuous activity? Broadie works her way to this at the very end of the paper, but she never considers where this leaves the distinction between G-type and R-type theories or their relationship with eudaimonism. She concludes: "It only remains to point out that once the conscientious agent recognizes virtuous dispositions, and the virtuous activities expressive of them, as goods, she will be under powerful pressure from precisely her own conscientiousness to put these latter ahead of all else, thereby identifying the *summum bonum* with virtuous activity" (58).[34]

This is where Broadie's paper ends, but I think it raises problems for her distinction between R- and G-type theories, identifying ancient theories with the latter type. In this final sentence she is describing a progression, according to which the "conscientious agent" comes to see virtuous activity not only as good, but as the highest good. Let's translate the position into our terminology. All along, the conscientious or decent person has adhered to the Superseding Practical Principle, the Supremacy of Virtue, which, as we have seen, says that the virtuous or right action trumps any other end one might have. This is the ethical principle that for Broadie and Hursthouse governs doing what is right. Broadie's point, up until the end of the paper, has been that the *summum bonum* is the highest good and that in the "ancient style"[35] this is to be understood not as a "standard of right action," but simply as an account of what makes all good things good. And so, in my terminology, it would be understood as a Prudential Practical Principle. If I am a hedonist, I seek to, let's say, maximize or optimize my pleasure; but if I am also, in Broadie's words, a "decent" or "conscientious" person, I live by the Superseding Practical Principle, the Supremacy of Virtue. So, when considering whether to break a promise that is now unpleasant, I do not deliberate based on my hedonism, but based on what I think is right or according to virtue. When "the right" is not at issue, as it were, I go back to judging goods and my pursuit of them based on my hedonism. This is just what it is on Broadie's account to distinguish between a G-type and R-type theory.

But what happens to the distinction between G-type and R-type theories in this new situation where the good *is* right conduct? First and foremost,

---

[34] See also Broadie (2017), 160–165.
[35] As opposed to Mills' (and Kant's) misunderstanding of it: see Broadie (2005), n. 2.

there are no longer going to be separate spheres of deliberation, and separate practical principles, for actions pursuing the good and those concerned with right conduct. So, in the situation where the good (at least in part) *just is* engaging in right conduct, it would seem that the distinction between G-type and R-type theories has collapsed. Broadie does not address this collapse, yet it would seem to be very relevant for the assessment of the many Greek ethical theories that include right conduct—virtuous activity and the virtuous disposition from which it stems—as at least part of what the highest good is.

I add here that to say that the good is right conduct is not to supply, of course, a *standard* for right and wrong of the sort that hedonism on an R-type interpretation would be. For it does not resolve the outstanding "determining question," as I have labeled it, where that means we still have an open question about how to determine, epistemologically, what constitutes virtuous action tokens or even types.[36] While we might assume, perhaps mistakenly, that we can relatively simply see that one course of action is more pleasant than another, we are on arguably more controversial ground when we seek to determine what the virtuous course of action is.[37] We will have to return to this issue when we discuss the many ancient ethical theories—Plato's, Aristotle's, and the Stoics' most prominently—according to which virtue is an essential part of eudaimonia.

5. The Third Role of Eudaimonia: As Motivation

Before we turn to consider aspects of Terence Irwin's eudaimonism, let us explore a bit further what I posited in the Introduction as the "third role" for eudaimonia, as a motivation for acting virtuously. As is well known, the Greeks acknowledge three classes of goods: of the soul, of the body, and material possessions. On the Socratic/Platonic account, however, there are not only goods *of* the soul, but there are also goods *for* the soul, because the soul is an independent locus of harm and benefit.[38] Socrates and Plato hold that the good state of the soul is incomparably more important than the good

---

[36] See Chapter 2 below and Vasiliou (2008), ch. 4.
[37] For example, Socrates notoriously thinks that one must figure out what virtue is.
[38] This is a central Socratic ethical insight, as I argued in Vasiliou (2002) and elaborated in (2008); Polus in the *Gorgias*, for example, is depicted as a character that does not grasp that the soul can *itself* be in a good or bad condition independently of the body or of one's material possessions.

state of the body or the good state, if we speak that way, of one's material possessions. Healthy actions, such as eating well and exercising, generate and preserve a healthy body; similarly, virtuous actions generate and preserve a virtuous soul; unhealthy actions and vicious actions have the contrary effect. In a nutshell, this is the Platonic answer—laid out with increasing sophistication and detail in the *Crito*, *Gorgias*, and *Republic*— to "why be moral/virtuous?" Without an excellent soul, one has no prospect of happiness, of living well, whatever else happiness may include. Therefore, one is always better off doing virtuous actions than actions that are contrary to virtue, since the latter harm the most important and valuable part of oneself; and no benefit to one's body or possessions could compensate for a harmed or corrupted soul.

The connection between actions and the condition of one's soul is a necessary one. Every time one does something that is contrary to virtue one harms one's soul; every time one does what is virtuous one benefits one's soul.[39] The upshot is well known: it is wrong to think that one can, for example, cheat on an exam and have that be a simple one-off act, which, provided that one is never caught or punished, has no effects except for the gain of an undeserved high grade. Even if one is never caught or punished in any way in this life or any afterlife (not even "internally punished" by feeling guilty), one has still harmed one's soul, the most valuable part of oneself, by acting contrary to virtue. One has not only cheated but has made oneself, to some extent, a cheater, thereby affecting one's character for the worse.

If we accept this argument, however, what does it achieve and how does it achieve it? Let us begin with what it does *not* do: it does not provide an ultimate end of virtuous action. It would be incorrect to say that one acts virtuously *for the sake of* having and maintaining an excellent soul. The virtuous person acts virtuously for its own sake (or, as Aristotle says, for the sake of the fine [*kalon*]). Nor does this argument *justify* virtuous actions; that is, it does not provide an account of *why* this or that token action or this or that action-type is virtuous. What the argument from action to character does is to provide someone who wondered why one ought to commit to being virtuous (the content of which is metaphysically and epistemologically determined offstage) with a *motivation* to do so: namely, only by being and acting

---

[39] This need not exhaust all our actions. Many deliberate, non-acratic actions may be neither virtuous nor contrary to virtue; in Chapter 7 I shall argue against traditional scholarship that even the Stoics recognize "intermediate actions."

virtuously (whatever that genuinely consists in)[40] does one preserve and maintain the excellence of the most important part of oneself.

How significant is this information—the information that actions (that are virtuous or contrary to virtue) necessarily affect our character? I call it "information" since I maintain that Plato and Aristotle deny that it constitutes a justification for virtuous action. One reasonable thought would be that this information, since it purports to indicate a necessary beneficial connection between action and character, would be enormously important in an agent's motivational economy. So, one might think that it ought to convince a skeptic of the necessity of acting virtuously or at least give them a good reason for acting virtuously. On further reflection, however, this becomes considerably less clear. There is no benefit visible from the perspective of someone who already doubts either the incomparable value of the state of one's soul (as compared with one's body or possessions) or doubts that the genuinely virtuous actions are in fact genuinely virtuous. This is because, as the *Republic* clearly recognizes, for the person acting justly in unfortunate circumstances, there are no benefits either for their body or for their possessions; indeed, there may well be significant harms or losses in both of these categories. Thus, if a person does not *already* have at least some love for genuine virtue, it is difficult to see how this argument would motivate them at all. If I don't already appreciate to some extent why cheating on an exam is contrary to virtue and why it is shameful and wrong, merely being told that it will contribute to making me a cheater would have no motivational appeal for me.[41] If I am already reluctant to cheat, appreciate that it is contrary to virtue, but then think that perhaps I can simply do it without negative repercussion, then perhaps I can be further motivated not to cheat by an argument about its effect on my character and the sort of person I want to be.

We need to keep in mind that although everyone wants to live well and do well, not everyone wants to pursue virtue. The latter requires a special education and upbringing to inculcate, in Aristotle's language, a love of the *kalon*. Both Plato and Aristotle spend significant time discussing education, habituation, and upbringing (e.g., Plato, *Republic* 2–3; Aristotle, *Nicomachean Ethics* II.1–4) and its critical importance. While I agree that appeal to eudaimonia and to one's being "better off" in this attenuated sense

---

[40] Thus, Socrates's search for what virtue *is*, which is ultimately discovered in knowledge of forms: see Vasiliou (2008) and (2015).

[41] As we shall see below in §7, the Kantian parallel would be an appeal to my rational autonomy in order to motivate me to follow the Categorical Imperative.

can be a source of motivation to commit to the Supremacy of Virtue for one who already has some love for genuine virtue, it will not provide the sort of motivation that could plausibly persuade a variety of skeptics, such as Polus, Callicles, and Thrasymachus, to do so. I think nevertheless that we have identified a role that eudaimonia *does* play in Greek ethical theory beginning with Socrates. Unlike Vlastos's "eudaimonist axiom," which according to him Socrates staked out for the rest of Greek philosophy, I believe that this argument about the soul being an independent locus of harm and benefit, which is harmed or benefitted in turn by vicious or virtuous actions, is the genuine Socratic/Platonic contribution to the subsequent tradition.[42]

In Section 7 below, I will return to these issues and raise some doubts about whether such a role is sufficient to call an ethical theory eudaimonist by comparing Plato's reasoning to Kant's. Let us turn first to a brief account of some aspects of Irwin's eudaimonism.

6. Irwin's Eudaimonism

The thesis that emerges from Terence Irwin's three-volume work, *The Development of Ethics*, is that the naturalist version of eudaimonism that appears in Aristotle and Aquinas, properly understood, is the most philosophically defensible moral theory in the history of Western ethics. For Irwin, eudaimonism can bring together moral considerations and considerations of self-interest (or well-being) into a philosophically harmonious and well-defended whole. The biggest challenge is to explain how to bring in moral considerations—considerations about others for others' own sakes, encapsulated in virtues such as justice and in the love of another in a genuine friendship—within a framework that is egoistic, but, it is argued, not objectionably so. As Irwin puts it while criticizing Schopenhauer's rejection of eudaimonism as a moral theory: "We might change our minds about people's character if we realize that their apparently virtuous actions were really aiming only at some selfish advantage for them; but should we change our minds if we simply believe that they care about the virtuous action for its own sake and regard it is as part of their own happiness?"[43] Irwin implies that we should be persuaded to answer "no."

---

[42] I will further explore this role and its appeal in Plato in Chapters 2 and 3.
[43] (2009), vol. III, §1044, 256.

It is clear that for Irwin eudaimonia is comprehensive or all-inclusive, in two senses. We saw in our consideration of Broadie's position that the *summum bonum* is comprehensive in the sense that it is the ultimate explanation of the goodness of all good things. Nevertheless, Broadie does not hold that the *summum bonum* in and of itself gives us either a Superseding Practical Principle or a Comprehensive Practical Principle. Something's being superlatively good (e.g., pleasurable, in the case where pleasure is the *summum bonum*) does not necessarily mean that one would pursue it. On Irwin's account, by contrast, the highest good, eudaimonia, is comprehensive in both its *content*—it includes all goods within it as parts or components—and in its *role* as a practical principle. As he says: "We will deny that the ultimate end is comprehensive if we deny that all our practical principles are subordinate to it."[44] So, Irwin agrees with Vlastos that eudaimonia must operate as a Comprehensive Practical Principle; if it did not, it would fail to explain the rationality of all of our (deliberate, non-acratic) actions, which, according to Irwin and Vlastos, is part of the point of eudaimonism. Thus, eudaimonia is comprehensive in the scope of its content, including all goods, whether instrumental or valuable in themselves, within it, and it is comprehensive as a practical principle insofar as it is always the ultimate aim of *all* of our actions.

In addition, Irwin explains how our moral or other-regarding actions can be given rational basis by appeal to our own good, without that becoming objectionably egoist in a way that spoils the idea that certain acts (e.g., just acts) are not only valuable in themselves but also done for the sake of another. Consider the following passage (Vol. II, §710, 535–536):

> Aquinas ought to agree with Butler's claim that conscience is distinct from self-love. The considerations that weigh with conscience are those that make an action morally right. Aquinas and Suarez recognize these considerations in their discussion of the *honestum*. Considerations of my own happiness do not necessarily appear in the deliberation that is required for identifying the morally right action; and, since a virtuous person takes the rightness of an action as a sufficient reason for doing it, virtuous people do not need to consider their own happiness in deciding what to do, when moral questions are involved.

---

[44] (2007), §273, 494. See also, §§68, 72, 243. See too §387, 687: "Aquinas believes that reference to some single comprehensive end is necessary for rational willing."

Irwin is treating the split in deliberation we considered at the start of the chapter. For Butler considerations of conscience concern what is morally right, in a way similar to Aquinas's and Suarez's treatment of the *honestum*.[45] A virtuous person, looking to what is morally right, does not "necessarily" bring in consideration of her own happiness in deliberation that attempts to identify the morally right action. With the "necessarily" I take it that Irwin wants to preserve a sense in which deliberation about what is right *could* bring in consideration of one's own happiness:

> It does not follow, however, that conscience weighs reasons that are entirely outside the scope of self-love. [. . .] Self-love has good reasons to accept the claims of conscience, on the strength of this argument: (1) Self-love takes a holistic view of my interest, referring to my nature as a whole; that is why action on self-love is natural. (2) My nature as a whole requires me to accept the place that conscience accords to the legitimate demands of other people, since my nature requires me to regard myself as a responsible agent making legitimate demands on them. (3) Therefore, enlightened self-love also accepts this prescription of conscience. (Vol. II, §710, 536)

Enlightened self-love, which one can find in Aristotle and Aquinas (according to Irwin), stands opposed to narrow self-love; the latter does not consider other-regarding actions or actions in support of the common good, but the former does, since it takes a naturalistic and "holistic" view of the self and its interests, according to which one sees oneself as one agent among many connected by various "legitimate demands" and responsibilities. Narrow self-love is one side of the Sidgwickian thesis of the dualism of practical reason into reasoning about prudence or self-interest ("narrow self-interest" or "egoistic self-love," in Irwin's terms); practical reasoning about morality and the common good, which is an impersonal sort of reasoning, is the other. While Sidgwick sees these competing sets of deliberative reasons as on a par, Butler holds the supremacy of conscience.

Irwin, however, argues that we can bring these two types of practical reasoning together by recognizing a split between the principle that is the overriding guide of action and the principle that decides on the overriding guide; he calls the latter a "higher-order deliberative point of view."

---

[45] Throughout this discussion I simply take Irwin's interpretations of the figures in question for granted.

Acceptance of Aristotelian eudaimonism requires some revision in Butler's doctrine of the supremacy of conscience, but does not require him to abandon this doctrine entirely. From the Aristotelian eudaimonist point of view, conscience is supreme insofar as it is the overriding guide to action, but self-love is supreme, insofar as it is the principle that decides on the overriding guide to action. Perhaps one might say that conscience is supreme from the practical point of view, but self-love is supreme from a higher-order deliberative point of view" (536).

By distinguishing between levels of deliberation, Irwin allows that one does not deliberate about what to do (e.g., in some moral case) by deliberating about one's own happiness. Rather, the virtuous or moral person, on the first-order level, deliberates about what is right and virtuous, while, on a higher-order level, she appreciates that being the sort of person who deliberates about what it is morally right to do for its own sake is the best sort of person to be, and so indirectly, as it were, by making virtue the overriding guide of her action, she turns out also to be benefitting herself.[46] Irwin's position, then, maintains that one does not determine what to do by reference to one's own good narrowly construed; rather, what one has most reason to do is what is objectively right (Irwin's realism and objectivism enter here).[47] On the other hand, through this split of deliberative level, what it is most in one's self-interest to do (one's "enlightened self-love" or "non-selfish egoism") is to be the sort of person who, when acting, deliberates in a first-order way about what is right, independently of what is in their self-interest.

It is one thing to query why some token action, apparently self-sacrificing but required by virtue, is worth going in for here and now; it is another to step back and reflect on why being a moral or virtuous person is worth going in for overall. This is the point of Irwin's different levels of deliberation: deliberating about what to do in the here and now versus stepping back in "a cool hour" (vol. 3, p. 885) and deliberating about what reasons one has for being the sort of person who acts for the sake of virtue above all. It is in the latter reasoning, according to Irwin, that we find ultimate reasons grounded in a conception of eudaimonia (in turn grounded in a conception of what we are as rational human beings).

---

[46] This comes out as well in Irwin's discussion of Prichard (vol. III, sec. 1400), esp. 885.
[47] See, e.g., vol. 3, ch. 93, for defenses of objectivism against critics. Skorupski (2012), esp. 322–323, 339–332, challenges the appropriateness of Irwin's attribution of versions of realism.

7. Plato and Kant: Two Eudaimonists?

What has emerged as a central part of eudaimonism on Irwin's account is the idea that what grounds the rationality of acting virtuously is that an action is either an instrumental means to or a constituent of the agent's own good, their eudaimonia. One rejects a critical component of eudaimonism, therefore, if one holds that the ultimate grounds for acting virtuously are not in the agent's own good. So, notoriously, Kant would be an obvious opponent of eudaimonism, for reason alone determines what one's duty is and binds one, qua rational agent, to that duty. Since, as we have seen, Plato attempts to supply an argument that a person is better off or happier acting justly (i.e., morally) than unjustly, it can seem clear that Plato is an egoist (even if of a non-selfish variety), seeking to ground morality in the agent's own good, and so too a eudaimonist.

But is this right about Plato? We do not need a lot of detailed textual exegesis to appreciate that the idea that what is just (or right) is grounded in the agent's own good is not in fact Plato's. For it is basic Platonic metaphysics that an action (or a person, for that matter) is just or courageous or beautiful because it (or they) participates in the Form of Justice or Courage or Beauty. It is nothing about the agent or the effect on an agent of acting virtuously that *makes* a certain token or type of action virtuous; that is a matter of an independent metaphysical relationship between the sensible instantiation of some token action and the transcendent Form in which it participates. After all, not only is Plato a realist about morality, he is a Platonist! The epistemology follows suit. What it takes for an agent to know that an action is just, in the best case, is for her to know the Form of Justice and then to determine whether (and to what extent) a token action participates in it. However unsatisfactory that may sound, it is clearly the Platonic view; indeed, it is precisely the role of the Philosopher-Kings in the *Republic* to learn how to apply the knowledge of Forms they have acquired through their rarefied and sophisticated education to the sensible world in the course of fifteen years of applied training.[48]

Recalling this should be sufficient to see that for Plato it is no part of the metaphysical or epistemological determination of the justice or rightness of an action to examine or discover something about what is the good of the agent. So, if we think this is necessary for eudaimonism, then Plato, in the

---

[48] For details, see Vasiliou (2008), ch. 8, and (2015).

Republic at least, is not a eudaimonist. But, of course, Plato is *also* asking whether the person who acts justly is somehow for that reason happier or better off, even though if she were benefitted in some way that benefit would neither be what *makes* the action just nor the *justification* for her pursuit of it. And the answer to that is, manifestly, yes: by doing (genuinely) excellent actions one produces and maintains a genuinely excellent and healthy soul, and the soul is the most important part of a person's well-being or happiness, incomparably more important than her physical health or her material possessions. Without looking at the argument for this claim, let alone whether it is a good argument, this is sufficient to see that Plato does agree, of course, that a person is better off acting justly than unjustly, for the former has the effect of benefitting the soul, while the latter harms it. So, acting virtuously *does* confer a benefit on the agent after all, despite the fact that what acting virtuously is is not grounded in or justified by appeal to the human good. Further, I argued above in Section 5, being made aware of this beneficial connection may well play a motivational role in committing to the Supremacy of Virtue, at least for agents in a certain condition. Is *this* sufficient, then, to make Plato a eudaimonist?

I think the answer is "no," and we can see this by considering Kant. Fortunately, as in the discussion of Plato, we do not need to get into detailed Kantian exegesis. For Kant, one's duty is not grounded in one's own good; rather, it is grounded in the Categorical Imperative. Using the Categorical Imperative Procedure, we can (somehow) determine whether token actions are contrary to duty. This may be as difficult (or not) to understand in detail as Plato's idea of participation in Forms, but that is neither here nor there. The crucial issue is to appreciate the parallelism: neither for Plato nor for Kant is the moral action determined, metaphysically or epistemologically, by anything to do with its relationship to the agent's own good. But what about the Platonic idea that the agent is, in acting morally or justly, in a way benefitted, since just action turns out to benefit the soul? Does that have a Kantian parallel? I think it does—or at least could. For Kant, what is special about human beings and what gives them dignity and the status of ends in themselves is their rationality. When one acts from duty, one is acting as an autonomous rational agent. To shirk one's duty would be to act heteronomously, following one's inclination rather than one's reason. Thus, when I act morally and from the motive of duty, I act in the only way that displays my (best) self as an autonomous, rational being. If that is my "I" then aren't *I* obviously *better off* behaving according to duty than not?[49] If so, do we want to say that Kant is a eudaimonist and an egoist?

Furthermore, it is arguably not the case that the fact that such and such an action would be an exercise of my rational autonomy that *makes it the case* that it is my duty.[50] The latter is something that is revealed to me *via* the exercise of my reason, just as an exercise of my autonomous reasoning can reveal to me that the internal angles of a triangle are equal to two right angles while of course this is not *made true* by my reasoning. And my reasoning discovers what is the case by looking at triangles or actions, not by reference to rational autonomy. For Plato, as I have said, it is the action's participation in the Forms that makes it the action it is; and knowledge of the Forms is the (best) way for a person to identify whether an action is just or not.[51]

Now Kant's, as well as Plato's, notion of what it is to be better off is a specialized and moralistic one and clearly does not fit smoothly with an ordinary, selfish egoist, who, say, wants money, pleasure, or power. Nevertheless, the parallelism at this level of the theory remains: why think I am better off behaving morally/virtuously? Kant has one answer: because it is only then that I exercise my rational autonomy; Plato has another: only then do I maintain and generate a healthy soul. But how does this make one of them a eudaimonist and the other not? Thus, if we are going to say that this is sufficient to make Plato a eudaimonist, then Kant will be one as well.[52] My suggestion then is that this argument ought to be understood as a *reductio* of the idea that merely maintaining that acting according to what is objectively right in some way benefits the agent is sufficient to make an ethical theory a version of eudaimonism. Nevertheless, on my account both Plato and Kant have something they could say to someone who asks how she would be benefitted by acting virtuously/morally.

---

[49] While this interpretation of Kant may be disputed, it is an interpretation defended by scholars and not simply a fancy; see White (1999), 210–211; also Wood (2008) and Uleman (2010) and (2016).

[50] Here recent "realist" or "anti-constructivist" readings of Kant are relevant: see, e.g., Langton (2007), Wood (2008), and Merritt (2017).

[51] The point is the same for any philosopher who thinks the content of virtue is objective and independent of the attitude of the agent. So, Aristotle places the content in the *kalon*, which the practically wise person (the *phronimos*) knows.

[52] I have presented considerations that would lead one to doubt whether Plato is a eudaimonist, given certain similarities between his ethical outlook and Kant's. I offered a *modus tollens*: if Plato is a eudaimonist, so is Kant. But Kant isn't (or else, I suggested, we have lost any substantive conception of what eudaimonism is). So, neither is Plato. But as the saying goes, one person's *tollens* is another person's *ponens*—or something like that. According to Irwin (see, esp. 2009, vol. 3, ch. 71), by contrast, even the traditionally notorious anti-eudaimonist, Kant, could usefully take elements of eudaimonism on board as a supplement and support for his moral theory.

I mean to draw this parallel between Plato and Kant seriously, but also provocatively. While I am serious about the potential parallelism (at least on a certain defensible reading of Kant), I am not saying that Plato and Kant have the same agenda.[53] Plato is explicitly attempting to argue about how a person is better off and happier by being just, and he does this not only at length but, in particular in the *Republic*, in significant detail in describing justice in a person as a harmony in the tripartite soul; he then also describes in great detail in *Republic* 8 and 9 how characters falling short of virtue in various ways are correspondingly miserable to varying degrees. Kant, by contrast, has no such agenda; he is not interested in explaining how a person is better off by following the Categorical Imperative, let alone "happier". In these terms, of course, he would reject the description. All I am saying is that, in fact, if a person asked Kant (or a Kantian) whether they are in any way better off acting from the motive of duty, he could reasonably appeal to the rational autonomy they thereby display.

That said, let us consider practical principles of action. Kant would never say that the *aim* of one's action is to exercise one's rational autonomy; one's superseding practical aim is to do one's duty. It is the same, I claim, with Plato. One does not aim in action to make one's soul healthy; one aims at doing the right thing. But in both cases it will, as a matter of fact, turn out to be the case that by doing one's duty or acting virtuously this will have a beneficial effect on one's (best) self. Of course, whether this effect is at all sufficient to plausibly call such an agent *happy* is another matter. One could certainly disagree as to the value of acting in a rationally autonomous way (or, on the other hand, about the harm of acting heteronomously following sensuous inclination). Plato, as I said, spends considerable energy describing in detail what sorts of benefits and harms accrue to the virtuous and vicious agent.

Both Plato and Kant, then, believe that virtuous action or duty trumps any other end we may have in acting, and so, as good and moral people, we ought to commit ourselves to the Supremacy of Virtue or the Categorical Imperative as our Superseding Practical Principle. Our reason for making this commitment is appreciated in the course of appreciating *that* an action is genuinely virtuous (via our knowledge of Forms) or that it is genuinely our duty (via an exercise of our pure practical reason). So, Plato and Kant hold, for virtue and duty, respectively, that the genuinely virtuous or moral person acts from virtue or duty: no other motive is needed. What I have suggested,

---

[53] I thank Matt Evans for pressing this point.

however, is that while no further motive is needed, it turns out, on each of their accounts, that as a matter of fact an agent's best self accrues a benefit by committing themselves and acting in this way because it involves acting in a way that for Plato preserves and maintains an excellent state of soul and for Kant consists in an exercise of rational autonomy.

8. Conclusion

I agree with and defend the position, then, that ancient Greek ethics, beginning with Socrates, has views about the effects of acting virtuously on the agent: an action that is genuinely virtuous and done for the sake of the *kalon* necessarily affects the agent in a certain way. Acting virtuously is at the same time to affect one's soul and contribute to its becoming and/or maintaining its virtue. Further, the Platonic-Aristotelian tradition, followed in this respect by the Stoics and Epicureans, holds that one's soul or character is the most important part of oneself, compared with one's physical or material well-being (as the Kantian holds that it is our capacity for rational autonomy that gives human beings their distinctive dignity). So, in this narrow respect, then, acting virtuously or morally has a beneficial effect on the agent. I say "in this narrow respect" to highlight the fact that such beneficial effects, as so far described, leave open that a person may be quite miserable in other respects: they may be harmed physically, psychologically, and materially—and of course in an extreme case even be killed—while still being (or having been) benefitted with respect to their soul (or their rational autonomy). The critical point is that appeal to the putative benefit of moral action for the agent is not meant to provide the *aim* or ultimate *end* of virtuous action nor is it supposed to be the justification either for token virtuous actions or for the commitment to be the sort of person who acts in that way. What it does do is answer an appropriately conditioned agent who wonders whether there is some self-interested reason for acting as virtue dictates. Am I *in any way* better off or, as the Greeks would put it, happier, by acting virtuously rather than not? While I think that the answer for both Plato and Kant is "yes," I have argued that that "yes" is insufficient for eudaimonism. We need therefore to reexamine the ancient philosophers' works in detail, keeping explicitly in mind the different roles that eudaimonia might play in a theory with the label "eudaimonism," before we can justifiably claim that Greek ethics, as "eudaimonist," is a radically distinct way of doing moral theory.

2
Socrates and Eudaimonism

1. Introduction: Ethics and Deliberation in the *Apology* and *Crito*

I have argued at length elsewhere that when one examines the so-called Socratic dialogues without what I might in this context call a "eudaimonist prejudice," what one finds is an overwhelming focus on virtue, not eudaimonia.[1] Socrates's attention to virtue has two emphases. The first, and primary one, which we have already seen in the Introduction, is his commitment to a Superseding Practical Principle "The Supremacy of Virtue (SV)." Socrates claims that he has always adhered to the principle, which says that doing the virtuous action trumps any other end one might have in acting, and he calls on his fellow Athenians and interlocutors to do the same. Recall that SV operates in two ways: first, as a positive principle that requires that one explicitly deliberate about what the virtuous action is in some circumstance, especially in cases we might characterize as moral dilemmas. So, for example in the *Crito*, Socrates deliberates about whether escaping from prison is just/right; in this case, doing the right thing is his explicit aim, and not simply avoiding wrongdoing.[2]

In other contexts (indeed in most contexts), commitment to SV manifests itself as a limiting condition on one's actions, captured in Socrates's dictum that it is never right to do wrong. While one may act for a variety of ends in any given situation, if a certain action is contrary to virtue, however that is determined, then it must not be done, no matter what external goods may be gained or lost.[3] As we have seen, this is the most plausible way of construing the ubiquity of SV, the idea that it is *always everywhere operative*, which is

---

[1] See Vasiliou (2008). "Socrates" as throughout refers to the character in Plato's works, not the historical figure.
[2] In his own voice *and* in the voice of "the Laws," Socrates states that no end—not his own life, not care of his children, not the well-being of the city—ought to be put above the end of doing the right thing (48b, 54b). Discussed in detail in Vasiliou (2008), see esp. Intro and chs 1 and 2.
[3] As we shall see later, however, external goods have a significant role to play in deliberation that seeks to determine what the virtuous action *is* in some situation.

suggested by Socrates's own frequent formulation of the principle as "it is never right to do wrong."

Next, we need to appreciate the difference between "aiming deliberation" and "determining deliberation." Socrates's declaration of his commitment to SV in the *Apology* has been interpreted as meaning that Socrates has no interest in consequences. Julia Annas comments as follows, referring to *Apology* 28b: "In reply to an imagined critic who faults him [Socrates] for behaving so as to be risking death, he says that we should not consider the consequences of our actions at all, even death, but only the issue of whether the action is just or not."[4] But Socrates never says that we should not consider the consequences of our actions "at all." He does say that *if* an action is contrary to virtue, then it must not be done—no matter what other benefits one might get by doing it. But in the process of *determining* what the virtuous action is, he leaves open, perfectly reasonably, that we will want to consider the consequences of different courses of action. When he says one ought to do the virtuous thing above all, he is saying that there is no external good—pleasure, money, health, even life—that supersedes doing the virtuous action *as an end*. What he is *not* saying is that life, health, money, and so on are irrelevant in a different deliberation that seeks to determine what the virtuous action *is* in some circumstance.[5] Here is where the distinction between aiming and determining questions becomes crucial. For Socrates health is not a competitor with virtue in a deliberation that seeks to decide what one's supreme aim should be (i.e., in answering the aiming question). External goods, however, *will* be relevant in a determining deliberation, where what is sought is to determine what the virtuous action is. Who gets what material goods, who lives or dies, who is physically hurt or helped, and so on, are all considerations in a deliberation about what the right or virtuous thing to do *is*. This opens up what sort of ethical deliberation one might engage in—and in a philosophically productive way. For example, in the *Crito* Socrates considers all sorts of reasons for and against escaping from prison, raising considerations that we might classify as deontological, consequentialist, pragmatic, and so on. No consideration or type of consideration is ruled out a priori as irrelevant in a deliberation that seeks to determine what the right

---

[4] Annas (1993), 33.
[5] In the context of "determining deliberations" and "determining questions," I am concerned with determining in the epistemological, not metaphysical, sense. Unsurprisingly, these are related: we need to figure out (i.e., determine epistemologically) what is really the virtuous course of action (i.e., determined metaphysically). In full-blown Platonism what determines metaphysically what is truly virtuous is participation in the relevant Platonic Form; see Chapter 3 and Vasiliou (2015).

thing to do is. What manifestly *is* ruled out by Socrates is that anything— his reputation, his life, the life of his children, the welfare of the city, and so on— should count as a competing *aim* of his action.[6]

Nothing I have said here so far makes the *Apology* or *Crito* incompatible with some form of eudaimonism; I have merely outlined what I take to be the central part of the ethics as presented in them, with their explicit focus on virtue. In these dialogues Socrates treats both what I have called "aiming questions"—questions that consider competitors, such as survival and pleasure, to his own answer to what the Superseding Practical Principle should be—and determining questions, most notoriously via the Socratic "what is F?" question. With these distinctions in mind let us turn to consider the arguments for attributing eudaimonism to Socrates and, further, to consider what roles eudaimonia is taken to play in Socratic ethics.

2. The Eudaimonist Approach and Its Discontents

Commentators defending the attribution of eudaimonism to Socrates invariably gather their evidence piecemeal from passages scattered across the dialogues.[7] The most prominently cited are from the *Lysis* and *Euthydemus*, with support from the *Gorgias* and *Meno*. It is striking that no one text commits Socrates to eudaimonism in any of its most prominent forms; the best its defenders muster is that some places suggest it—again the *Lysis* and *Euthydemus* most prominently—and other passages are compatible with it. Socrates's remarks, suitably cobbled together, can thus be made consistent with eudaimonism.

I have significant sympathy, then, with the remarks by Nicholas White, who comments on Irwin's attribution of eudaimonism to Socrates, for example, in the *Apology* and *Crito*, as follows:[8] "What seems most striking about [Irwin's] argument, however, is that it is so ingenious and unobvious, and that it must make such heavy use of premises from passages that are

---

[6] See Vasiliou (2008), ch. 2.

[7] For example, Brickhouse and Smith (2000), 128, cite these, and only these, four passages—*Lys.* 219–220; *Gor.* 467–468; *Meno* 77e–78b; *Euthyd.* 278e—as the evidence that supports the "Principle of Eudaimonism: Happiness is everyone's ultimate goal, and anything that is good is good only insofar as it contributes to this goal." I shall consider each of these passages in detail below.

[8] White (2002), 178, n. 68. It is important to realize, though, that Irwin relies most heavily on the very same passages as Penner (2010), Brickhouse and Smith (2000), Bobonich (2010), and Vlastos (1991), so I think this comment by White is applicable far more broadly.

widely separated both from each other and from the *Apology*. The supposition that a reader would be likely to put these passages together to see the reasoning leading to eudaimonism seems to me to gain much of its plausibility from the prior assumption that Greek thought was imbued with eudaimonism."[9] Much of White's argument shows that nothing that Socrates says in the *Apology* or *Crito* (and then he goes on to consider *Euthydemus* and *Meno* as well) *requires* that Socrates (or Plato) be interpreted as holding the very strong claims of eudaimonism. White diagnoses this tendency as simply part and parcel of a prior assumption that Plato *must* take eudaimonism for granted.[10]

Combine White's careful criticisms (these passages do not "entail" eudaimonism), however, with the generally cautious claims of the defenders of eudaimonist readings (e.g., in passages that seem to attribute the Supremacy of Virtue to Socrates, they point out that nothing he says is "incompatible with" eudaimonism, and so on),[11] and it can seem that to some extent each side is talking past the other. Moreover, almost all of the defenders of eudaimonist readings are explicit about the weaknesses in Socrates's eudaimonism. But such weaknesses in Socrates's (and Plato's) positions are explained and excused by the fact that they are, after all, the originators of the "eudaimonist framework."[12] To the frustration of anyone trying to attribute eudaimonism to Socrates, excellent and obvious questions—like "would a virtuous person be any less happy if he were in excruciating pain than if he weren't?"— do not seem to have a clear answer. Is Socrates a Stoic or an Aristotelian on these issues? The fact that many of the texts are indeterminate or even apparently conflicting on questions that seem basic and central to more "mature" eudaimonism, as it appears in standard readings of Aristotle or the Stoics, does not incline the defenders of the eudaimonist reading of Socrates to abandon it or at least set it aside;

---

[9] See White (2002), 177, n. 3, for similar criticism of Vlastos's argument that Socrates is a eudaimonist.
[10] See White (2002), 183.
[11] E.g., see Bobonich (2010), 298–299.
[12] Recall from the Introduction, Vlastos (1991), 203: "[The Eudaemonist Axiom] once staked out by Socrates, becomes foundational for virtually all subsequent moralists of classical antiquity." Annas (1999), ch. 2: "We are more at home with arguments which press the claims of virtue *as opposed to* happiness. But the indications that Plato is a eudaimonist are unmistakable. We must, then, try to see how Plato can see the Socrates of the *Apology* as a seeker for happiness" (40). On the question of the relationship of external goods to happiness, Annas writes, "there seems to be a deafening silence" in Plato (42). Nevertheless, she maintains that Plato holds that virtue is sufficient for happiness, like the Stoics (44–45); further, he himself does not grasp the radical implications of this thought, but "this is not surprising; Plato is pioneering a eudaimonistic theory" (45).

rather, the assumption is precisely that we are seeing eudaimonism in its infancy and so these questions remain to be sorted out more carefully, first by Plato, but then really by Aristotle and the Hellenistic Schools.[13]

Given this state of affairs, a productive way forward may be to ask what philosophical work the attribution of the eudaimonist framework to Socrates is doing for our understanding of Socratic ethics. While I agree with White that it would not occur to anyone to attribute eudaimonism to Socrates merely on the basis of the Socratic dialogues (generously construed) without the subsequent history of Greek ethics (and, as White emphasizes, the modern history of its interpretation), let us agree in a conciliatory fashion that one *could*.[14] I shall argue, however, that Socrates' remarks about eudaimonia do not support commentators' more ambitious claims about its centrality to Socratic ethics. Further, I shall show that a myopic focus on the eudaimonist framework has warped our understanding of Socratic virtue, his defense of it, and Socratic deliberation.

3. Virtue, Wisdom, and the Eudaimonist Hope

With only one exception I know of, scholars take Socrates's ethics to be essentially eudaimonist.[15] Moreover those scholars who attribute the eudaimonist framework to Socrates hold that Socrates thinks that virtue is knowledge (i.e., wisdom), full stop. In two arguments that are key support for the attribution of eudaimonism to Socrates—*Meno* 87d–89a and *Euthydemus* 278e–282d[16]—we learn that wisdom is the only independent good; all other so-called goods are, at most, only good if they are used correctly; and only wisdom will make us able to use them correctly. Since happiness is a matter of securing good things, wisdom (i.e., virtue) must be a component of or causal means to happiness.[17] If one lacks wisdom (virtue), one lacks the sole

---

[13] See Irwin (1995) on admitting that the eudaimonist framework is not explicit, even in Plato. Annas (1993) omits consideration of Plato completely; but see previous footnote.

[14] In the Epilogue I suggest that we find the eudaimonist framework in full-bloom in Cicero; of course, a primary aim of this book is to argue that commentators have too quickly read it back into the ethical philosophy of the Classical and early Hellenistic periods.

[15] White (2002) is the exception; eudaimonist interpreters include: Vlastos (1991), Irwin (1995), Brickhouse and Smith (1995) and (2000), Annas (1999), Penner and Rowe (2005), Reshotko (2006) and (2011), Penner (2010), and Bobonich (2010).

[16] Discussed in detail in §§4–5 below.

[17] Positions vary. Brickhouse and Smith (2000) are outliers within the group that attributes eudaimonism to Socrates. The fact that Socrates does not possess wisdom (and so does not possess virtue, since wisdom is virtue) means that if wisdom is necessary for happiness, then Socrates is not happy. But, they argue, Socrates is described as happy, so wisdom must not be necessary for virtue.

independent good, and one also lacks all the other things that would be made good or at least beneficial by the possession of wisdom (i.e., health, wealth, beauty, strength, and so on).

Christopher Bobonich calls these arguments about the importance of wisdom: "Socrates' most radical and philosophically interesting defense of the importance of virtue."[18] Such a view is typical among commentators on Socratic ethics. Wisdom is necessary and sufficient for right action, where "right action" means action that leads to or constitutes happiness; wisdom involves the "correct" use of health, wealth, and so on, so that the latter become goods (i.e., beneficial) for the agent. I shall argue that this is at best a partial understanding of Socratic virtue and at worst a deeply skewed one. The eudaimonist interpreter (henceforth "the eudaimonist") holds that something is a virtue if and only if it benefits the agent; *eudaimonia* is what confers goodness on virtue (and everything else) and *also* what is the decisive consideration for action.

Let us look in more detail at two specific formulations of eudaimonism in the context of Socratic philosophy:

(1) Brickhouse and Smith (2000, 128): "Principle of Eudaimonism: Happiness is everyone's ultimate goal, and anything that is good is good only insofar as it contributes to this goal."

(2) Bobonich (2010, 296): "The Principle of Rational Eudaimonism: It is rationally required that, for each person, his own (greatest) happiness is the decisive consideration for all his actions." Bobonich distinguishes this from "The Principle of Psychological Eudaimonism: Each person pursues (and tries to act upon) his own (greatest) happiness as the decisive consideration for all his actions."

At least initially, each of these sounds rather different from Vlastos's formulation quoted in the Introduction, as well as from each other. Brickhouse and Smith's formulation contains two claims: the first a psychological one about human beings and their ultimate goal, and the second about happiness as the source of the goodness of all things. In Brickhouse and Smith's formulation, there is no mention of action or decision. Presumably, if happiness is my ultimate goal, then, rationally speaking, I ought to pursue it. But merely to say that happiness is my *ultimate* goal is not to say that I do not

---

[18] Bobonich (2010), 324.

have other goals, which may or may not be subordinate to that ultimate goal; nor is it to rule out the possibility that sometimes other demands—for example, requirements of virtue or perhaps of love—may supersede my pursuit of happiness, as I discussed in the "common-sense" philosophical account treated in Chapter 1. So, as far as Brickhouse and Smith's formulation goes, my happiness does not necessarily supply me with more than a Prudential Practical Principle. But presumably the second part of their formulation is meant to help with this. If the *only* things that are good are good insofar as they "contribute" to my happiness, then, of course, if something does not contribute to my happiness then it is not good (for me). If, then, we think that it is constitutive of rationality that I do what is good (when I recognize it and am able), then the principle is going to amount to something much closer to Vlastos's idea that happiness is the ultimate goal *of all my rational acts* and so operate as a Comprehensive Practical Principle.[19] But this leaves open where, to put it in more contemporary terms, "the right" stands. While it may not be good (for me) to do a certain action, the rightness (or virtue) of that action may require it.

Bobonich's formulation differs somewhat. There we have an idea of happiness functioning as an end that trumps any other end I might have in action, which is how I argued Socrates treats virtue above.[20] For Bobonich, happiness is explicitly and overtly *practical*; it serves as a guide to action, and a decisive one at that. Since it is by reference to happiness that our actions are or are not the ones we ought to do, if we knew what happiness was, we could then determine what we should do: namely, whatever would lead to happiness. Given this description of eudaimonism, it is unsurprising that Bobonich holds what I labeled the "Eudaimonist Hope": we can determine the content of virtue by figuring out what genuinely benefits us (i.e., what our good is, i.e., what eudaimonia is); virtue consists in the actions and character-states that either lead us to or constitute our genuine benefit. As Bobonich says in the same essay: "A rational eudaimonist should also want to explore whether happiness can help *give content* to other important ethical (and political) ideas. As our analysis of virtue showed, happiness gives

---

[19] As we saw in Chapter 1, this is also how Annas and Irwin understand eudaimonia as a practical principle.
[20] There is also the idea of maximization, which I won't discuss further except to say it seems undesirable to build it into the definition of eudaimonism, given that there is only one place in all ancient ethics—the Hedonist Argument in the *Protagoras*—where there is some sort of hedonic calculus that suggests the idea of maximization. See §6 below.

content to the notion of virtue since my action is just if and only if it is best for me overall" (my italics).[21]

In Bobonich's formulation, we thus find an additional role for eudaimonia, beyond being the ultimate aim of all our actions: as something that can give content to our notion of virtue, conceived of as virtuous action. For Bobonich, it is part of eudaimonism to maintain that the content of virtue is determined by the content of eudaimonia. And so, having discovered what eudaimonia is, we can identify which action tokens and action types are the virtuous ones. Bobonich builds into the abstract structure of eudaimonism the rejection of the idea that virtue has its own nature, independently of eudaimonia. Presumably part of the power of such a eudaimonism is that it allows us to avoid the question that Socrates and his interlocutors find so difficult—"what *is* virtue?"—and replace it with the presumably more tractable question, "what is eudaimonia?" Once we have an answer to this, we have a way of determining (both metaphysically and epistemologically)[22] what virtue is. Thus too Bobonich's eudaimonism not only has eudaimonia play the role of providing the content of virtue (the Eudaimonist Hope) but thereby it also supplies the ground, justification, and motivation for our pursuit of virtue. Thus, assuming we have a solidly justified conception of eudaimonia, from which our conception of virtue or right action follows, we then have a firmly grounded notion of virtue as well. Once such a fullfledged eudaimonism is in place, it no longer makes sense to launch an investigation into what the moral or ethical or virtuous is, for that has no content that is independent of a conception of what the best life for a human being is.

Note too that providing content for ethical concepts is clearly stated as something that should apply presumably to any rational eudaimonist; it is not presented as a peculiarity of the Socratic position. The hope expressed here is that one could, for example, rule out an action as just if one determines that it is not best for one overall. Since the second sentence contains an "if and only if," Bobonich is leaving open the other direction as well: if I can determine that an act is unjust, then I would also know that it is not best

---

[21] Bobonich (2010), 328.
[22] Again, as in the previous chapter, all I intend here is to disambiguate the term "determine" between a metaphysical sense—what determines whether a liquid is water is whether it is H20—and the epistemological sense—I identify water as the liquid the comes out of the tap. One could use the essence of water to determine epistemologically (i.e., to identify) what liquid is water, but of course ordinarily one does not do that.

for me.[23] But the emphasis here, which is what I see as the essence of the Eudaimonist Hope, is that the notion of the best good, of happiness, will be the side of the biconditional that aids us in giving content to our notion of virtue. Since it is apparently so difficult to find out what virtue is—recall the failure of all of the dialogues of definition—we might make some headway by turning to the notion of the best and working from there.

We should note right off, however, that the Eudaimonist Hope sounds distinctly *un*Socratic and *un*Platonic. As we saw in outline in Chapter 1, what *makes* an action just (as opposed to what makes an action good for me) for Socrates and Plato does not have anything to do with the action's relationship to *me* but with something about the nature of the action *itself*, namely, whether it "has" (in the "early" or "Socratic" dialogues) or "participates in" (in the "middle" dialogues) the form of justice. I certainly do not deny that Socrates and Plato believe that one is benefitted by acting virtuously (and therefore by being virtuous), but that benefit is what Aristotle would call a "necessary coincident" of acting rightly; it is not what *makes* an action right.[24]

I shall argue that we look in vain in these dialogues for an account of benefit that can independently ground our account of virtue. For Socrates and Plato, knowing the answer to what truly benefits us turns out to be *just as problematic* as knowing what the virtuous action is.[25] Ultimately, this should cause us to question the charity and plausibility of thinking that Socrates shares the Eudaimonist Hope.

Before turning to the texts, it may be useful to summarize some primary points of difference between the eudaimonist readings of Socrates and my own:

1. Socrates does not aim at happiness (or "the beneficial") in action, either explicitly or as a limiting condition; rather, he aims at virtue, which is achieving knowledge and psychic health internally, and doing virtuous actions and refraining from actions contrary to virtue externally.

---

[23] But, as I say in what follows, it would run against the rationale of the Eudaimonist Hope to think that one could figure out what is unjust independently of what benefits one, since the latter is what provides the content of the former.
[24] See Chapter 1, §5.
[25] For additional argument, see Vasiliou (2008), ch. 3.

2. The positive benefit of virtuous action (its effect on the soul) is, as we have seen, a "necessary coincident" of acting rightly (i.e., virtuously; again, ch.1, §5).
3. One cannot define acting virtuously in terms of an independent concept of benefit. For Plato and Socrates what genuinely benefits us is as problematic as what virtue is.
4. Moreover, what makes an action just (as opposed to what makes it a good for me) does not have anything to do with the action's relationship to me, but with something about the nature of the action itself (and its relationship to forms, i.e., the essences of the virtues, whether we conceive of those metaphysically as transcendent or immanent).

Eudaimonism is attributed to Socrates often on the basis of passages in the *Euthydemus* and *Meno*, which I turn to first (Sections 4 and 5). The most significant discussion of happiness in the "early" dialogues, however, is arguably in the *Gorgias*, supplemented by a passage from the *Lysis* (219–220), which I consider in Sections 7 and 8. In between (Section 6), I examine the Hedonist Argument from the *Protagoras* as the exception that proves the rule. The *Euthydemus* and *Meno* are interesting and significant for what they say (and what they do not say) about the relationship between happiness and virtue. As we shall see, however, they say very little in a substantive way about what happiness consists in (beyond what we shall see is a generic formulation of it as consisting at least partly in having good things). To the extent that these dialogues address the issue of a practical principle at all, it should come as little surprise that Socrates appeals to virtue, as always, as the Superseding Practical Principle. What will be more surprising to the eudaimonist interpreter, however, is that Socrates seems to advocate for our commitment to the Supremacy of Virtue even in cases where virtue requires that we forgo the very goods in which we plausibly take happiness to consist.

4. *Euthydemus*

In 278e–282d, Socrates offers an example for his sophist interlocutors of the sort of protreptic argument he would like them to provide for the young Cleinias. The argument is explicitly aimed at how to persuade a boy that "one must devote oneself to both wisdom and virtue (χρὴ σοφίας τε καὶ ἀρετῆς ἐπιμεληθῆναι)" (278d1–2).²⁶ As mentioned, on most interpretations, Socrates's view is that there are not really two things here, wisdom *and* virtue; rather, it will turn out simply that wisdom *is* virtue. This has some truth to it, but I will argue that it is not the whole story, for it omits any concern with virtuous action.

Socrates first establishes the claim that he describes as ridiculously obvious: that all people wish to do well (εὖ πράττειν) (278e3–5). A second "even more simple-minded (ἔτι εὐηθέστερον)" statement is that people do well by possessing "many good things" (279a3), such as wealth, health, beauty, power, good birth, honor, moderation, justice, bravery, and good luck.²⁷ In fact this second claim is not so obvious after all: it is not merely the *having* of good things that makes us happy, since good things by themselves would be of no advantage to us if they were not also *used*. So, to be happy, a person must *have* and *use* good things (280e3). 280e–281e then argues that a *sine qua non* of these supposedly good things providing a benefit to the person—and so genuinely being goods—is that they are not merely used, but used "rightly" (ὀρθῶς). If they are used incorrectly, they will actually be harmful (and so bad) for the user. More accurately, then, all of the things that Cleinias called "goods" earlier in the argument are really neither good nor bad in themselves, but are good or bad depending on whether they are used "rightly." Of course, it is knowledge that enables one to use the so-called goods "rightly." So, the familiar conclusion is that wealth, health, and so on are not goods in themselves or by nature but they are rather, as scholars call them, "dependent goods"—dependent on wisdom for their goodness; by contrast, wisdom alone is the sole independent good.²⁸

---

[26] Russell (2005) says it is Plato's "declared aim in the *Euthydemus* to investigate what happiness really consists in" (37), but that is not true. Regardless of what Plato's aim (as author) may or may not be, this is not even Socrates's aim. His declared aim makes no explicit mention of happiness, but instead to provide an example of protreptic to convince young Cleinias to care about virtue and wisdom. An exaggerated and aporia-inducing claim such as wisdom *is* good luck would certainly provoke such interest. See next note.

[27] A notorious argument follows in 279d–280b in which Socrates argues that wisdom *is* good fortune, so that if one is wise, they have no need of good luck. I think there are obvious textual clues that Socrates is not serious about this argument (e.g., Socrates admits that the conclusion that a wise man needs no good luck is reached "finally—I don't quite know how" [280b1]), but I shall discuss that here. This argument is central to Russell (2005), 30–31, 36–37, 42. He hinges his "directive conception" of happiness, wherein it is the exercise of wise rational agency as such that is happiness, on the claim that wisdom is good luck is clearly Plato's view, which the "additive conception" of happiness cannot take seriously, "even if we find that it stands in need of further articulation and defense" (37).

[28] A "Moderate View" holds that the ordinary so-called goods, such as health, wealth, beauty, and even courage and temperance are in fact goods when they are conjoined with wisdom, while wisdom is the only good all by itself. An "Extreme View" by contrast holds that that the "Dependent goods" are not goods at all; the one and only good thing is wisdom; the only good is wise use of other things,

Commentators then connect (and argue about) what follows from The Dependency Thesis about the relationship between virtue (conceived of as wisdom) and happiness.[29] Most scholars hold that Socrates argues that wisdom is necessary and sufficient for happiness; Russell Jones argues, by contrast, that Socrates maintains that wisdom is only necessary, but not sufficient, for happiness.[30] While I agree with Jones on this point, my primary focus lies in a different place. The argument claims that knowledge brings about right use. Socrates motivates this idea with typical examples from the *technai*; for example, knowledge of carpentry brings about correct use with wood (281a1–4). He then goes on to extrapolate to the cases of using "wealth, health, and beauty" rightly; knowledge would again lead to correct "action" (281a6–b1). But what is the "right use" of, say, a chainsaw? Clearly it is not merely knowing *how* to operate a chainsaw, but it would involve cutting the right things at the right times in the right way. In some extreme circumstances, perhaps it would be "right use" of a chainsaw to use it as a weapon.

In one way, the eudaimonist appears to have a clear answer to what right use is: using something rightly is to use it in a way that truly benefits me (i.e., that contributes as a means to my happiness or else is a component of it).[31] Of course this answer has substantive content only insofar as we have an independent account of what happiness is (I'll come back to this later in the chapter). But let's set the Eudaimonist Hope aside for a moment, and recall a frequent sense of virtue for Socrates, which is at work in these passages, but which is generally neglected by eudaimonist interpreters: virtuous action. When Socrates talks of using health, wealth, and beauty "rightly" or well, he clearly means using them justly and virtuously. Ignoring for the moment whether wisdom (i.e., virtue) is necessary or sufficient for happiness (an issue that Socrates does not actually explicitly address in this dialogue), the more central Socratic claim, and the one that is more obviously established in the argument under consideration, is that virtuous *action* will require one

---

which are not good themselves and do not thereby become good. This distinction is not important for my discussion.

[29] Bobonich (2010), 324–326; Price (2011), 12–16. See too Jones (2013), 1: "The sufficiency thesis explains why Socrates is so interested in wisdom (which is the same as being interested in virtue, according to Socrates)."
[30] Jones (2013).
[31] See Bobonich (2010), 328 (cf. 330): "As our analysis of virtue showed, happiness gives content to the notion of virtue since my action is just if and only if it is best for me overall."

to *have* virtue in the sense of possessing wisdom; for wisdom about what the virtuous thing to do is is necessary for non-accidentally correctly identifying the proper action. To use my wealth "correctly" is to use it in the right way at the right time toward the right objects, and so I need to know what the right time, the right objects, and the right way is. Moreover, this point is entirely apposite to the protreptic aim of the argument: it supplies Cleinias with an argument for why he ought to pursue wisdom and virtue.

We cannot make good sense of the argument, however, if we focus only on the idea of what it is to *be* virtuous (i.e., to possess wisdom). The wisdom or knowledge has to be *about* something (cf. *Charmides* and many other Socratic dialogues). If using something "rightly" is using it "wisely," then we want to know what it is to use it "wisely"; we need to know what the wisdom is *about*. I think, in common with eudaimonist interpreters, that Socrates holds that acting virtuously is, in fact, always in the agent's interest.[32] But Socrates never deliberates (in the *Apology*, *Crito*, *Euthyphro*, etc.), nor does he recommend deliberating, by considering what benefits us—as though that were a simple matter of fact we could then use to determine what constitutes "right" action. There is no textual evidence that Socrates shares the Eudaimonist Hope. The *Euthydemus* argues only that *if* x is used wrongly, then x harms the user; *if* x is used rightly, then x benefits the user. There is no claim, however, that *what it is to use something rightly* is to use it in order to benefit oneself. The claim is instead that using x rightly will make x a benefit for you. The former makes it sound as though the problem that is being solved is "what benefits me?" and then whatever that is will be "right use." (This is how the eudaimonist argues.) I am arguing that the latter, though, is the properly Socratic position: "using something rightly" *is* "using it virtuously." So, what we need to figure out, as Socrates explicitly stresses in so many places, is how to use x—our wealth, health, strength, or whatever—*virtuously*. Then, using it virtuously, which will be an objective matter concerning what ought to be done with my, say, wealth, I will be benefitted because at the end of the day I ought to commit to doing the virtuous thing above all (i.e., to SV as a Superseding Practical Principle).[33]

---

[32] Morrison (2003) denies that Socrates is an egoist. So does Ahbel-Rappe (2010); she does not cite Morrison, though she appeals to overlapping passages.

[33] The self-interested reasons for being thusly committed are offstage in the *Euthydemus* and *Meno*, but, as we shall see in this chapter and the next, they are explicit in the *Crito*, *Gorgias*, and *Republic* in terms of the effects of just actions on the well-being of our souls. Recall the general point from Chapter 1, §5.

A passage near the end of the first protreptic provides a summary that dovetails smoothly with this interpretation:

> Since we all desire to be happy (ἐπειδὴ εὐδαίμονες μὲν εἶναι προθυμούμεθα πάντες), and since we appear to become such from using things and using them rightly (ὀρθῶς), and knowledge (ἐπιστήμη) is what furnishes rightness (ὀρθότητα) and good fortune, it is necessary indeed, as it seems, that every man in every way prepare himself for this: to be as wise as possible. Or not?—Yes, he said.
>
> And surely it is necessary for one who thinks this to get [wisdom] much more than money from his father, and from his guardians and his friends and others and from those who claim [to be his] lover, either foreigners or citizens, begging and beseeching [them] to hand over wisdom, it being neither shameful nor fit for indignation to serve and to be a slave to either a lover or any man for the sake of this, **being willing to provide any of the noble services whatsoever in desiring to become wise** (ὁτιοῦν ἐθέλοντα ὑπηρετεῖν τῶν καλῶν ὑπηρετημάτων, προθυμούμενον σοφὸν γενέσθαι). (282a1–c1)

Here it is clear that happiness is not, as expressed in the formulations of eudaimonism by Bobonich and Brickhouse and Smith above, "the decisive consideration for all one's actions," nor would it be the case that "anything that is good is good only insofar as it contributes to this goal [i.e., happiness]." For although wisdom or knowledge is necessary for happiness, a person should only do anything *fine/noble* (*kalon*) to get it. This implies that doing virtuous actions trumps (or constrains) the pursuit of happiness: one should forgo the knowledge that is necessary for happiness, and so forgo happiness, which everyone desires, if the only way to get it is by acting ignobly (*ou kalōs*); thus, it is false that Socrates here holds that eudaimonia is either a Superseding (or "decisive") Practical Principle of our actions or a Comprehensive one.[34] In itself this view is nothing surprising: just another statement of the Supremacy of Virtue, which I have argued is Socrates's Superseding Practical Principle throughout the dialogues. Further, even

---

[34] A deflationary reading might interpret "noble services" as simply taking a conventional line with respect to erotic practice, but the philosophical point still holds; Socrates is not one to be squeamish, following the argument where it leads (recall the example of the insatiable catamite in the *Gorgias*). It is clear that if you abandon what is the "highest good" for the sake of something else (and incontinence is not at issue) then what is purportedly the "highest good" must not be "highest" after all.

if Socrates agrees that what eudaimonia is (or at least what it requires) is obtaining wisdom *virtuously*, he must not share the Eudaimonist Hope, for we do not have the requisite independence between the notion of acting virtuously and acting beneficially. Virtue has an objective content, which one needs to know in order to use things "correctly" and which cannot be reduced to what harms or benefits us in the ordinary sense. By "in the ordinary sense" I mean what procures for us the standard list of external goods, what are here described as "dependent goods," such as health, wealth, and beauty. We shall see a similar point made in the *Meno*.

My interpretation better fits Socrates's second engagement with Cleinias as well. There Socrates asks: "Well, what sort of knowledge would we acquire if we went about it rightly (ὀρθῶς)? Isn't the answer simply this, that it would be the one which would benefit us?" (288d9–e2). Importantly, it is not knowledge of *what* would benefit us—that is not the *object* of the knowledge. Rather, the knowledge would be knowledge of something *else*, and *that* knowledge would itself be beneficial to us. Thus, in the example that follows Socrates humorously asks whether the knowledge might be knowledge of where gold is buried (or of how to turn stones into gold). This supports my way of reading the argument: knowledge is *of* where gold is buried, and the facetious suggestion is that *that* knowledge would clearly benefit us (by making us rich). But it is not, as on a eudaimonist reading, a matter of knowing *that* gold benefits us and thus concluding that we should obtain it in order to be happy. Of course, the eventual investigation of the *basilikē technē* ends in failure, because they cannot say what the knowledge that they are seeking is *of*, even though they think that such knowledge would "provide and produce happiness (ἡ εὐδαιμονίαν παρέχουσά τε καὶ ἀπεργαζομένη)" (291b6–7). But here, again, note that the sought-after knowledge would "provide and produce happiness," but it is not knowledge *of* happiness. So, we find here the familiar claim from Chapter 1 that a virtuous person is better off, that is, happier, in virtue of their virtuous actions and, as I argued there, this may, for a good young person like Cleinias, supply him with some motivation to seek out what virtue is after all.

5. *Meno*

Now let's turn to what I claim is a similar argument in the *Meno* (78c3–79a2). Socrates and Meno agree that no one wants to be miserable and unhappy

(78a4–5); everyone wants to be happy. As in the *Euthydemus*, the next premise is that one becomes happy by acquiring (genuinely) good things. So, one person is "better" than another by being better at obtaining the good things, which everyone desires. Thus, virtue is tentatively defined as the ability to procure good things: for example, health, wealth, gold, silver, civic honors, and positions of power (78b9–d1). (The *Euthydemus*' concern about *using* good things only arises later in the *Meno*.) Socrates then asks Meno whether he thinks it important that these goods be acquired justly and piously or whether it doesn't matter *how* they are acquired. Meno agrees that one is virtuous only if these things are acquired justly. Commentators then mostly focus on how this derails Meno's definition, since he ends up employing the *definiendum* in the *definiens*.

Consider instead, however, what this says about Socrates's alleged eudaimonism. Why would *how* one secures goods have anything to do with whether one is happy? If happiness is simply having good things, why is there the *ad hoc* addition that one must acquire them justly, and so on? Socrates is drawing out Meno's (unsurprising) commitment to virtue as an end that supersedes any other in acting; Meno is not going to agree that one ought sometimes to act contrary to justice. So, regardless of how this argument counts against Meno's definition of virtue, we should notice that what is being agreed to is, if anything, apparently in tension with eudaimonism. According to this argument, one should indeed *forgo* good things, and so the happiness that allegedly comes with their possession, if they can only be acquired unjustly (contrary to virtue). Just/virtuous action supersedes what would, prima facie, make one happy. So, this parallels the point at the end of the first protreptic in the *Euthydemus*, when Socrates says Cleinias should do whatever *fine* things are necessary for him to procure wisdom, again cutting against the idea that happiness, the highest good, must be the decisive consideration in action, conceived of independently of virtue.

The second argument from the *Meno* (87d–89a) raises issues similar to those in the *Euthydemus*. Again, we have the question of what the knowledge of "right use" is and how it works to benefit the agent. What is it to *use* one's strength or wealth "correctly"? To perform right actions, where that means virtuous actions. Meno, even more so than Cleinias in the *Euthydemus*, is happy to agree that virtue is beneficial—that it is good for the one who possesses it.[35] We understand that with wisdom things such as wealth,

---

[35] After all, Meno has given speeches on virtue "thousands of times" (80b).

strength, and so on become goods for us. So, we want to become wise; but what sort of wisdom will we acquire? It cannot be the knowledge that wealth is good, since by itself it is not; it must once again be the knowledge of how to use wealth correctly. And correct use for Socrates is clearly *virtuous* use. Socrates concludes that virtue "in the soul" (88e5–6) is, in whole or part, wisdom (89a3–4).

But if we step outside of this argument, we will see that the *Meno* too is concerned with *virtuous action* and not merely with virtue as a state of soul. This comes up after the discussion of the lack of teachers of virtue. Socrates says something surprising for those who think he simply equates virtue with wisdom: "For it is ridiculous that it escaped our notice that it is not only under the guidance of knowledge that things are done well and correctly by people (ὡς ἡμᾶς ἔλαθεν καταγελάστως ὅτι οὐ μόνον ἐπιστήμης ἡγουμένης ὀρθῶς τε καὶ εὖ τοῖς ἀνθρώποις πράττεται τὰ πράγματα)" (96e3–4).

Socrates adds that perhaps this is the reason that he and Meno did not understand how good men come to be. He then says something troubling for the eudaimonist. The good person must be beneficent, but Socrates makes clear that the good person's beneficence will not merely be self-directed but a matter of "whether they guide *us* rightly in affairs (ἂν ὀρθῶς ἡμῖν ἡγῶνται τῶν πραγμάτων)" (97a3–4). As in the second exchange with Cleinias in the *Euthydemus*, which culminates in a failed search for the *basilikē technē*, Socrates is pointing toward political leaders who are going to lead others "correctly." Now of course this is not incompatible with eudaimonism (leading others correctly may, in some way, benefit oneself), but for present purposes the point is that leading others correctly will be a matter of directing others toward virtuous actions.[36] So, even though knowledge is a better state of soul, both it and true opinion (*doxa*) are sufficient to correctly identify what needs to be done. The wisdom or true opinion is *about what the virtuous action is*, because it is this that governs using the dependent goods correctly, so that

---

[36] It turns out, of course, that true opinion as well as knowledge can guide correctly, and that this passage is focusing on the epistemological point. While Socrates (or Plato) thinks much less of true opinion than knowledge, the possibility that true opinion can "guide correctly" brings out the idea that true opinion can be sufficient for doing the virtuous action. Vasiliou (2008), chs. 7 and 8, argues that true opinion plays a key role in the *Republic*. The citizens of the lower classes have true *doxai* instilled by the philosopher-rulers, who, of course, have genuine knowledge, about what they should do and how the Kallipolis ought to be. Thus, the lower classes in the *Republic* are in fact guided "rightly," as the *Meno* here claims would be the result of a good person's beneficence.

they may in fact benefit one. It is not wisdom about what eudaimonia or the good is.[37]

So far, then, in these arguments Socrates explicitly endorses the idea that without being virtuous (i.e., possessing wisdom) one cannot be sure to use other putative goods "rightly" (i.e., virtuously), which is necessary for their actually being beneficial to us. We only generate and maintain excellent souls (characters) insofar as we engage in genuinely excellent actions and avoid actions contrary to virtue, as, I have emphasized, we learn in the *Crito*, *Gorgias*, and *Republic*. Socrates clearly seems to think that being virtuous and acting virtuously is a necessary component of the happy life. As far as practical principles go, Socrates adheres in the *Euthydemus* and *Meno*, as he does everywhere, to the Superseding Practical Principle, Supremacy of Virtue. There is no hint that he thinks of eudaimonia as supplying us with a new or different practical principle, such as a Comprehensive Practical Principle, of the sort endorsed in the scholarly descriptions of eudaimonism we have seen previously in this chapter and in Chapter 1.

6. The *Protagoras*'s Hedonist Argument: The Exception that Proves the Rule

The "Hedonist Argument" in the *Protagoras* (351b3–358c)[38] ought to be notorious for more than its apparently anomalous endorsement of hedonism.[39] Others have recognized that the idea of maximizing pleasure via some sort of calculation occurs only here in all of Greek ethics.[40] My focus is on the nature of the eudaimonism that is in play. Nowhere else in Plato do we have an explicit statement (whether *ad hominem* or not) of what the good life consists in combined with an examination of how that conception affects

---

[37] I take it that these arguments in the *Meno* and *Euthydemus* are in part also expansions of Socrates's idea in the *Apology*, *Crito*, *Laches*, *Charmides*, and many other places that one ought to listen not to the majority but to the one who knows. Why do you listen to the one who knows? Because she gets what is to be done *right*.

[38] It can be difficult to say where the argument ends, since this would be determined in part by what claims one believes are covered by the argument. Does it just include the relationship between hedonism and the Denial of Akrasia or does it also include positive ideas about the source of the "salvation of our lives"?

[39] See the long-running debate about whether Socrates (or Plato) is endorsing the hedonism presented in the argument or whether Socrates adopts it merely *ad hominem*: See Zeyl (1980), Taylor (1991) Rudebusch (1999), Russell (2005), Denyer (2008), Price (2011), 253–269, and Shaw (2015).

[40] See, e.g., Nussbaum (1986), ch. 4, and Annas (1993).

our understanding of action and the content of virtue. A remarkable feature of this argument is that for the only time in Plato (or Aristotle or the Stoics), we are presented with an account of eudaimonia that does not, in some way or other, essentially involve virtue and acting virtuously.[41]

Socrates abruptly interrupts his argument with Protagoras about whether courage and wisdom are the same and asks, in a seeming non-sequitur,[42] whether Protagoras believes that "some human beings live well (εὖ ζῆν) and others badly (κακῶς)" (351b3–4). As we have seen, Socrates asks the same question in the *Euthydemus* (278e3–6) and *Meno* (78a4–5).[43] While in those dialogues Socrates then discussed the role of the possession (and, later, the proper use) of goods for living well and happily,[44] here in the *Protagoras* he immediately queries the role of pleasure and pain. Protagoras agrees that someone who is living in distress and physical pain would not be living well, but someone who lived out his life pleasantly would seem to have lived well (351b4–7). Socrates then tries to secure agreement immediately to the idea that therefore living pleasantly is good and living unpleasantly bad, but Protagoras balks, adding that a qualification is needed: assuming one takes pleasure "in noble things (τοῖς καλοῖς)" (351c1).

This is a familiar moment in the dialogues: driving a wedge between the noble or the virtuous, on the one hand, and what is pleasant or what seems to yield happiness, on the other. Meno agrees with Socrates that being excellent (and so becoming happy) is a matter of "securing good things," when Socrates follows up by asking whether a person ought to secure those things justly and not unjustly. When Meno assents, he agrees that virtue should act as a limiting condition on his actions. Here Protagoras similarly suggests that the *kalon* ought to act as a control on which pleasures are to be pursued and, presumably, to what extent. Without this, Protagoras, like Callicles in the *Gorgias* (494b–495), could be driven to concede that shameful actions,

---

[41] A caveat, which will be examined in Chapters 3 and 5, is that both Plato and Aristotle explore, and to differing extents and in differing contexts endorse, conceptions of the good life, which we might call "intellectualist." The good life conceived of as theoretical contemplation, however, is still one where virtue is essentially involved, except that it is not ethical virtue, but intellectual virtue that is deemed most excellent. Of course, the Epicureans, considered in Chapter 6, have the closest similarity insofar as they adopt hedonism, although of a critically different type.

[42] The rationale for the sudden topic switch is revealed later when, with the conclusions of the Hedonist Argument in hand, Socrates returns to the question of the relationship between courage and wisdom (359a, cf. 353b).

[43] Indeed, the character of Socrates in the *Protagoras* and *Euthydemus* seems rather similar, although I cannot argue that here; perhaps it is the engagement with sophists that brings out Socrates's particularly wily and prickly side.

[44] As also at *Symposium* 204e–205a, discussed in Chapter 3.

like that of the catamite, are nevertheless good insofar as they are pleasant. But Socrates here affects surprise that Protagoras would go along with this view, which, he says, is shared by the many. Most people, then and now, do not think one should pursue pleasure (or avoid pain) past what is right or noble into what is wrong or shameful (or at least they would, then and now, be embarrassed to admit this), such as taking pleasure at another's expense by betraying them or causing them pain. Socrates often uses this implicit commitment to the Supremacy of Virtue by interlocutors such as Crito, Euthyphro, Gorgias, Meno, and others to motivate the urgency of inquiry into what virtue is;[45] but he does not do so in the *Protagoras*, which, as we shall see, plays with its own avoidance of the infamous "what is F?" question. Instead, Socrates will repeatedly challenge the many, and implicitly Protagoras, to provide some—*any*—other criterion for good and bad besides pleasure and pain (353c–355b). When they fail to do so (or when he and Protagoras fail to do so on their behalf), he proceeds to treat them as committed to hedonism.

Socrates briefly attempts to qualify what he means: pleasant things are those that are themselves pleasant or that generate pleasure (351d7–e1). Given that, Socrates asks, are pleasant things, insofar as they are pleasant, to that extent good? Protagoras suspends judgment on this, claiming that they should examine it further. The complex order of the subsequent argument is confusing and, I think, has distracted scholars from what is going on. Once Protagoras says that he wishes to investigate whether the hedonism Socrates has presented is correct, Socrates asks Protagoras whether Protagoras also agrees with the many about knowledge (just as Socrates has accused him of agreeing with the many that pleasure is good, only insofar as one takes pleasure in "noble" things). Here Socrates presents his Denial of Akrasia (352b–e): knowledge is sufficient for right action and, when it is present in someone, rules them; it is not the case, as the many believe, that knowledge is "dragged around like a slave" by pleasure, pain, lust, fear, and so on, as is claimed in putative cases of incontinence.[46] Protagoras, perhaps disingenuously,[47] agrees with Socrates about this against the many who believe in incontinence.

---

[45] See Vasiliou (2008), ch. 4.
[46] As noted by Denyer (2008), 183, the word *akrasia* and its cognates do not occur in *Protagoras*.
[47] See Shaw (2015), 126.

Socrates then, via apparent cases of incontinence, directly returns to the question of hedonism, arguing in sum that anytime one calls a pleasant thing bad or painful thing good, one is not talking about it qua pleasant or qua painful, but, in a kind of shorthand, instead referring to its supposedly pleasant or painful consequences. So, he would suggest that no one calls cigarette smoking bad because of the pleasure it gives someone who likes to smoke, but because of the pain from ill effects of cigarette smoking later on. Essentially, Socrates repeatedly challenges "the many" (and, therefore, Protagoras and all the others present) to provide some reason for calling a thing good or bad other than its being pleasant or painful or its leading to pleasure or pain. In fact, he asks them at least five times whether they can come up with *any* other criterion for a thing's being good or bad.[48] Before the fifth and final offer, Socrates supposes that the many would be getting impatient with his continual harping on the same point and imagines replying to them (in an awkwardly literal translation):

> Pardon me, I would say. First it is not easy to show what in the world you all call "being defeated by pleasures"; next, all of the demonstrations are in this [i.e., depend on this point about pleasure being the good]. But still, even now, it is possible to retract [your position] if you in some way are able to say that the good is something other than pleasure or that the bad is something other than pain; or is living out your life pleasantly without pains enough for you (ἀρκεῖ ὑμῖν)? If it is enough and you are not able to state anything else as good or bad that does end in these things [pleasure or pain], listen to what [comes] after this. (354e8–355a5)

Five times in a little over one Stephanus page, then, Socrates virtually begs anyone to come up with some candidate for a thing's being good or bad other than pleasure or pain; but none of the sophists present (and certainly not his poor benighted beloved, Alcibiades) can.[49] To anyone who has read other dialogues, this is quite striking. Surely one might have suggested that it is

---

[48] 353e6–354a1, 354b5–c2, 354d1–3, 354d7–e2, and 354e8–355a5.
[49] Moss (2014) reads this differently, understanding the repeated querying of the claim that pleasure is the good as a sign of Socrates's seriousness about it and a somewhat unique scrupulousness on his part to avoid foisting a thesis on "the many" that they do not hold. My interpretation focuses more on what this repetition is supposed to indicate to the reader/hearer of the dialogue: namely, to think of an alternative conception of the good. I entirely agree with Moss, 290, however, on the conditional nature of the argument and its complete dependence on hedonism. See too Kamtekar (2017).

bad or wrong to betray someone or to run away in battle, one might think, because it is unjust or cowardly, regardless of the pleasure or pain incurred. In that case, as in many dialogues, this would immediately trigger an investigation into what virtue *is* after all and how it would benefit us independently of whether it generated pleasure or pain; of course, the *Republic* takes up just this question for justice or, as we might say, morality. Further, at the end of the *Protagoras*, Socrates says precisely this when he expresses his dissatisfaction with what they have all achieved (again, translating literally): "Seeing clearly that all these things are terribly scattered topsy turvy, I am eager to make everything clear and I would like us, having gone through these things, to go through also in regard to virtue, *what it is*, and then again to take up about it whether it is teachable or not teachable" (361c2–6).

Among other reasons, this is a remarkable passage because it calls attention to what has been done in the dialogue. As we shall see, they *have* in fact said what virtue is: virtue (as a state of a person) is knowledge of the measurement of pleasures and pains, and a virtuous action is the action that maximizes pleasure (the good), which the virtuous person would be able, because of her knowledge/wisdom, to identify correctly. At the end of the dialogue Socrates undermines their conclusions: hedonism, and the account of virtue it supplied, leaves everything upside down. The superficial reason for this is that Socrates and Protagoras have appeared to switch positions without meaning to (which is taken as evidence of their confusion). But another reason the argument might be thought unsatisfactory—an explanation that fits with "Socrates" in other dialogues—is that the Hedonist Argument's assumption of hedonism makes it seem to be the case that "the good" and "the beneficial" can be characterized *independently of the content of virtue*. Of course, this is what makes the Hedonist Argument perfect for someone who holds the Eudaimonist Hope: having defined the good *independently* of any conception of moral virtue, virtue, now hollowed out of content, can be defined as *whatever* state leads to the good: in this case, knowledge of measurement of pleasures and pains.

While it is true and recognized that this is the first (and only) example of a hedonic calculus in Greek ethics, what is more important for our purposes is that it clearly displays how the Eudaimonist Hope might work and overwhelmingly rejects it. Since eudaimonia is essentially tied up with moral virtue, it cannot provide an independent account of harm and benefit, bad and good, which could *then* supply content for our notion of virtue—just as we saw the attempt fail in the *Euthydemus* and *Meno*.

While altogether this is, I think, strong evidence that Socrates is arguing merely *ad hominem* in his presentation of hedonism, what is more important here is to see the limited and particular effect that this advocacy of hedonism has on the conclusion and the nature of the eudaimonism that is presented.[50] As Socrates says above, *the whole argument* relies on adopting hedonism. And, as I have emphasized, there has been no positive argument for its truth other than repeatedly asking "the many" whether they could come up with any additional reason for a calling a thing good or bad independently of its pleasure or pain (or its pleasurable or painful effects). We must remember that there has been *no argument* to show that Protagoras was wrong to maintain that what is *kalon* and what is pleasurable may come apart. Socrates has just challenged any of them to come up with a simple counterexample: stealing someone's sandwich with impunity may be pleasant and not painful, but it is still a wrong and bad action. Why? Because it is unjust. But what is injustice and why is it bad, if it isn't itself painful or doesn't result in pain? We must turn to the *Republic* for a reply. Here in the *Protagoras*, the usual Socratic and Platonic dialectical connections are interrupted, and Socrates trades on the many's (and the sophists') inability to defend a notion of good and bad that is independent of pleasure and pain.

We are now in a position to appreciate that within the confines of the Hedonist Argument we are on radically new ground: first, with respect to *akrasia*, as Socrates immediately moves to show, but even more profoundly with respect to the nature of virtue and its relationship to happiness. First, as I have argued previously,[51] nothing in the argument shows that incontinence, as a phenomenon, is impossible, except insofar as psychological hedonism is true.[52] Socrates's Denial of Akrasia, as argued for here, depends on stereotypical examples of incontinence as examples of knowledge "being defeated by pleasure"—indeed, this is the way he describes the phenomenon repeatedly. "Being overcome by pleasure" can mean either: (1) being overcome by a *greater* pleasure, in which case one is doing what one ought to do, since

---

[50] Of course, the "what is F?" question concerning virtue has not been discussed at all in the dialogue. In violation of his "priority of definition," Socrates immediately discussed whether virtue was teachable, and then moved on to whether all the virtues were one, without ever trying to say what virtue itself is. But matters are even a bit more complicated, for, as I say above, Socrates *has* answered what virtue is within the confines of the Hedonist Argument. But this final comment betrays the idea that it has entirely missed the genuine nature of virtue. See below.

[51] Vasiliou (2008), 163–165.

[52] See Kamtekar (2017), who argues that it is only in the context of the Hedonist Argument, where Plato argues for psychological eudaimonism, based on ethical hedonism; otherwise, the centerpiece of Plato's moral psychology is the natural desire for the good.

things are good insofar as they are pleasant and so *a fortiori* no akrasia is involved; or (2) being overcome by a *smaller* pleasure, which means one has made a mistake, which, at a minimum, is irrational: why would one choose a smaller over a larger pleasure, since, *ex hypothesi*, the smaller cannot be better in any other way? Without psychological hedonism, however, there is no reason to think that I might not be irrationally moved by, say, pity, to forgo a greater pleasure; and so, it would be a type of incontinence involving a failure to stick by what maximized one's own pleasure.[53] Regardless, in context, wrong or bad action (i.e., action that is more painful or results in more pain) must be worse and so irrational; only someone who is ignorant about which action was the most pleasurable would voluntarily do such a thing. "If our doing well (τὸ εὖ πράττειν) depended on this— namely on acting on and achieving large quantities, while avoiding and not acting on small quantities—what would seem to us the salvation of life (σωτηρία ... τοῦ βίου)? (356c8–d3).

Socrates concludes, then, that "the salvation of our life" consists in an art of measurement (ἡ μετρητικὴ τέχνη) rather than the power of appearance (ἡ τοῦ φαινομένου δύναμις) (356d4). Given that hedonism is true, what we are measuring, upon which the happiness of our lives depends, is obviously pleasures and pains. So, knowledge of the measurement of pleasures and pains becomes sufficient for right action (357a–b).[54]

This is a significant achievement: we have ended up with the knowledge about what right action is, what virtue is, which eludes Socrates and his interlocutors in so many other dialogues. The wisdom that would provide knowledge of "right use," sought after in the *Euthydemus* and *Meno*, would be the *technē* of measurement of pleasure and pains. Virtue, on this account, is the wisdom that is the *technē*, while the virtuous action —that is, the right action, the action that ought to be done, which is the same as the right use of, say, my wealth and other dependent goods—is the use that maximizes

---

[53] This possibility is also near the surface in the rejection of hedonism in the *Gorgias*; see Vasiliou (2008), ch. 3.

[54] Again, not necessarily psychologically sufficient, but rationally, unless psychological hedonism is true—and there has been no argument for that. The further assumption that a person who knew what was most pleasurable would do it is taken for granted because of the obvious motivational power of pleasure; indeed, the inability of anyone present to offer another reason to call something good or bad other than by reference to its being pleasant or painful suggests that they may implicitly adopt psychological hedonism as well. We might also note here, however, that *even if* psychological hedonism were true, that does imply that a human being *could not* act for some reason other than pleasure; it only says that human beings, as a matter of fact, do not. Here is where I part company with Kamtekar (2017), since I doubt that psychological eudaimonism is being argued for; see further Vasiliou (2021).

my pleasure. We now have an answer to what virtue is; the outstanding determining question that Socrates seeks to answer in the "dialogues of definition." Since the Hedonist Argument provides an independent account of the good, it is clear what the sought-after wisdom is *about*, namely, what is most pleasurable, which is precisely what we never discover in the *Euthydemus* or *Meno* at parallel points in the argument.

Most importantly we should appreciate, however, that the wisdom that Socrates has allegedly discovered here is *not* wisdom or knowledge *that hedonism is true*; rather, it is that the knowledge of the measurement of pleasures of pains, *on the assumption that hedonism is true*, will be of the utmost benefit to human beings.[55] By being wise one can be sure to do what most benefits one, but one does *that* (according to this argument) by measuring pleasures and pains; the *technē* of measurement tells us what the virtuous action is. The Hedonist Argument thus offers a neat example of what the wisdom that is virtue would be like *if* we had a distinct conception of the good; a conception of the good that does not essentially involve "doing the virtuous thing."[56]

But this apparent argumentative success comes at significant cost. Virtue, what is right, is what maximizes the good, which is pleasure. Ordinary virtue, the virtue that Socrates investigates in so many dialogues and that he argues in the *Apology* he has always tried to act in accordance with by, for example, not agreeing to try the generals at the battle of Arginusae as a group or not helping to bring in Leon (32a–d), has been replaced by a formal, contentless notion of virtue as excellence, which is then filled in by the independently established content of the good. Thus, the Hedonist Argument realizes the Eudaimonist Hope perfectly. In order therefore to act rightly and virtuously one must know how to measure pleasures and pains; acting wrongly is to measure pleasure and pain incorrectly. This is far from the notion of wrongdoing prominent throughout the dialogues, where doing wrong, acting unjustly, is vividly described, for example, in *Republic* 2 and explicitly associated with what are taken to be pleasant actions. Indeed the point of the argument of *Republic* 2 is to look at the

---

[55] And so, as we have seen, the *technē* of the measurement of pleasures and pains would be "the salvation of our lives (ἡμῖν ἡ σωτηρία τοῦ βίου)" (357b6–7; cf. also 356d3, 356e2, 356e5–6, 356e8–357a1).

[56] This parallels the gold example from the *Euthydemus*: it is knowledge of where gold is that will be of the greatest benefit to me, *on the assumption that* possessing gold is of the greatest benefit to me.

effect of just actions on the soul, independently of just such pleasant or painful consequences, stretching so far as to remove even rewards or punishment in the afterlife.[57]

But if Socrates does not adopt hedonism,[58] then we are back to the Supremacy of Virtue as his Superseding Practical Principle and left without any clear sense of how to determine what the virtuous action is. The critical point here is that figuring out what to do—and the wisdom that would enable us to do that knowledgeably—is *not* knowledge of how acting virtuously benefits us; it is knowledge of what the virtuous action *is*. A major problem with interpretations of eudaimonism that involve the Eudaimonist Hope for understanding Socratic ethics is that it makes it appear as though Socrates thinks that that question may be sidestepped. Instead of needing to figure out (wisely) which action is virtuous and which is not, we can look wisely at what benefits us and what the good for us is and use *that* as a criterion for right action. This may be fine in theory, but for this approach to have some substance one must assume that it is clear (or at a minimum, clearer) what genuinely benefits us, but I have argued that, at least in the *Euthydemus* and *Meno*, what genuinely benefits us is just as problematic as what virtue is.[59] While we do get an answer in the *Protagoras*, it is a highly questionable one and at odds with all of Socrates's, Plato's, and Aristotle's subsequent treatment of the issue. But it is valuable nevertheless as a foil that shows us what it would be to fulfill the Eudaimonist Hope, where the problematic notion of virtue can be given content by the more straightforward account of the good.

---

[57] See Vasiliou (2008), ch. 6, for a detailed defense of this interpretation.

[58] And I do not think he does, not even in the *Protagoras*; Moss (2014) holds that he does not accept hedonism as the many understand it, namely on an ordinary view of what pleasure is (namely, some sort of positive bodily feeling), but that he does accept what she calls "Socratic Hedonism," which involves a different, Socratic understanding of pleasure as identical to what the many understand as good/fine (e.g., standing firm in battle or exercise).

[59] Recall the Bobonich quote earlier, 328: "A rational eudaimonist should also want to explore whether happiness can help *give content* to other important ethical (and political) ideas. As our analysis of virtue showed, happiness gives content to the notion of virtue since my action is just if and only if it is best for me overall" (my italics). This idea is what I have labeled "The Eudaimonist Hope." In fact, however, Bobonich himself concedes two pages later in the same article that the Eudaimonist Hope is in fact dashed in the case of Socrates (330): "I shall close by noting what I think are perhaps *the two most serious gaps in Socrates's views* that mark issues to which Plato and the rest of Greek Ethics were sensitive." There is no detailed account of what is good for human beings. Socrates's account of human nature (i.e., psychological eudaimonism) is "not sufficiently detailed to provide a substantive account of the human good. *Moreover, without such a substantive account, it is quite difficult to see why (as Socrates clearly expects) a person seeking happiness would follow, at least in large part, ordinary judgments about what is and is not virtuous*" (my italics).

7. *Lysis*

The argument at *Lysis* 219–220 is disproportionately cited as evidence for Socrates's eudaimonism.[60] In fact it establishes one point that is, for example in the *Symposium* and in Aristotle's *Nicomachean Ethics*, repeated in relation to eudaimonia, but that is far short of supporting eudaimonism. The discussion in the *Lysis* concerns what a friend or what something that is dear or loved (the translation of φίλος into English in this dialogue is notoriously awkward) is; it makes no explicit mention of happiness or the happy life at all.[61] In the course of the argument at 219–220, Socrates points out that sometimes one thing is dear to a person for the sake of another thing. So, for example, medicine is dear (or loved by or a friend) to someone who is sick. But, Socrates points out, it cannot be the case that we love x for the sake of y, and y for the sake of z, and so on ad infinitum. The "chain of desire" must come to an end somewhere in some "first principle (ἀρχή)" (219c6), which should be called the "first friend (πρῶτον φίλον)" (219d1) or primary object of desire, for the sake of which all of the subordinate things in the chain are desired/loved. The idea that desire terminates in something that is desired for its own sake (only) and not also for the sake of something further is well known as one of the formal criteria for happiness in Aristotle (see *NE* I.2; I.7). In the *Symposium* (204d–e) as well, which I will consider in the following chapter, there is a quicker version of the *Lysis*'s argument about desire, but there it is explicitly connected to the idea that happiness is a terminus of desire: it makes no further sense to ask why one desires happiness.

Of course, it does not even require argument to support the claim that the idea that desire terminates in something that is desired for its own sake, something "final (*teleion*)," is not sufficient evidence that Socrates (or Plato) is advocating eudaimonism. No scholar would say such a thing; nevertheless, this passage is frequently cited (barely a Stephanus page long) as part of the evidence for Socrates's and Plato's eudaimonism. If, however, we are not antecedently convinced that they are eudaimonists and so examine the evidence critically, then the passage looks considerably less substantial. In particular, as we shall see, it does not follow from this argument that there is only *one* such terminating chain of desire, so that there is a desire for *one* thing

---

[60] See, e.g., Penner and Rowe (2005) and Price (2011), ch. 1, as well as earlier citations from Brickhouse and Smith (2000).

[61] Price (2011), 9, opens his discussion of Plato on eudaimonia with this passage, dismissing the possibility considered in footnote 1 that there might be more than one "ultimate" end.

that explains *all* of our subordinate desires.[62] If there were, it would be laying important groundwork for the idea of a Comprehensive Practical Principle.

Instead, in the example in the *Lysis* (219d6–220a1), Socrates imagines what a father would care about in relation to his son, who had just drunk hemlock, arguing that wine (as a supposed cure for the poison) would then be "dear" to the father. Further, the cup that the wine is in would also be dear to/loved by the father (presumably because without the cup the wine would spill and be lost, and so the cure would be lost, and so the son would be lost). He then argues that these three things—the son, the wine, and the cup—are not on a par but stand in subordinate relations to one another. In this example, then, the son is what is desired for its own sake; he is the "first dear thing" that explains why the wine and cup, in turn, are also dear to/loved by the father. While this example illustrates the distinction between caring about or desiring something for its own sake versus for the sake of something further, there is no argument that the father's son is the *only* thing he cares about for its own sake; perhaps he has two sons, a polis, and engages in philosophy, and cares about them all for their own sakes, which clearly need not imply that he cares for them all equally.

It is important here, as throughout, to remember that just because living well and doing well are a universally desired end, does not mean that one does *everything* that they do for the sake of that end. So, the *Lysis*, while articulating the distinction between desiring something for its own sake versus desiring it for the sake of something further and the idea that any (rational, coherent) chain of desire must terminate in something desired for its own sake, does not offer support for the idea that happiness is a Comprehensive Practical Principle.

8. *Gorgias*

Scholars often cite the *Gorgias* as a crucial text in support of Socrates's eudaimonism.[63] In the Polus episode, Socrates tries to get Polus to understand the soul as an independent locus of harm and benefit.[64] There is also,

---

[62] See, e.g., Price (2011), 9ff., for a very different view.
[63] The difficulties for specifying its view of eudaimonism, however, are many; see, e.g., Price (2011), 9–10, and Russell (2005).
[64] The argument is straightforward in outline, and I have analyzed it before in detail: see Vasiliou (2002), (2008), ch. 3.

74 VARIETIES OF HAPPINESS

however, significant discussion of whether a person is happy. Let me begin with a couple of summary points. Socrates argues that one's soul, body, and possessions (money) can all be in better and worse states. For each there is a corrupt (*ponēria*) state: injustice, disease, and poverty (477b8–c2). Since doing injustice and being unjust (the two go together, see, e.g., 479a–b, where each is mentioned) harm the soul by making it unjust, and the soul is the most important part of a person (implied eventually by Polus's concession that harm in the soul is "most shameful" [477c2–4]), a person is made most miserable by being unjust and doing injustice. Throughout the discussion with Polus, it is clear from the many uses of comparatives and superlatives that being happy (or being miserable) is not an either/or option (see the comparative options at 469a–b; cf. 509b–c). Most miserable is a person who is unjust but never pays the penalty; one who is unjust but pays the penalty (on the running medical analogy, the one who receives the treatment for his disease) is less miserable; correspondingly, the one who is happiest is the one who never commits injustice, while the one who gets rids of the injustice in his soul by paying the just penalty is "second" (478d–e).

The clear upshot of the argument is that anyone who wants to flourish and be happy must, at least, avoid injustice and never act contrary to virtue. That is, any person who wants to be happy, as everyone does, ought to adhere to SV. There is no discussion here about whether that is sufficient or identical to happiness; the implication of many passages is that it is simply necessary, although others seem to imply sufficiency. What is clear is that the doer of injustice (and especially the doer of injustice who never pays for it, like Archelaus) has no prospect of happiness. That said, as Socrates remarks, he would want neither to suffer nor to do injustice, although if it *had* to be one or the other, he would choose suffering it (469b–c). What this makes clear is that Socrates, plausibly, considers suffering injustice also to be bad, despite the fact that this obviously does not harm one's soul. So, while harm and benefit to the soul is of incomparably more value than harm or benefit to the body (or to one's possessions), it doesn't mean that the latter are not harms or benefits at all. Otherwise, Socrates would be indifferent to suffering injustice. This suggests, what will be argued for in the *Republic*, that while the just person is better off and so "happier" than the unjust person who escapes punishment, there is no claim that such a person is happy.

Assuming this is, in brief outline, the view being presented in the *Gorgias*, what does it say about Socrates's eudaimonism? As a practical principle of action, Socrates continues to endorse virtue as the superseding end of one's actions. What we learn further in the *Gorgias* (echoing claims in the *Crito* and *Republic*) is that actions have certain effects on the soul—just actions have good effects and unjust actions harmful effects. I have argued in Chapter 1, however, that this is a relatively weak claim: if one holds a certain conception of what a person most importantly *is* (her soul, say, or her rational autonomy), she is then benefitted by acting virtuously/morally. It is not to say that such a person is happy, even if it is to say that a person has no prospect for happiness if they are unjust or immoral. So, we have some partial account of a conception of eudaimonia: at a minimum, being virtuous and acting virtuously is a *sine qua non* of being happy (correspondingly, doing unjust actions and therefore being unjust prevents one from being happy). Happiness, however, is not functioning here as a practical principle of action: we do not act in order to promote or to achieve our happiness. We ought to be guided in action by SV either as an explicit aim or else as a limiting condition. There is likewise no indication that happiness is supposed to operate as a Comprehensive Practical Principle: Socrates never speaks in the Polus episode of happiness as the end of all our actions. Rather, he appeals to our happiness as part of an explanation of how, as a correlate of SV as a limiting condition (the claim that it is never right to do wrong), it is true that doing injustice is worse for the agent than suffering it.

Further, there is no hint that happiness, consisting as it does at least partly in a good condition of our soul, provides the *content* of virtue or justice. I cannot look to such a conception of happiness in order to figure out what to do: whether, for example, it is just or unjust for Socrates to escape from prison or to participate in laying siege to Potidaea. What determines whether those actions are just has nothing to do with a conception of eudaimonia. Thus, the idea that the conception of eudaimonia can fix the content of virtue, as one who endorses the Eudaimonist Hope holds, is nowhere in evidence in the *Gorgias*.

The fact that the Eudaimonist Hope is not in play shows that in answering the determining question in any particular situation—is it just to put this person to death here and now?—one does not look to a conception of eudaimonia to find the answer. Presumably, for Socrates, one looks to one who has knowledge of the form of justice to find out whether this would be just; and so, however that is to work, whether a token action is or is not just is an objective fact about the situation, not a function of how performing the action would affect the agent's soul. In this sense, the *reason* or *justification* of this token action's being just would refer to the account of justice itself, that is, to an account that explains how this token action is an instance of the general form. Therefore, the reason that the action is just has nothing to do with the agent's eudaimonia.

Nevertheless, if one is seeking a reason *to be the sort of person* who is committed to SV above all as one's practical principle, learning purported facts about the effects of just actions on one's soul, and the purported fact that the condition of one's soul is a necessary and most significant factor in one's happiness would clearly be significant. Thus, eudaimonia here operates as a reply to a certain kind of moral skeptic. Not a skeptic about what the virtuous action is (or whether a person could ever know what the virtuous action is) but perhaps a skeptic like Polus who challenges not the specific content of "ordinary" virtue, but the value of committing to it above all in the first place. This is an important type of argument, but, as I argued in Chapter 1 (see, esp., §5), less than what most scholars have taken to constitute eudaimonism.

While the issue addressed with Polus concerns why a person would ever prefer suffering injustice over doing it, the question at issue with Callicles, once "justice by nature" is on the table, turns to how we are supposed to live (500c). The positions in outline, anyway, are reasonably clear. Callicles proposes the life of unrestrained appetitive gratification. A person possessed of intelligence and courage does not constrain their appetites, but allows them to grow and has the power to fill them: that is the best life, albeit a life that many people may not have the power or ability to achieve. The inferior many thus develop and endorse the institutions of ordinary justice—what Callicles calls justice by *nomos*—in order to constrain those who are naturally superior and prevent them from achieving what is their proper, natural end of having more than their fair share. Socrates, consistently with the views he expresses while engaging Polus, advocates the position that no one who engages in injustice and is unjust has a prospect of a happy life. Refraining from injustice and keeping oneself orderly in some fashion or other are necessary for happiness and a flourishing life. In other words, Socrates advocates adherence to ethically virtuous action and being an ethically virtuous person.

This is not a surprise, but Socrates's position remains vague in the sense that he has not offered a way of determining what is just or unjust.[65] He explains and endorses a particular conception of how just actions—whatever they are—mark and develop the sorts of persons we are. So, in the vivid account he offers near the very end of the dialogue (523a–527a), the *logos* he

---

[65] As I argue in Vasiliou (2008), ch. 3.

says Callicles will understand as a *muthos*, he analogizes the soul to body, as he has throughout the dialogue, and just as the effects of actions on the body remain marked on the body and determine its condition—fat, thin, scarred, deformed, and so on—so the actions a person undertakes while alive analogously "mark" the soul. All of a person's unjust actions will leave "scars," and mutilate their soul and this, in the parable, will be visible to the divine judges once one is "stripped" of the body so that the condition of the soul is laid bare. This is a familiar argument by Socrates: just and virtuous actions make the soul just and virtuous, while the opposite have the opposite effect. The condition of one's soul is of incomparable value to the condition of one's body or state of one's material possessions. There is no possibility of living well with a corrupted soul, and so one should always act virtuously or not contrary to virtue if one wants any prospect of happiness.

What emerges here with respect to eudaimonia and eudaimonism? As one would expect, there is no doubt that Socrates's and Callicles's clashing conceptions of flourishing lives yield conflicting practical demands. But what sorts of practical principle do these conceptions of eudaimonia yield? First off, we should note that neither Socrates nor Callicles really presents something robust enough to count as a full conception of eudaimonia. As I have argued above, Socrates merely presents following SV and being committed to it as a necessary condition for happiness. At various points, as noted, he speaks of different degrees of happiness (or misery); the doer of injustice who pays the penalty is less miserable (and so happier or better off) than the doer of injustice who avoids punishment. What's more, Socrates here (and in the *Crito* 47e) suggests that life with a sick body is an unhappy one, albeit on the way to the point that living with a "sick" soul is incomparably worse. Nevertheless, this seems to imply, plausibly, that one's physical condition has an effect on one's happiness. Similarly, as noted above, Socrates says he positively does not want to suffer injustice, although this does not cause him the most grievous type of harm; he is not, then, simply indifferent to suffering injustice, but plausibly leaves it open that it may affect his happiness, even if not in a way comparable to harm done to his soul.

Furthermore, while anyone hoping to be happy should always act justly and never contrary to justice, whatever that actually involves, this fact shows that, unsurprisingly, the Superseding Practical Principle for Socrates remains, as always, SV; in particular, it has not been replaced by some conception of eudaimonia. Indeed, just as there is no clear and specific position on the impact of bodily harm or benefit or loss or gain of possessions on one's happiness, there is correspondingly no proffered practical principle governing when and how to pursue or avoid such putative goods, except for the ubiquitous restriction on never acting contrary to virtue.

Callicles's own conception of happiness, such as it is, also leaves many details unclear, especially given Socrates's criticisms. While unrestrained appetitive gratification, pursued with intelligence and vigor, is the rough outline of his account, just what this involves remains crucially underdetermined. Does Callicles advocate utterly unconstrained pursuit of pleasure, as his acquiescence to the example of the catamite suggests (494e–495a)? Or, is he more serious later, after Socrates's arguments against the idea that any and all pleasures are good, when he claims to be joking, saying that of course he (like everyone else) agrees that some pleasures are better and others worse (499b)? If this is his position, Callicles never gives any hint as to what makes them better or worse. What sorts of appetitive gratification will his superior person pursue?[66] The only thing we do know, which is sufficient to distinguish it from Socrates's position, is that the pursuit of happiness will not be constrained by ordinary, ethical virtue, such as temperance or justice. But it is not clear what the supreme aim of my actions is on the Calliclean view: unlimited pursuit of food, drink and sex? Or political power? What about the inevitable conflicts that would arise? These details are not sorted out.

So, readers of the *Gorgias* are presented with two contrasting sketches of lives, each claimed to be the happy one by its advocate. Of course, as discussed in the Introduction, a true conception of the happy life must have some practical impact on the life of a rational agent. Thus, in some way, the Calliclean will pursue appetitive gratification unconstrained by concerns with ordinary justice; the Socratic will unwaveringly commit to SV and then do the best they can to acquire the knowledge of what in fact is just so that they will never go wrong. As far as SV is concerned, however, as a Superseding Practical Principle, the Socratic may act however they please in cases where virtue does not make a specific demand, subject to the ubiquitous constraint of never acting contrary to virtue; SV says nothing about that one way or the other.

---

[66] Barney (2011) argues that Callicles has a full-blown positive immoralism, in contrast to Thrasymachus. Although I cannot argue for this fully here, I think we need to be careful in assessing just where Callicles's account remains incomplete. It seems from Thrasymachus's immoralist speech, and the rewards of the tyrant it lauds, that his conception of happiness ultimately turns on appetitive gratification in a way very similar to Callicles's.

As in the *Protagoras*, Calliclean hedonism does operate by providing (however vaguely, especially if Callicles genuinely agrees that there are better and worse pleasures) the content of virtue, and so, unlike the Socratic and Platonic positions, it seems closer to fulfilling the Eudaimonist Hope. For Callicles the content of virtue is determinable from the content of harm and benefit, which is a matter of fact.[67] So from the fact that taking the cattle benefits Herakles and from the fact that he is strong enough to take them with impunity, we can determine that it is just (by nature) that he take them, thereby acquiring the benefit of the cattle at the level of material possessions and appetitive gratification at the level of the soul. What gratifies (or frustrates) appetite is also, for Callicles, a simple matter of fact; it can be read off from one's desires. One could (begin to) determine what it is right to do, on the Calliclean view, by figuring out what constitutes unrestrained appetite gratification. That is, the conception of the good will provide content for the conception of virtue, as Bobonich includes in his definition of eudaimonism. As we have seen, however, this fails to work for the Socratic position. Even if committing to SV is necessary for being a happy person (as we have seen Socrates argue), and, even if the explanation of this is the general effect of just and virtuous action (and their opposites) on our souls, we cannot look to our souls or their condition to determine the content of virtue. Socrates and Plato (and Aristotle as well) believe that certain action tokens are in fact the ones that are required or in fact the ones that are contrary to virtue; these are the ones that the knower of what virtue is can properly identify. It is, then, the doing or refraining from these actions that generates a healthy soul, which is a prerequisite, in turn, for a person's being happy.

Finally, it is clear that Socrates *is* explaining how commitment to SV can make the agent herself better off. As the *Republic* will elaborate in much more detail, Socrates describes how a person is benefitted by just action, even when they are being harmed with respect to their bodies or possessions. Does this mean that it is the justification for acting virtuously? I have argued in Chapter 1 that it does not. It is information about the sorts of effects certain sorts of action have on our characters or souls. There is, in fact, something beneficial for a person in doing the right thing, which of course may not be apparent to people such as Socrates's interlocutors in the *Gorgias* or *Republic*. That said, there is no suggestion that *the reason* to do the virtuous thing or to refrain from acting contrary to virtue is because of the benefit that

---

[67] See Vasiliou (2008), ch.3 for a detailed account of Callicles' position.

will accrue to one's soul. Thus, the reasoning is not: my ultimate end is happiness. To get happiness I have to have a healthy soul. To have a healthy soul I have to commit to SV. So, my reason for committing to SV is for the sake of my happiness. I have argued that this is not the form of argument that we actually find in the *Gorgias* or the other Socratic dialogues.

3
Plato and Eudaimonism

1. Introduction

What has emerged from our study of the role of eudaimonia in the "Socratic" dialogues will be consistent with what we find in the rest of Plato's dialogues. There is an interest in different conceptions of eudaimonia and in assessing lives and characters as more or less happy, more or less miserable. Further, continuing the strand of argument first seen in the *Crito*, Plato will argue that by committing to virtue (and the knowledge that requires), a person will always, in the most important respect, be better off. Without virtue and, at least some relationship to wisdom,[1] a person has no prospect for happiness. That said, there is no role for happiness as a practical principle, as the end or goal that decides our deliberations or governs our actions, whether because it somehow supersedes any other end or because it is comprehensive and contains all subordinate ends with it. Additionally, happiness does not function as a guide to the content of virtue. As discussed in Chapter 1, for Plato the content of virtue is something fixed objectively by the Forms, not determined by its relation to (human) eudaimonia.

The two most relevant and most referenced dialogues in regard to Plato's eudaimonism are the *Republic* and *Symposium*. Compared with the "Socratic" dialogues, however, where we saw that the *Apology, Crito, Lysis, Euthydemus, Gorgias, Protagoras*, and *Meno* were all adduced in various ways to support the claim that Socrates is a eudaimonist, it is really only the *Republic* and *Symposium* that supply arguments relevant to assessing Plato's position as a eudaimonist.

But perhaps one might think that the *Philebus* is also crucial. The dialogue opens as a debate about what is the best good: pleasure and enjoyment or knowledge and understanding. Socrates further describes the argument as one wherein "each of us will be trying to prove some possession or state of the soul to be the one that can render life happy for all human beings"

---

[1] I say this because I do not think that Plato holds that a person must themselves be wise in order to have any prospect of happiness. See Vasiliou (2008), chs.7–8 and (2011b); contrast Bobonich (2002).

(11d4–6). In Socrates's dream at 20b ff., he secures agreement that the good is both most complete (τελεότατον) and sufficient (ἱκανόν) (20d; cf. 60a–e). These criteria rule out the possibility that the good is either pleasure alone or wisdom alone, since either, entirely bereft of the other, would fail to be most choiceworthy. Therefore, the best life must be some sort of mixed life. In the final argument, a very Platonic, intellectualist account of the good is given: the good consists in truth, symmetry, and beauty, which, somehow, are to be considered a unity (65a). Given this, it turns out that *nous* beats out pleasure in each case, being more akin to truth, symmetry, and beauty than pleasure.

The *Philebus*, then, is clearly about what eudaimonia *is*: what is the best life for a human being? It turns out to be a life of a sort of mixture of wisdom and pleasure, with intelligence playing the most important role in the mixture of the two.[2] This doctrine, while interesting in its own right, is not particularly significant for attributing eudaimon*ism* as a type of ethical theory to Plato. For it says nothing about the role of eudaimonia as a practical principle of action, it does not attempt to provide content for virtue in terms of the good, nor does it explain the relationship between ethically virtuous action and the good in a way that attempts to motivate commitment to the former.[3] It was central to the argument of the Introduction and Chapter 1 that the mere discussion of what eudaimonia is, what human well-being consists in, is insufficient to make a philosopher or an ethical theory eudaimonist. For these reasons, then, I shall set the *Philebus* aside and assess Plato's eudaimonism by focusing on the *Republic* and *Symposium*.

2. The Just Person Is Happier than the Unjust

The most well-known way that happiness appears in the *Republic* is in the dialogue's overarching aim to show that a just person will always be happier or better off than an unjust person. Glaucon and Adeimantus challenge Socrates to show what possible benefit can accrue to a person who acts justly and avoids acting unjustly, even when she can get away with injustice. Glaucon pushes this challenge to the limit by declaring that in order to see whether there is any such benefit, the just person must be imagined to seem

---
[2] Indeed, the rather grudging addition of pleasant sensation may just be a function of our human limitation (22c); see Irwin (2007), §56, 98.
[3] The same holds for the *Laws*.

unjust and the unjust person just. "In this way both [the characters sketched] will reach the extremes, the one of justice, the other of injustice, and we'll be able to judge which of them is happier (εὐδαιμονέστερος)" (361d2–3). Thus we can be sure that only the value of justice or injustice in themselves comes to light, rather than any of their "consequences," such as physical harms (or benefits) or material gains (or losses) including social advantages (e.g., one's reputation and social standing), and risk of punishment and blame by others or even by the gods.

Adeimantus sums up what is wanted:

> You agree that justice is one of the greatest goods (τῶν μεγίστων ἀγαθῶν), the ones that are worth getting for the sake of what comes from them, but much more for their own sake, such as seeing, hearing, knowing, being healthy, and all other goods that are fruitful by their own nature and not simply because of reputation. Therefore, praise justice as a good of that kind, explaining how it benefits its possessors itself by itself (αὐτὴ δι' αὑτήν) and how injustice harms them. (367c5–c4, Grube/Reeve, modified)

Here is a sharpened version of the challenge raised in the *Gorgias*. Socrates advocates adherence to SV, but why should someone commit to this practical principle, when it so obviously seems to leave them less well-off with respect to their physical well-being, material possessions, and appetitive gratification? I have discussed the argument of *Republic* 2 in detail previously, arguing that the only notion of benefit and harm for the soul that the many possess concerns, at bottom, appetitive gratification or frustration (again, similar to the *Gorgias*).[4] In the description of the shepherd who possesses the so-called Ring of Gyges, the emphasis is on how such a person could do whatever he wants, have whatever he wants, and so on, strikingly similar to the conception of the best life advocated by Callicles.

The response is straightforward enough, at least in outline. Socrates will argue that there is a hitherto unsuspected way in which the soul can be benefitted (or harmed) that has nothing to do with appetitive gratification.[5] In fact, as Socrates in the *Gorgias* had already stated and then illustrated in his "myth" at the end of the dialogue, there is a state of psychic health for

---

[4] Vasiliou (2008), ch. 6.
[5] See Vasiliou (2008), chs. 7 and 8.

the soul. In the *Republic*, as is well known, this health has to do with each of the soul's three parts or kinds playing their proper role: reason ruling, spirit assisting, and appetite obeying. What we learn further in Socrates's reply in *Republic* 4 is that such a state of soul is created and maintained by doing virtuous and just actions (443e–444a). The form of the reply is the same as in the *Crito* and *Gorgias*: by doing virtuous actions and avoiding actions contrary to virtue, one benefits the most important part of oneself, one's soul. And, further, no one has the prospect of being happy if their soul is unhealthy and corrupted.

This familiar line of argument, of course, stops well short of supplying any conception of eudaimonia; it is relevant to what I have identified as the third role of eudaimonia, supplying motivation to an agent (at least of a certain sort), as to why she ought to commit to SV. As we shall see below, insofar as the *Republic* presents a positive account of eudaimonia, it very closely resembles what we have seen in dialogues like the *Euthydemus* and *Meno*. But the main thread of the *Republic*—the argument that the just person is happier than the unjust person—at most gives us a necessary condition for happiness.[6] As scholars have been careful to note, Socrates does not argue that the just person on the rack is *happy* but rather *happier* than one whose soul is corrupted and diseased, but who has physical pleasure, reputation, material possessions, and so on. In the response to Glaucon and Adeimantus, Socrates is arguing that a person is better off, and so more *eudaimōn*, by being just and acting justly, but as I emphasized above, there is no overall account of what eudaimonia *is*. Thus the *Republic* does not provide a full account of eudaimonia, does not set eudaimonia up as a Comprehensive Practical Principle or as a Superseding Practical Principle (which is occupied by virtue, as always in Plato); nor does it, of course, suggest that the content of virtue can be determined by reference to some conception of eudaimonia—it is the transcendent Forms that make actions and persons just, courageous, and so on. What we have instead, as I argued in Chapter 1, is a weaker claim, shared even in a way by Kant, that there is a benefit that always accrues to the agent, on some conception of what the agent most importantly is (such as their soul or their rational autonomy), from virtuous or moral action.

---

[6] Irwin (1995), §134, argues that in the *Republic* Plato never endorses the idea that being a just person and acting justly is sufficient for happiness: "Plato gives no reason to deny that the external goods lost by the just person are genuine goods."

3. Eudaimonia in the *Republic*

While the argument about whether the just person is happier than the unjust is reasonably the most well known, the *Republic* does discuss eudaimonia outside of that context, from which we can gain hints about the conception of eudaimonia at work. What is striking, I shall now argue, is how ordinary that discussion is: happiness will turn out to consist in having and using good things, even if, as the interlocutors may slowly concede, one must be just or virtuous before one could gain the requisite benefit, and so gain happiness from such things.

The three classes of the Kallipolis have been delimited when Adeimantus objects at the start of Book 4 that the best citizens of all, the rulers, will not be made very happy by the system that has been set up: they will have no pay, in fact not even be allowed to touch money, and they will simply work and watch over things with only their subsistence provided. They will not have all the typical luxuries—such as large, well-furnished houses, travel, the ability to host guests—of people that are typically called happy (419a–420a).

Socrates's often-noted reply is that their aim (as founders) is not to make any particular class or group of people outstandingly happy, but the city as a whole. This is, however, a rather remarkable response. One might expect, particularly if examining eudaimonia was a central feature of Plato's project, that Socrates would use this objection as a chance to reject such a common, ordinary account of happiness, clearly involving contentment, material possessions, and physical pleasure as components, and contrast it with an alternative account of genuine happiness tied in some essential way to virtue. But this is not what Socrates does. There are a few phrases, which might indicate a hesitation about the conception of happiness being appealed to in the objection, such as reference to things that are "thought to" make some happy or those "seeming" to be happy (cf. 419a9, 420a7). Furthermore, Socrates begins his response by saying that he would not be surprised if the guardians, deprived of these ordinary goods, did not turn out after all to be "the most happy" (420b5). But, that said, Socrates in fact basically concedes Adeimantus's point. As he elaborates in his response, it would be easy to make people happy by letting them work when they want, dressing the cobblers in purple robes, letting people feast, and so on. He could also make the rulers happy similarly, as is actually considered later in Book 7 by letting them philosophize to their heart's content (I will come back to this), but then no group would be likely to do their own work, on which the happiness and well-being of the city depends. As Socrates says this may not be a big deal when it comes to potters and cobblers, but when it comes to the rulers, they must rule excellently, for the well-being of the city depends on it.

Elaborating on the happiness of the individual classes, Socrates next says something rather surprising. Their job as founders is to look to the happiness of the city as a whole, which depends on compelling and persuading each of the groups to "do their own work," but then "they ought to leave it to nature (ἡ φύσις) to provide to each group a share of happiness" (421c3–5). How should we think about such comments in the context of thinking about the role of eudaimonia in eudaimonism? Socrates reiterates (420b) that their task is to find justice in a city, and their hypothesis is that justice would be found in a well-governed one and injustice in a poorly governed one. As founders, they are looking to the well-being or happiness of the city as whole with a view to how to determine its political structure, what founding laws to establish, what overall principles (such as each person should do his or her own work) to follow, and so on. Looking at such a city, as they will do later in Book 4, they will claim to find justice within it—that is, what it is for a city to be just. Nevertheless, Socrates is explicit here that the practical principles that individuals follow within the Kallipolis will not be principles aimed at their own (as individuals or as a class) happiness. Rather, they will need to do what is right and just, what virtue requires, which may or may not give them a share of happiness. It will, if the overarching argument we canvassed in the previous section is correct, leave them *better off* than they would be if they shirked their duty and acted in unjust ways, but whether that will make them *happy*, Socrates leaves to nature to provide or not.

So, eudaimonia does not play a significant role as a practical principle for the citizens of the Kallipolis.[7] Furthermore, while designing the best city is designing a happy city, the *Republic* is not offering any particular conception of individual happiness, beyond the claim that being a just person and doing just actions are necessary for it. The idea that nature will need to provide happiness for the individual groups seems to be in harmony with an "ordinary" conception of eudaimonia, which includes fortune and other external goods as components of it. Whether some individual lives a blessed or happy life is not something that Socrates, as founder, is trying to achieve for the individual citizens of the Kallipolis, nor is their own happiness something that individual citizens of the Kallipolis should aim at in their own actions,

---

[7] Aside, perhaps, from being a Prudential Practical Principle, see below.

either as a Superseding Practical Principle or as a Comprehensive Practical Principle.

Let me elaborate a little on the last point. Each individual in the Kallipolis should aim at virtue and not act contrary to virtue. The particular actions that constitute acting virtuously or not will differ, of course, depending on the class one is in. For example, it would be contrary to virtue for the cobbler to try to rule or for a ruler who has a "bronze" child to object to its being in the lowest class, and so on. Socrates here casually concedes that an individual cobbler might be happier amassing some money and then spending his time feasting and relaxing, but, the reasoning goes, that would not be what he should be allowed to do, *even if it would make him happier*. This is sufficient to show that happiness is not operating as a Superseding Practical Principle: one's own happiness does not trump any other aim one might have in acting. This issue will arise again in Book 7 when it comes to the Philosopher-Kings: it is conceded there that they would be made happiest by not ruling, and spending their time doing philosophy instead. But once again, this cannot be the Superseding Practical Principle of their action: rather, they must do what virtue requires, which is for them to take their fair turn at the onerous task of ruling.

Moreover, eudaimonia is not operating as a Comprehensive Practical Principle. When Socrates leaves it to nature to provide happiness to individuals, it is clear that he does not think that all of an individual's actions are (or ought to be) aimed at their eudaimonia. As we just saw, many of the actions required of all classes, and explicitly of the ruling class, may run contrary to what would make them most happy.[8] Thus the role of eudaimonia here in the *Republic* as a practical principle is as a Prudential Practical Principle of the sort we saw Sarah Broadie defend as the concept of the *summum bonum* in Chapter 1. A conception of eudaimonia might tell an individual in what her highest good consists and so, when the demands of virtue do not intrude, may guide her rational pursuits. The Philosopher-Kings are the perfect example once again. When they are ruling, they act in a way that does not maximize or optimize their individual happiness because they have an obligation not to do so. But when they have served their turn at ruling, they are explicitly allowed to go back to contemplation, in which their happiness consists, and they will, it is suggested, be rewarded

---

[8] This runs counter to Kamtekar's (2004), 133, 142, claim that it is "foundational" to Platonic political philosophy that the political goal is the "happiness of the citizen."

by going to the Isles of the Blessed after they die, where they can engage in contemplation eternally (540b–c). Thus, the role of eudaimonia functions as something it is rational to pursue, *when* the demands of virtue do not intrude. It is a Prudential Practical Principle, telling us what our good is (for the philosophers, contemplation), and so they should pursue their good so much as is permitted and so much as, in Broadie's phrase, a "decent person" would do. But engaging in contemplation is not their Superseding Practical Principle, nor is it their Comprehensive Practical Principle, as though all their actions, for example their obligatory turn at ruling, were really *for the sake of* contemplation.[9]

The opening of Book 4 is recalled in the midst of Book 5 (465b–466c), when Socrates claims that the shared property of guards and auxiliaries will guarantee a lack of dissension or lawsuits over wives, children, property, and so on, and lead to a happier life than the life of Olympic victors. Socrates returns to the objection that despite the fact that the guards were the most elite and best of the citizens, they would least be able to partake of the things that generate happiness (419a ff.). Recalling that their concern then was not to make any particular group happy, but to make the city as a whole as happy as possible, Socrates now claims that in fact the guards will plausibly be very happy—happier than Olympic victors. What is important for our purposes is to look at what Socrates cites as evidence for this claim: the guards' "victory" is more noble (καλλίων), and the public upkeep for themselves and their children is more complete. After all, their victory is nothing less than the preservation of the whole city and their reward is all the necessities of life for them and their children, and a worthy burial. Socrates then emphasizes that the sort of happiness provided for the guards is not the sort that would make them cease to be guards; it is a moderate and stable life and, "as we say," best (466b). They are not providing the sort of life for a guard, analogous to having the shepherds wear purple robes, that would undermine their performing their role as guards. Finally, Socrates warns that if a "foolish and adolescent (ἀνόητός τε καὶ μειρακιώδης)" conception of happiness takes hold of some guard and leads him to appropriate everything in the city for himself, then he will learn the

---

[9] It will not be a coincidence that when we examine Aristotle's own intellectualist conception of eudaimonia as *theoria* in Chapter 5, I will argue that he is presenting a revised conception of the best sort of eudaimonia, but not a conception of eudaimonia that is supposed somehow to supplant the conception of eudaimonia as morally virtuous activity in its role as a practical principle of action. The thought that he is has led to making his introduction of eudaimonia as *theoria* most confounding.

truth of Hesiod's aphorism that "the half is worth more than the whole" (466b–c).

What's significant here is the *conception* or perhaps *conceptions* of happiness that are put forward. Socrates's argument that the guards do, after all, have a very happy life is based on ordinary considerations: they are doing invaluable work by preserving the Kallipolis, and they and their children are provided for by a complete, if moderate, welfare system—a quantity of external goods that "as we say" is sufficient for a happy life. But here again there is no idea that being virtuous or knowledgeable is by itself sufficient for happiness. Happiness consists in doing good, excellent work, with a virtuous character, and having adequate external goods to live comfortably and then to be well buried: what an ordinary, plausible conception of happiness! While Socrates acknowledges that others may think happiness requires more extravagant lifestyles, he warns that a happiness of that sort, given to the guards, would destroy their capacity to function as guards/rulers, and so destroy the Kallipolis. (Indeed, he will explain what happens to the city when its rulers go wrong in Books 8 and 9.) And, again, Socrates seems to bring this up almost as point of information against those who would charge that the guards have been made miserable. But the happiness he does attribute to them is neither their motivation for acting as they do nor the justification for it. What's more it is not the goal or aim of their actions. It is simply the effect of their living and performing the role of guards in the Kallipolis as Socrates has outlined it. So, happiness here is not playing any sort of ultimate practical role at all in the deliberations of the guards themselves. Of course, a conception of a happy life, and the belief, for example, that it requires adequate upkeep, is playing a role in Socrates's decisions about how to arrange the lives of the guards, but this is only *one* factor; paramount is the fact that they must remain *guards* and fulfill their necessary role.

The issue of the happiness of the guards returns once again in Book 7. By this point we have learned that the rulers must be philosophers, and that philosophers, left to their own devices, "would not act" and prefer simply to contemplate, thinking that they had already reached the Isles of the Blessed while still alive (519c). In order to avoid this, the philosophers must be compelled to take their turns at ruling.[10] Glaucon then objects to Socrates's idea that the philosophers must return to the "cave," saying that he is making

[10] A view that was in fact foreshadowed in Book 1, 347b–d.

them live a "worse" life when they could live a better (*ameinon*) one. There is, of course, a notorious crux here: if the philosophers, by fulfilling their just commitments (argued for at 520a–d), are in fact made less happy than they would otherwise be by shirking their duty to rule and simply engaging in philosophical contemplation, then doesn't that undermine the overall argument of the *Republic*, which is that an individual is always better off and happier acting justly than unjustly? When Socrates begins his response by reminding Glaucon of what he said at the opening of Book 4, namely that they are not trying to generate the most happiness for any one class in the city, but for the city overall, he seems to miss the point. While that may be a reasonable and laudable goal in the design of the Kallipolis, it fails to respond to Glaucon and Ademeimantus's Thrasymachean challenge to the supreme value of acting justly from Book 2; rather, it seems precisely to concede that, at least in this case, the philosophers would be better off, and happier, if they remained out of the "cave," in contemplation.

To address this problem fully and to canvas the many solutions scholars have offered would lead us too far from our focus.[11] What's important for us is first that the notion of happiness at work is once again emphatically ordinary, based at least in part on the idea of whether the party in question will be satisfied. There are things that the philosophers will want to do, which they will be prevented from doing, which will generate frustration and leave them unhappy. Similarly, back at the start of Book 4, before anyone had an inkling that the rulers would need to be philosophers, Adeimantus imagines that rulers would again be frustrated at their inability to travel, buy lovely houses, and procure lavish gifts for their lovers. Socrates clearly recognizes the challenge and the prima facie conflict between the demands of virtue and justice and an individual's happiness.[12] In all these contexts eudaimonia is a matter of giving the class in question *what they want*—including fulfilling the philosophers' rarefied desire to contemplate. Happiness, conceived of as living well and doing well, is assessed as providing a satisfying overall life, beyond the necessity of being virtuous and acting virtuously.[13] Eudaimonia is not operating as a Superseding or Comprehensive Practical Principle.

---

[11] See Vasiliou (2015) for discussion, and references to relevant secondary literature.
[12] See White (2002), ch. 5.
[13] See too the rewards that (normally) accrue to the just person, described in Book 10 (612b–614a), once Socrates has been released from the requirement to restrict himself to giving an account only of what justice *itself* does to a person.

Even if we suspend judgment on the adequacy of Socrates's overall response, we know that the philosophers in the Kallipolis will spend most of their time doing philosophy (πρὸς φιλοσοφίᾳ) and then take their turn at ruling when it comes (540b2). Although it is not explicitly said, this is clearly part of the philosophers' lives being happy ones: while they must fulfill their just duties as rulers, they will also gain the rewards of satisfying their desire to philosophize.

Overall, then, the views of eudaimonia and the roles it is being asked to play in the *Republic* do not differ far from what we found in the "earlier" dialogues. Happiness requires being just and virtuous (or at least striving to be) and seems to consist in having and using good things correctly. Of course, eudaimonia is an object of universal desire: everyone wants to be happy. Further, as we have seen, the happiness of the city as a whole is relevant to the design of the Kallipolis, but also the happiness of individual classes is given consideration, and the charge that they are being made less happy is addressed, particularly in the case of the upper two classes who are officially deprived of the external goods ordinarily associated with happiness. That said, while the citizens in the Kallipolis will seem to live for the most part happy lives, their happiness, as a practical principle, is neither supreme nor ultimate. Rather, all the citizens, including the philosophers, are ultimately governed by the necessity to do what is just, given who they are and the class they occupy.

4. Eudaimonia in the *Symposium*

Eudaimonia is first introduced in Diotima's speech in connection with the gods. She is trying to explain to Socrates why, in fact, he too does not believe that Eros is a god (202c4). Socrates is surprised at this, and Diotima responds as follows:

> Tell me, don't you say that all the gods are happy and beautiful (εὐδαίμονας εἶναι καὶ καλούς)? Or would you dare to say that there is some one of the gods who is not both beautiful and happy (καλόν τε καὶ εὐδαίμονα)? – No, by Zeus, not I.
>
> **Indeed don't you state that the happy [people/gods] are those possessing good and beautiful things (εὐδαίμονας δὲ δὴ λέγεις οὐ τοὺς τἀγαθὰ καὶ τὰ καλὰ κεκτημένους)?**—Very much so.

But haven't you agreed indeed that Eros on account of [his] need of good and beautiful things desires these things themselves of which he is lacking?—I have agreed.

Then how would a god be one without a portion of beautiful and good things?—In no way at all, as it seems.

You see therefore, she said, that you too do not believe that Eros is a god. (202c6–202d7)

In the context of the overall argument, Diotima is aiming to show that Eros is a *daimōn*, between mortal and immortal, just as a philosopher is between knowledge and ignorance (204b), both of which are contented, static states (I'll come back to this). But more locally she sets up some basic tenets regarding eudaimonia. The tenet that the gods are noble/beautiful and happy is of course a traditional one: who would "dare" to say that they are shameful/ugly or ill-fated and unhappy? The sentence in bold, however, seems to express a general thought that applies to human beings as much as to gods: **the happy are those possessing good and fine/beautiful things.**[14]

Diotima returns to the topic of happiness a couple of Stephanus pages later, after she has described Eros's parentage. There is an odd back and forth, given the argument we have just had (translating literally):

[The question] is clearer this way: the lover of beautiful things loves [i.e., feels erotic desire]; what does he love [i.e., feel erotic desire for] (ἐρᾷ ὁ ἐρῶν τῶν καλῶν· τί ἐρᾷ;)?—And I said, that he have [them] [i.e., the beautiful things] (γενέσθαι αὐτῷ).

But, she said, the answer longs for a further question, like such: what will the person who has beautiful things have?—I am not very easily able, I said, to answer this further question.

But, she said, what if someone asked by switching things around and using "the good" instead of the "the beautiful"; come on, Socrates: the lover loves [i.e., feels erotic desire for] good things; what does he love [i.e., feel erotic desire for] (ἐρᾷ ὁ ἐρῶν τῶν ἀγαθῶν· τί ἐρᾷ;)?—I said, that he have [them] (γενέσθαι αὐτῷ).

And what will the person who has good things have?—This is easier, I said; I am able to answer: that he will be happy (ὅτι εὐδαίμων ἔσται).

---

[14] As we have seen in Chapter 2, this claim is subject to some examination in both the *Euthydemus* and *Meno*, where it is not the possession, but the use, and in particular the *correct use*, of putatively good things that leads to/is happiness.

For, she said, the happy are happy by possessing good things and it is no longer necessary in addition to ask: what does the person wishing to be happy wish *for*? But the answer seems to be final (κτήσει γάρ, ἔφη, ἀγαθῶν οἱ εὐδαίμονες εὐδαίμονες, καὶ οὐκέτι προσδεῖ ἐρέσθαι "Ἵνα τί δὲ βούλεται εὐδαίμων εἶναι ὁ βουλόμενος; ἀλλὰ τέλος δοκεῖ ἔχειν ἡ ἀπόκρισις).— True, I said.

This wish and this love, then, do you suppose it is common to all human beings and that everyone wishes to have good things always? Or what do you say?—I say this, I said, that it is common to all. (204d5–205a8)

Let's set aside the faux humility of Socrates's initial confusion, since it seems particularly egregious given that, as we have seen above, he has just agreed that the gods are happy by possessing good and beautiful things.[15] What is clear is that we get assurance in this argument that the earlier passage (202c–d) was indeed meant to cover both gods *and* humans: possession of good things is what makes people happy, and their being happy is then the endpoint of their desiring. The latter is of course another very familiar point about eudaimonia in both Plato and Aristotle. We desire x for the sake of y, and y for the sake of z, and so we have answers to the question "why do we desire x?" and "why do we desire z?," but at some point this must come to an end, which we desire for its own sake.[16]

But saying that the question "why does one want to be happy?" is final and has no further answer is not to say that happiness is the end of *all* of my actions (as if it were a Comprehensive Practical Principle); nor does it say that it trumps any other end I might have in acting (as if it were a Superseding Practical Principle). For example, I might desire to possess good things in order to be happy, but then it turns out that the only way I can possess them is to act in ways that are contrary to virtue: this is precisely the situation described in the *Meno* (as we saw in Chapter 2). If I think that my happiness trumps the end of acting virtuously, I will act one way; if the other way around, I will act otherwise. A third possibility, of course, would be to revise my conception of happiness beyond merely "possessing good things" to something like possessing good things so long as I acquire them virtuously

---

[15] We might see this faux humility as part and parcel of the fairly transparently fictional (within the fiction of the dialogue itself) device of Socrates's purporting to relate a speech of Diotima, given that "she" obviously refers to things that have just occurred in the dialogue, such as the fact that on Aristophanes's account lovers are searching for their "other halves" and a description of Eros that is pointedly opposed to Agathon's.

[16] See the discussion of *Lysis* 219–220 and *Gorgias* in Chapter 2.

(or not contrary to virtue). But then this addition would require argument, for we have lost the plausibility of the premise that Socrates here readily assents to: that possessing good things makes a person happy.

So, I call attention to the weakness of this "finality claim," which is simply that there is no further question to be asked, such as, "why should I be happy?" This is quite different from a stronger finality claim that says: this is the end of *everything* that I do or I do *all* that I do for the sake of happiness.[17] Up to this point, then, what we have are minimal claims about action and desire and the familiar claim that one is happy by possessing good (and beautiful) things.

The argument then takes a turn. Diotima introduces the idea of immortality via possessing good things "always," leading to the conclusion that what the lover wants is to possess the good forever (206a11–12). For our purposes, let us note two things. First, the introduction of two things—immortality and the idea of having the good "forever"—has seemed notoriously *ad hoc* to commentators. The treatment of immortality, particularly with relationship to the soul, is singular in the *Symposium*, for there is no mention of the soul as immortal; rather, the infamous point is that mortals participate in immortality via generative acts, whether having children for those "pregnant in body" or in creative or political works for those "pregnant in soul" (208e ff.). This process is in keeping with how mortal things maintain and sustain themselves, namely, by replacing old things with new ones, whether it is parts of the body, new human beings, or replacing forgotten knowledge with new study. Second, we should note that explicit discussion of happiness has dropped out. At 208e the word *eudaimonia* occurs for the last time in the Diotima episode, when she says that those pregnant in body think that by having children they will forever achieve "immortality and remembrance and happiness (ἀθανασίαν καὶ μνήμην καὶ εὐδαιμονίαν)" (208e4).

The teleological structure typically associated with eudaimonism, however, arises in the transition to the "higher mysteries" and in the account of the mysteries themselves. First, we are told that all the literal and figurative giving birth that occurs in what comes to be called, by contrast, "the lower mysteries," which Diotima says that "even" Socrates could be initiated into, have a higher purpose "if someone goes about them correctly" (210a2). Evidently, then, there are two ways of pursuing the activities of procreation and production: one seems to be more or less at random, as ordinary people

---

[17] As Sheffield (2012), 136, well argues.

do in having children and as even great people like Homer and Solon do in writing epic poetry or making laws. In the first type of case, people are driven by their "pregnancy" to "give birth in (the presence of) the beautiful" (206e) and then mistakenly believe that their happiness and immortality consist in their children or artworks or laws. But in the second case, a person has an appropriate guide leading them up the ascent and going beyond anything that the lower mysteries by themselves envisioned. This is what Diotima is unsure Socrates can achieve. Given how well known these passages are, I shall not go through them in detail. The primary point is to note that for someone who engaged in the activities of the lower mysteries *properly*, the earlier mysteries are really *for the sake of* the higher mysteries (210a1–5).

> Even you, Socrates, could probably come to be initiated into these rites of love [i.e., into the "lower" mysteries involved in childbirth and cultural productions]. But as for the purpose (ὧν ἕνεκα) of these rites when they are done correctly—that is the final and highest mystery, and I don't know if you are capable of it. (209e5–210a2, Nehamas and Woodruff, modified)

The same *hou heneka* language is repeated (210e5–6 and 211c2), but now *within* the higher mysteries, to indicate that these mysteries themselves end, of course, with knowledge of the Form of Beauty. The infamous description of not only what the Form of Beauty is like, but more importantly what the life of one who grasps it is like, makes clear that it by itself makes life worth living:[18]

> And there in life, my friend Socrates, said the foreigner from Mantinea, there if anywhere is life worth living for a human being (βιωτὸν ἀνθρώπῳ), beholding that Beauty. If you once see that, it won't occur to you to measure beauty by gold or clothing or beautiful boys and youths—who, if you see them now, strike you out of your senses, and make you, you and many others, eager to look at (ὁρῶντες) the boys you love and to be with them (συνόντες) forever, if there were any way to do that, forgetting food and drink, everything but looking at them (θεᾶσθαι) and being with them (συνεῖναι). But how would it be, in our view, if someone got to see the Beautiful itself, absolute, pure, unmixed, not polluted by human flesh or colors or any other great nonsense of mortality, but if he could see the

---

[18] Anticipating Aristotle's notion of the self-sufficiency of happiness, see Chapters 4 and 5.

divine Beauty itself in its one form? Do you think it would be a poor life (φαῦλον βίον) for a human being to look there (ἐκεῖσε βλέποντος) and to behold it (θεωμένου) by that which he ought, and to be with it (συνόντος αὐτῷ)? Or haven't you considered well, she said, that there alone, when he looks at Beauty in the only way that Beauty can be seen – only then will it become possible for him to give birth not to images of virtue (because he is in touch with no images), but to true virtue (because he is in touch with the true Beauty). The love of the gods belongs to anyone who has given birth to true virtue and nourished it, and if any human being could become immortal, it would be he. (211d–212b, Nehamas/Woodruff trans., modified)

While there is no explicit mention of happiness or the happy life here, it is clear that Diotima is saying that the life that culminates in the grasp of the Form of Beauty[19] is a life that is the most happy one; it makes life "worth living (*biōton*)" (cf., of course, *Ap.* 38a5–6: "the unexamined life is not worth living for man (οὐ βιωτὸς ἀνθρώπῳ)"). Further, we have the rhetorical question: "do you think this would make a *phaulon bion* ... ?"

What is being put forward here as the "higher mysteries" is an intellectualist conception of the happy life.[20] I have argued elsewhere that Plato makes clear in this passage and in other places that he conceives of the grasp of the Forms as a kind of stasis, a final endpoint.[21] In the *Republic* Plato says that without active intervention to compel the philosophers to "return to the Cave," those who have spent their whole lives being educated and become philosophers and grasped the Forms "will not willingly act (τοὺς δὲ ὅτι ἑκόντες εἶναι οὐ πράξουσιν), thinking that they have arrived at the Isles of the Blessed, while still alive" (*Rep* 519c4–6). Here too Diotima suggests that nothing would be missing from the life of contemplation of the Forms. There is obviously a lot in common here with the intellectualist conception of eudaimonia that Aristotle puts forward in *NE* X.7–8—the primary differences being that for Aristotle the forms contemplated are not transcendent entities (but they are forms) and that contemplation is a type of *energeia*, which is one of Aristotle's primary innovations beyond Plato.[22]

---

[19] Which may well be the Form of the Good, given the exchange between *to agathon* and *to kalon* throughout the arguments leading up to it.
[20] See Sheffield (2012).
[21] Vasiliou (2015).
[22] See Chapter 5.

These larger questions aside, however, for present purposes let us reflect on what sort of eudaimonism the *Symposium*'s conception of eudaimonia suggests. We already have our answer: The practical role for eudaimonia as a description of the best life is not as a Comprehensive or Superseding Practical Principle, but a *summum bonum* in Broadie's sense and a Prudential Practical Principle. A leader guides the initiate up the steps of the ascent toward grasp of the Form of Beauty. There is no discussion of the ways in which these activities and actions *may or may not* be superseded by ethical demands. (For example, while on the ascent, what if one's polis is attacked and courage demands that one defend it?) Nor is there a claim that the activities and actions in the ascent are somehow all-encompassing or comprehensive—that is, explaining why we do *all* that we do. On the contrary, even if considerably vague and confusing in its details (to the frustration of scholars), the ascent describes a very particular regimen designed to lead to a very particular goal, which, it is claimed, will constitute a happy life. Thus, we can ask the same questions about the conception of eudaimonia here that scholars ask about Aristotle's intellectualist conception: what is the proper relationship of this intellectual virtue, wisdom, that makes life worth living for a human being in the *Symposium*, and the ordinary moral virtue of the type that Socrates champions in his adherence to SV? Our discussion of Aristotle over the next two chapters should clarify just this issue.

4
Aristotle and His Interpreters on Eudaimonia

Aristotle's *Nicomachean Ethics* is taken to be *the* work of eudaimonist ethics. This chapter aims at a broad understanding of the primary ways in which the role of eudaimonia in Aristotle's ethics has been interpreted. Aristotle is pulled in two directions. On the one hand, he is committed to a version of his Socratic legacy, according to which the Supremacy of Virtue ought to be one's Superseding Practical Principle. Thus, as the ultimate practical end of one's actions, virtue understood as a Superseding Practical Principle deserves the label *eudaimonia*. On the other hand, discussions of what the best life for a human being is in terms of what constitutes a genuinely happy life are part and parcel of both philosophical and broader cultural discussions about eudaimonia. Moreover, the concept of virtue, so important to Plato and central to Aristotle's ethics, is broader than what I have been calling the "moral virtue" primarily at work in the Socratic application of the Supremacy of Virtue. In particular, one might wonder, as Plato and Aristotle do, what is the *most excellent* human excellence? They both agree that this will have to do with what is most divine. And in both cases as well, it is therefore connected with philosophy and its object: understanding (*nous*).

In the next chapter, I consider the text of the *Nicomachean Ethics* in detail and provide a novel interpretation of how we ought to understand it. Here, however, I focus primarily on prominent lines of scholarly interpretation with the aim of foregrounding the assumptions at work in various kinds of readings and the conceptual tensions that emerge. For, as I hope to show, interpretations of Aristotle are deeply affected, and in some cases driven, by scholars' conceptions of the eudaimonism he allegedly embraces. Moreover, as we have already seen with Plato, different scholars ask eudaimonia to play different roles within the eudaimonist framework. Since the scholarship on the *Nicomachean Ethics* is so abundant and familiar, I hope not to waste the reader's time reviewing overly trodden terrain. Rather, in this chapter, relying on references for background, I concentrate on presenting and critiquing the

Varieties of Happiness. Iakovos Vasiliou, Oxford University Press. © Oxford University Press 2025.
DOI: 10.1093/9780197645093.003.0005

main lines of interpretation. I also argue for the significance of elements of John McDowell's reading of the *Ethics*, developed primarily in the 1980s and 1990s, which has been dropped, so far as I can tell, as a serious contender by most students of Aristotle. What is especially valuable in McDowell's treatment is his intense focus on the role of eudaimonia as, in my language, a practical principle. He starts from this and tries to make the conception of eudaimonia as the best life fit with its role as a practical principle. While I argue that his view encounters difficulties with the text, which I address in the next chapter, nevertheless it is critical to one of my primary aims: undermining the idea that eudaimonia functions in Aristotle as a Comprehensive Practical Principle. Over the next two chapters I hope to show the damage this idea has wrought on interpretations of the *Nicomachean Ethics*.

1. Scholars on Aristotle on Eudaimonia

Discussion of eudaimonia in Aristotle is still dominated by debates between "inclusivists" or "comprehensivists" and "exclusivists" or "monists."[1] The former camp believes, roughly, that Aristotle thinks that eudaimonia consists of the set of (all) goods in themselves; these are pursued "for the sake of happiness" at least in the sense that they are constituents of happiness.[2] The latter identify eudaimonia with a single (type of) activity, for example, (morally) virtuous activity or (intellectually) virtuous activity (i.e., *theoria*).[3] How does this map on to the distinctions I have been tracking in this book? Before

---

[1] Heinaman (2002) strongly attacks the idea that eudaimonia is comprehensive: that is, that it contains all goods. I have been concerned throughout, of course, to attack the idea that eudaimonia functions as Comprehensive Practical Principle. Heinaman (2002), 101 and 101, n. 4, stresses and lists the frequent and unvarying definition of eudaimonia as virtuous activity in the *NE* (he claims the same for *EE* and *Politics*; I have doubts about the former, see Chapter 5). Heinaman (2002), 122–127, argues that Aristotle clearly maintains that there are degrees of happiness.

[2] Ackrill (1980) is the most important originator of this view; see refinements and further defense in Irwin (1985), (1986), (1991), and (2012a). Heinaman (2007) provides a detailed critique of the textual evidence in favor of inclusivist and comprehensivist accounts and supplies bibliographic references. Inclusivists maintain, essentially, that happiness contains parts or components, so that happiness consists in more than one (kind of) good; comprehensivists maintain that happiness includes all goods in the sense that it includes at least all kinds of goods (not, of course, every token good). Of course, many further distinctions can and have been made, but they are not relevant for our purposes; see references.

[3] Kraut (1989) and Lear (2004). A related but distinct interpretive strand, a "paradigm case account," championed especially by Charles (1999) and (2015), maintains that there is one central, focal account of eudaimonia (namely as *theōria*) and that other activities (such as morally virtuous activity) may also have value depending on its relationship to the primary activity; I consider this interpretation further below.

examining the text, we can appreciate that each interpretation gains some plausibility depending upon the aspect of eudaimonia we consider: its role as a practical principle or its being a conception of the best, most desirable life. The idea that the best, most desirable life consists *exclusively* in one good or one activity is prima facie implausible. It is difficult to believe that a life of any single type of activity would not be made better by the addition of, for example, some external goods, such as health or wealth or beauty rather than the presence of their opposites. External goods would, further, seem to add to the happiness of such a life not only instrumentally, but also in their own right, justifying their being labeled "goods";[4] moreover, as we will see in the following chapter, Aristotle himself appears to say just this. Thus, reflection on what constitutes a desirable life urges one to think of eudaimonia in an inclusive way: happiness would seem to consist in virtuous activity, over a complete lifetime, with at least a suitable amount of external goods.

But such an inclusivist account is difficult to square with the roles eudaimonia is asked to play within eudaimonism: (a) as a principle that guides and regulates action and deliberation; and (b) as a source for the goodness of things and activities. As defenders of exclusivist or monistic accounts have objected, a mere aggregate set of goods does not seem to have the sort of unity that can guide action and deliberation, nor is it able to explain clearly the goodness of the ends that are subordinate to it.[5] If eudaimonia consists in a single activity,[6] as the exclusivist maintains, it would be prima facie simpler for it to play a role as a principle for action and as a source of goodness. It is more difficult to see how a *set* of intrinsic goods could operate in the same way.[7]

---

[4] Precisely the claim the Stoics notoriously deny; see Chapter 7.
[5] See Kraut (1989), 8–9, 212, and Richardson Lear (2004), ch. 2. For responses and refinements, see Irwin (1991) and (2012b), who defends a comprehensivist position, and Sauvé Meyer (2011), 52, who discusses Richardson Lear.
[6] Heinaman (2007) musters strong evidence, much of which I will consider below, that Aristotle identifies eudaimonia with virtuous activity and argues persuasively that this undermines all varieties of inclusivism about eudaimonia; Heinaman also provides a good account of inclusivist views and arguments. Irwin's (2012b) defense of a comprehensivist view does not cite or discuss Heinaman (2002) or (2007). Heinaman (2007), 225, argues, as I will, that virtuous activity does not include activities that simply do not violate virtue(contra Irwin [1991]); he cites *NE* 1173a5–13 and 1173b26 as clearly showing that not all human actions are manifestations of virtue or vice.
[7] The typical strategy for the inclusivist is to argue that while happiness consists of virtuous activity, plus some other goods, virtuous activity has a priority or authority such that pursuing some

What has largely driven the defense of inclusivist or comprehensivist views, however, is not primarily textual evidence; on that score, the exclusivists have the advantage, as scholars have pointed out.[8] Rather it is the following two considerations. First, as we just mentioned, there is the prima facie implausibility of the idea that the best life could consist only of one single type of activity and the related rejection of the idea that one's life could not be made better, and so happier, by the presence of external goods. But equally influential, I shall argue, is the idea that eudaimonia functions as a Comprehensive Practical Principle and so must provide absolutely all of our (good, rational) reasons for action. As we shall see, this idea is typically assumed without argument by *both* inclusivists *and* exclusivists. The importance of this for our purposes is clear, for the idea that eudaimonia always or even typically functions in Greek ethical theory as a Comprehensive Practical Principle is one of the primary targets of this book.[9]

The debate between inclusivists and exclusivists on the role and nature of eudaimonia centers around two notorious issues: first, how to reconcile the conception of eudaimonia we get in Books II–IX, where eudaimonia consists primarily at least in morally virtuous activity, with the conception of eudaimonia as *theōria* presented in X.7–8; and second, the place of a "complete life" and external goods with respect to happiness.[10] Over the course of this chapter and the next I examine both issues.

---

other good, like wealth or health, should never be done at the expense of virtue. One problem is that it is difficult to find explicit support for this kind of hierarchical structure in the text.

[8] See Richardson Lear (2004) and Heinaman (2007).

[9] Even some of the most virulent and thorough critics of inclusivism, such as Heinaman (2002) and (2007), who argues that Aristotle countenances goods, and even goods in themselves, besides happiness and that these goods are not parts or components of happiness, nevertheless do not consider how that fact affects the role of eudaimonia as a practical principle. More recently, Charles (2017) offers a reading of the "Function Argument" that persuasively resists comprehensivist interpretations (although he does not put it that way), arguing, "many things that all and only humans do are unconnected with being a good human because they are not ones whose doing well marks out an excellent human being" (109). Charles offers walking upright, telling jokes, playing games, and smiling as some examples.

[10] Recall that by "moral virtue" or "morally virtuous activity" I refer to the virtues as exercised in action (*praxis*) (courageous action, just action, temperate action, and so on) as opposed to "intellectual virtue," which involves theoretical wisdom and contemplation. This is a slightly different distinction than the division of virtues in *NE* I.13, which divides virtue into virtues of character and virtues of thought; the latter includes *phronēsis* as well as *sophia*. The exercise of *phronēsis* is central to morally virtuous activity.

2. Aristotle on Eudaimonia as a Practical Principle

With the preceding as background, let me translate this debate into the terms of this book, focusing in greater detail on eudaimonia as a practical principle. One might think that the inclusivist/exclusivist distinction would line up neatly with the distinction between a Superseding Practical Principle and a Comprehensive Practical Principle, but matters are not so straightforward. It is clear that inclusivist views fit most easily with conceiving of eudaimonia as a Comprehensive Practical Principle, dovetailing with Vlastos's account of eudaimonism, which I discussed in the Introduction and Chapter 1.[11] If eudaimonia is a Comprehensive Practical Principle, it explains the rationality of *all* of my deliberate, non-acratic actions, which is rendered more plausible since eudaimonia contains within it all goods in themselves.[12] But exclusivists, such as Gabriel Richardson Lear, also defend a version of the idea that eudaimonia is a Comprehensive Practical Principle, claiming that eudaimonia is a "convergent end."[13] She writes: "Any activity not leading to that end [the convergent end that is happiness] would be, in an important sense, *outside the life of the human being*. Thus despite Aristotle's failure to argue that the good is a convergent end, there is every reason to expect that this is what he believes."[14] This is significant for us for two reasons. First, it shows that Lear, who defends a monistic account of eudaimonia,

---

[11] See Irwin (1991), 383: "Aristotle is a eudaimonist: in his view, I have sufficient reason to choose to do X only insofar as X is the best way to promote my happiness." This is an account of what it would be for Aristotle to be a eudaimonist; in context, it is not necessarily an endorsement of the attribution of eudaimonism to Aristotle, although Irwin does in fact think that Aristotle is a eudaimonist in this sense. In Irwin (2003), 97, he argues that at least some evidence would indicate that the author of the *Magna Moralia* may *not* be a eudaimonist; see further discussion in Chapter 5.

[12] Thus, given the obvious possibility of conflict among various goods, inclusivists must rely on the idea that there is some explicit hierarchy among them, such that the loss of certain kinds of goods cannot be any reason to forgo virtuous action; this will be an issue below.

[13] Lear (2004), 21–23, 29, n. 42; see also Kraut (1989), 229. This label stems from Richardson (1992), 334, 344–349, where he argues that the textual evidence for attributing a comprehensive end to Aristotle is inadequate. Overall, Richardson is arguing for a "structured inclusivism," so his view ends up far from mine.

[14] (2004), 23, my emphasis. As we have seen, for Vlastos (1991), 221, eudaimonism has a maximally wide scope, seeking to explain the rationality of all non-acratic, deliberate actions. Lear does sometimes seem to intend a more narrow scope than Vlastos by placing a qualification on the limits of the convergent end as encompassing "at least our most important" actions. See, e.g., Lear (2004), 22: "happiness is being treated as the name for whatever end is the terminus of *all* a person's choices (or all the important ones)" (her emphasis). She repeats the qualification, "or at least the most important ones," when she again defends the idea that happiness is a "convergent end" at 29, n. 42. Although she never provides examples of what the less important actions are, we might think they include examples like those Vlastos explicitly includes *within* the scope of eudaimonism, such as when to get a haircut or whether to walk to the bus. Despite her qualifications, however, Lear ultimately seems to attribute a similarly wide scope to eudaimonia.

nevertheless agrees with Vlastos, Irwin, and others that eudaimonia is the end of *all* of our actions. Thus, when she claims that eudaimonia is a "convergent end," she should be understood as claiming that it functions as a Comprehensive Practical Principle. Second, she concedes that Aristotle fails in fact to argue for this.[15] This is particularly important, since if the argument of previous chapters has been correct there is no textual evidence that eudaimonia is a Comprehensive Practical Principle in Plato. So, we might expect that this is an innovation of Aristotle's. But as we will see not only is there inadequate textual evidence for thinking that Aristotle's conception of eudaimonia functions as a Comprehensive Practical Principle, there are also good philosophical reasons for rejecting it.

Finally, we should consider David Charles's defense of what he calls "the paradigm case account."[16] On this view theoretical contemplation is the referent of "the highest good" in the sense that it is the central case of the highest human good, meaning that all other goods are good by being related (either analogically or focally) to this central good. Theoretical contemplation, however, is not simply to be identified with the highest good (as the exclusivists would have it), nor is it to be one distinct intrinsic good, which, along with others, together constitute the highest human good (as inclusivists would have it). On Charles's account there is no one feature shared by all activities that constitute the highest human good (e.g., their being examples of contemplation). Nevertheless, they are all unified insofar as their desirability and goodness stems from their being analogically or focally related to intellectual contemplation. So, here we have a third account of what eudaimonia is: an activity whose essence is theoretical contemplation, but which also allows for other activities that are focally or analogically related to the central activity to count as activities of the human good. These non-central activities, such as morally virtuous action, certain pleasurable activities, noble friendship, and so on, are not, as inclusivists or comprehensivists would have it, "parts" of happiness, nor do they constitute happiness.[17]

While this alternative to exclusivist/inclusivist interpretations is attractive in certain respects, it does not address the tension in the roles of eudaimonia that is my central focus; in particular, it neglects the role of eudaimonia as

---

[15] Again, picking up on arguments from Richardson (1992).
[16] (2015), 78. See too Charles (1999) and Scott (1999).
[17] Charles (2015), 73 and 79: "Inclusivists err when they assume that eudaimonia is itself a life (*bios*) rather than the type of activity which makes a life worth living. This conflation leads them to conclude that the relevant type of activity must itself have parts." See too below and Heinaman (2007) for related criticism.

a practical principle. When I act for the sake of the *kalon* or, what amounts to the same thing, act for the sake of eudaimonia by engaging in morally virtuous activity,[18] Charles's account supplies an explanation of how and why that activity is good: it is good and desirable and an instance of the highest human good insofar as it bears an analogical or focal relationship to the central good, theoretical contemplation. But how are decisions *among* competing goods made? In a situation where moral virtue demands one thing and contemplation another, how does one decide what to do?

In this context consider too Richardson Lear's position. According to her, the "for the sake of" relation includes a relation of "teleological approximation."[19] So, when one acts as practical wisdom (*phronēsis*) dictates (and so engages in morally virtuous activity), one still participates in the highest human good, identified as theoretical contemplation, insofar as the activity of discerning and acting on the *practical truth* about what the virtuous action is *approximates* the (best) activity of discerning and contemplating *theoretical truth*.[20] But the same issue threatens Lear's account when it comes to action. Given that theoretical contemplation is the best example or the essence of the highest human good, why, if one could avoid it, would one engage in activity that only *approximates* it or, as Charles would have it, is only focally or analogically related to it? When it comes to action, then, paradigm case accounts seem to fall into the same trouble as exclusivist or monist accounts. To take an example I follow over this chapter and the next, suppose that courage, a virtue exercised for the sake of the *kalon*, requires that one put one's life or health at serious risk. The paradigm case account explains well why that can nevertheless be an instance of engaging in the highest good—because it is either an approximation of it or else focally or analogically related to it. But how should the fact that it is not *the* highest good affect my deliberation about what to do? Why should I sacrifice my engaging in the highest good, as courage requires in this instance, for the sake of a mere *approximation* of that good? Inclusivists fare no better on this front: they must simply include an ad hoc claim that morally virtuous activity supersedes the pursuit of any other good. The standard interpretations fail, then, to explain adequately the role of eudaimonia as a practical principle.

---

[18] See, e.g., Meyer (2016), 50 and 58, for the idea that virtuous activity done for its own sake, for the sake of the *kalon*, and for the sake of eudaimonia amount to the same thing.

[19] Although she describes herself as defending an exclusivist account, Charles includes her among the defenders of paradigm case accounts, presumably because of her idea of "teleological approximation" described above.

[20] Lear (2004), ch. 5, esp. 103.

3. McDowell on Aristotle on Eudaimonia

In a series of articles mostly from the 1980s and 1990s,[21] John McDowell defends an account of Aristotle's ethics in general and of Aristotle's account of eudaimonia in particular, which, I think it is safe to say, has largely been either ignored or at least relegated to the margins by most scholars.[22] What makes his interpretation particularly important for my argument, however, is that, as I mentioned, McDowell emphasizes features of eudaimonia as a practical principle that go missing or are marginalized on other accounts. Nevertheless, it will emerge that his interpretation too drastically downplays certain manifest features of Aristotle's position, which is why it has been, to some extent correctly, criticized as not justified by the text.[23] It is important, however, that highlighting the aspects of Aristotle's account of eudaimonia upon which McDowell focuses makes ignoring other aspects of Aristotle's account virtually mandatory. Thus attention to McDowell's view, I shall argue, makes clear a tension in Aristotle's own work that is manifested in more mainstream contemporary accounts of his conception of eudaimonia, most notably in the debates we have just considered among inclusivists or comprehensivists, exclusivists or monists, and paradigm-account interpretations, particularly concerning the question of how to understand the role of external goods. This in turn will help us to appreciate how the desirability of eudaimonia operates in Aristotle's theory, for the desirability of a particular conception of eudaimonia turns significantly on the role of external goods.

In my view, two fundamental features of Aristotle's position drive McDowell's reading. The first is Aristotle's central and repeated insistence that eudaimonia is an activity (*energeia*) (e.g., 1098a16–18, 1098b31–1099a7,

---

[21] See McDowell (1980), (1995), (1996a), (1996b), (1998a), and, relatedly (1979). Most recently see his response to Irwin in McDowell (2006).

[22] For example, in R. Polansky (ed.), *Cambridge Companion to Aristotle's* Nicomachean Ethics (Cambridge, 2014), there are two references to McDowell (one of which is to a contemporary view of his from "Virtue and Reason"), while by contrast Broadie, Cooper, and Irwin each has twenty-odd references. McDowell is not cited in the recent Irwin (2012a), not discussed in Lear (2004), and not cited in Lear (2009), Heinaman (2002), or (2007).

[23] In addition, part of the difficulty of McDowell's work lies in the number of interconnecting topics he is treating in any given paper, ranging from philological details about the Greek text to very general philosophical questions about the grounding of ethical objectivity. Certain topics are distant from my concerns here. I shall therefore largely set aside the claims McDowell makes about interpretive anachronism, moral psychology, and ethical objectivity, which perhaps have distracted readers from appreciating the respects in which his position is a textually defensible interpretation of Aristotle.

1099a29–31, 1169b28–30).²⁴ Aristotle himself presents the idea that eudaimonia is an activity as a novelty of his own position. Despite the fact that eudaimonia, like its English renderings "happiness" or "well-being," is a substantive, qua *energeia* at any rate it is something we *engage in*, not something we possess. Aristotle rehearses the point in Book IX: "For it was said at the beginning that eudaimonia is a kind of activity (ἐνέργεια τις), and it is clear that an activity comes to be and does not belong [to a person] like some possession (κτῆμα τι)" (IX.9, 1169b28–30).

Much of McDowell's view stems from trying to adhere rigorously (critics might say too rigorously) to Aristotle's account of eudaimonia as an *energeia*.²⁵ Furthermore, and this is not controversial, the activity in question is virtuous activity: morally virtuous activity in the body of the *NE* and then contemplative virtuous activity in X.7–8. Of course, all scholars recognize that virtuous activity is somehow essential to Aristotle's account of eudaimonia. McDowell's reading is more extreme insofar as he makes "eudaimonia-activity" and virtuous activity the same.²⁶ We should remind ourselves not only of the textual advantage that the identification of eudaimonia with either morally virtuous activity or intellectually virtuous activity has, which exclusivist or monist accounts share, but also the philosophical advantage. If, as we must, we take seriously Aristotle's repeated insistence that the special mark of his own conception of eudaimonia is that it is an *activity*, it would simply be a category mistake to think that a *part* or *component* of eudaimonia could be the possession of some external good, like health or wealth or having a complete life.²⁷ For having some wealth or being healthy are simply not *activities*, and so it is a category mistake to think

---

²⁴ See Heinaman (2007) for additional textual evidence.
²⁵ See "Realism" (2009), 26–27.
²⁶ See too Broadie (1994), 41: "The connection between happiness here [conceived of as the central good of a happy human life] and excellent activity is as close as the word 'is' can convey." And yet in Broadie and Rowe (2002), 278, she claims that strictly speaking the activity is only the main component of happiness as a whole; in places where Aristotle seems to identify happiness and virtuous activity, it is in reality an example of synecdoche; see Heinaman (2007), 226, for an effective reply.
²⁷ As I will discuss further in the following chapter, the *Nicomachean Ethics* is particularly distinctive in this regard, compared with either the *Eudemian Ethics* or *Magna Moralia*. The latter two works do use the word ἐνέργεια but much less frequently and most often paired with χρῆσις. The *EE* and *MM* do make the point that the good life has to be active; we must not merely possess the good, but use it. The *NE*, by contrast, puts the idea of a *telos* being an *energeia* front and center right at the start (I.1). Also, the concept of *chrēsis* involves the idea of usefulness *for something; energeia* by itself in Aristotle represents the idea of activity that is itself complete at every moment (like seeing) and that can be its own end, that is, can be without any particular *chrēsis*. This fits the conception of eudaimonia in the *NE*.

that they could be part of happiness.[28] As we have discussed, what drives the temptation to interpret happiness in an inclusivist or comprehensivist way is the implausibility of the identification of happiness with a type of activity as a conception of the good life; for surely, such a life would be made better, that is, happier, by the presence of external goods.

The second key element of McDowell's interpretation is a focused attention on the role of eudaimonia as a practical principle. The perfect or most complete end (the "highest" good, 1095a16) is that for the sake of which everything else is done. On the first page of "The Role of *Eudaimonia* in Aristotle's Ethics [Role]," McDowell cites 1102a2–3: "it is for the sake of [eudaimonia] that we do all that we do."[29] At a minimum, this suggests that I cannot purposefully and correctly choose to act *against* my own eudaimonia, for there is no other end of action that could in theory supersede it. It will turn out to be correct, however, that I sometimes may act in a way that is not against my eudaimonia and yet without needing to be acting in a way describable as "for the sake of happiness"; if this is right, then Aristotle does not understand eudaimonia as a Comprehensive Practical Principle but as a Superseding Practical Principle.

As we have seen, however, almost all scholars believe that Aristotle *is* thinking of eudaimonia as a Comprehensive Practical Principle. McDowell explicitly rejects this:[30] "it seems plausible that an activity can be undertaken for its own sake (e.g., for the fun of it) without being undertaken for the sake of doing well (*eupraxia*), which seems to be the mark of *praxis*. 'For the sake of doing well' restricts us to reasons for acting that draw on a conception of human excellence; this is the point of the 'function' argument in *EN*

---

[28] See, again, Heinaman (2007) for the textual evidence; at 236–237 Heinaman makes a point similar to the one I make here in the context of eudaimonia and having health or friends.

[29] "Role" (1980/1998), 3–4. See also, I.1–2 and I.7, 1097a18–24, 1097b20–21: "happiness is clearly something complete and self-sufficient, being the end of our practical undertakings" (Rowe). Since the beginning of this book I have argued that this idea—a common trope: we do everything for the sake of happiness—should not be taken in a strict, literal sense, which implies that *every* action is ultimately done for the sake of happiness. This phrase, as we saw in the Introduction and the discussion of Plato, may simply mean that happiness is our most important goal and that we make every effort to achieve it, which should not be understood to rule out the possibility of actions that I may be required to do, for example by the demands of virtue, but that may run counter to my happiness (see also Chapter 1); in fact, as we shall see, Aristotle does not countenance such actions; but he will countenance actions that impede or prevent one from living a *happy life*; see Chapter 5. Also, importantly, there may be actions that are neither required by nor contrary to virtue, see Charles (2017), 109.

[30] As perhaps does Broadie (1991), 32. See too Richardson's (1992) criticism of textual evidence for the idea that eudaimonia is, in his language, a "convergent end"; as we saw above, Lear (2004) agrees too that Aristotle's language does not commit him to a "convergent end" view, although she ends up interpreting him this way.

I.7."[31] McDowell claims that we can engage in actions "for fun," which are not undertaken as instances of doing well nor are they instrumental means to doing well. Presumably, then, there could be instrumental means toward "fun" (I need to go get my surfboard) as well as instrumental means toward "doing well" (I need to go get my weapons to defend the polis, as courage requires). Similarly, there are activities that are good in themselves in each sort of case: surfing and engaging courageously in battle. Surfing, for some agent, is just what having fun *is* in some circumstance; and acting courageously in battle is just what virtuous activity, and so happiness-activity (i.e., doing well), *is* in some other situation.[32]

McDowell elaborates on, in my language, the rejection of happiness as a Comprehensive Practical Principle:

> The point of the concept of eudaimonia is not to suggest a general determination of what can be practically rational, on the basis of some idea like that of an optimal combination of items that can be seen to be elements in a good human life anyway, independently of a particular ethic. We need not credit Aristotle with such a monolithic, if comprehensive, conception of reasons for acting in general. In any case reasons for acting in general need be no concern of his when he discusses eudaimonia. The concept of eudaimonia marks out, rather, just one dimension of practical worthwhileness. Practical worthwhileness in general is multi-dimensional, and the considerations that occupy different dimensions are not necessarily commensurable with one another. The significance of the fact that eudaimonia is equated with *the* good is not that all possible reasons for acting (all goods, in one obvious sense: see *NE* 1094a1–3) are embraced under eudaimonia, but that worthwhileness along the dimension marked out by the concept of eudaimonia is worthwhileness *par excellence*.[33]

As we see, McDowell's view involves a reading of the completeness and self-sufficiency of eudaimonia according to which to claim that eudaimonia-activity is the highest, most complete, and self-sufficient good is to claim that it singles out a particular "dimension of worthwhileness *par excellence*." The Function Argument then identifies this distinctive worthwhileness with virtuous activity. The virtuous person sees virtuous activity

---

[31] (1998a/1998b), 25, n. 5.
[32] See also McDowell (1998a/1998b), 33, n. 19.
[33] McDowell (1998a/1998b), 41. See too his (1995/2009), 31–32.

(i.e., eudaimonia-activity) as a type of activity that demonstrates a *sui generis* value superior in kind to any other, making life "choiceworthy and lacking in nothing" (1097b15). On McDowell's reading, this pivotal phrase, "that which alone makes life choiceworthy and lacking in nothing," is not meant as some sort of comprehensive claim about every good. Rather, it claims a normative and practical preeminence for a particular type of activity: eudaimonia.[34] This is how McDowell interprets the idea of virtuous activity not "being counted in together with other goods" (1097b17). The demands of acting virtuously in some instance are not weighed against advantages and disadvantages along some other dimension of worthwhileness, such as pleasure or health or financial cost; those others are, instead, in McDowell's view "silenced":

> How this derivative employment of the "prudential" notions comes about can be explained as follows. To embrace a specific conception of eudaimonia is to see the relevant reasons for acting, *on occasions when they coexist with considerations that on their own would be reasons for acting otherwise*, as, not overriding, but silencing those other considerations ... There seems to be no obstacle to allowing this derivative employment of the "prudential" concepts to occur side by side with a more ordinary employment—except that there is a risk of confusing them.[35]

While the terminology is rather confusing, the point is that McDowell understands Aristotle as isolating a distinctive notion of the harm and

---

[34] See too (1995/2009), 26–28. This marks some similarity with an exclusivist or monist view, except for the important difference that defenders of this view without fail continue to treat eudaimonia as a Comprehensive Practical Principle, and so as something that embraces all reasons for action; we saw that this made difficulties for exclusivist/monistic interpreters. See also Heinaman (1988) and (2007). Although Irwin (2012a) vigorously defends a comprehensivist interpretation of eudaimonia as, all things considered, the best both philosophically and textually, he nevertheless concedes that the specific texts describing self-sufficiency and completeness in I.7 can be read so as to support an exclusivist or monistic interpretation; see also Irwin (2012b), 165.

[35] (1980/1998b), 17–18, my emphasis. While McDowell speaks of "silencing," I speak of "trumping" or "superseding." The upshot is the same insofar as the decision about what is to be done, from the perspective of virtuous activity, is settled and definitive. The term "trump" or "supersede" captures this, but without saying anything about the agent's moral psychology. The term "silencing" makes a moral psychological claim, albeit in metaphorical terms, which in part insists that the agent not feel any pull or attraction toward the non-virtuous action. McDowell wants this to be the case and thinks something like it must be the case for Aristotle, because only if the non-virtuous course of action is silenced for the virtuous person can her psychology be differentiated from the continent person's; the latter is someone for whom the temptation to act contrary to virtue is still quite "audible," as we might put it. For further discussion, see Vigani (2019) and (2020).

benefit conferred by virtue from "ordinary prudential reasons."[36] While the former "derivative prudential reasons" are those that are employed by the virtuous person and manifested in their conception of what doing well is, McDowell also maintains that "ordinary" prudential reasons are still operative alongside these special, derivative ones in the course of a person's life. These ordinary reasons, which may be hedonic, aesthetic, hygienic, and so on, operate as reasons in circumstances where doing well—the distinctive kind of action undertaken for its own sake as an instance of doing well—is not at issue. We thus see how stark the contrast is between McDowell's conception of eudaimonism and the conception presented by Vlastos and the dominant tradition, which seeks to embrace all actions under the comprehensive umbrella of eudaimonia.

In a particular circumstance, virtue may require that a person forgo a certain pleasure. For one who is virtuous and committed to acting virtuously as what doing well is, "ordinary" reasons—for example, the pleasure involved in an activity one must forgo—are superseded. But in a situation where, say, indulging in such a pleasure would *not* be contrary to virtue, "ordinary" reasons can have their ordinary force. So, when having a drink is neither intemperate nor contrary to some other virtue (e.g., one has not made a commitment to do something that requires alertness and sobriety), one could, for example, choose what to drink, a martini or a glass of wine, based on reasons of pleasure and taste. In such a case, choosing wine would not be thought of by McDowell's Aristotle as an action undertaken for the sake of the eudaimonia; doing well would be neither here nor there in such a choice, except insofar as it operated as a limiting condition.[37] If this is correct, then McDowell is understanding eudaimonia, in its role as a practical principle, as a Superseding Practical Principle (one that trumps, or for McDowell, silences, any reasons for acting contrary to what doing well, what virtuous activity, demands) and not as a Comprehensive Practical Principle, which aims to explain the rationality of all of one's deliberate, non-incontinent actions. If we combine McDowell's emphasis on eudaimonia as (virtuous) activity with the idea that it functions as a Superseding Practical Principle, then one gets a version of Socrates's Supremacy of Virtue as a conception of

---

[36] This is a point we have seen clearly in Plato in Chapters 1, 2, and 3. He argues that the virtuous person is always "better off" acting virtuously, but of course this does not mean that the virtuous person is better off in any "ordinary" sense—that is, physically healthier, more beautiful, wealthier, and so on.

[37] Broadie (1991), 31, briefly mentions a similar idea.

what eudaimonia is, where virtue is explicitly understood as virtuous activity undertaken for its own sake. Eudaimonia *just is* engaging in virtuous activity (and never engaging in activity that is contrary to virtue), case by case.

Relatedly, Susan Sauvé Meyer also explicitly rejects the idea that, in my language, eudaimonia functions as a Comprehensive Practical Principle.[38] Rather, she sees acting for the sake of eudaimonia, or what is equivalent for Aristotle, acting for the sake of the *kalon*, as often operating as a limiting condition or constraint on action.[39] Meyer writes:

> It is clear upon reflection, that the ethical person's commitment to adhere to the standards of the *kalon* is not sufficient to determine or explain all of his actions, or even all of his subordinate goals. To be sure, there are some situations in which his commitment to the *kalon* makes it clear what he must do (or not do). This is the case, for example, when standing his ground in battle and risking his life is called for and fleeing his post would be shameful; or when being agreeable to a tyrant, laughing at a particular joke, or failing to take offence would be shameful. However, many more situations, perhaps even most of situations in which an ethical person acts, are ones in which nothing admirable or shameful is at stake. Which socks shall I wear this morning? Shall I go to the movies tonight or stay home and read a book? Shall I become a doctor or a dentist? Should I marry George? Shall I have tea or coffee with my breakfast? Should I accept the job in Toronto or New York? [...] We may call this the "space of permissions" left open by that ultimate commitment [to the *kalon*].[40]

Here Meyer expresses an understanding of Aristotle's practical injunction to commit to doing what is *kalon* above all that fits with McDowell's account and what I have argued is also Socrates's and Plato's understanding of the Supremacy of Virtue, explicitly rejecting the wide scope of a Vlastos-like, comprehensive account. Socrates's commitment to SV, and his urging others to commit similarly, often leaves agents in the "space of permissions" relative

---

[38] Meyer (2011). While Lear (2004) maintains that a comprehensive interpretation has to be part of the idea that eudaimonia generates the goodness of everything that is good, Meyer argues, contrary to Lear, that what I have been calling the "limiting condition" role of *to kalon* shows that it need not regulate our life the way that a "general's goal regulates the activity of the cavalry" (59). Meyer makes no mention of Heinaman (2007), although her position would be supported in certain respects by his arguments against inclusivist accounts.
[39] See Introduction, Chapters 1 and 2.
[40] Sauvé Meyer (2011), 58.

to the demands that virtue makes, either positively by presenting an action as what virtue requires or, more typically, in its role as a limiting condition by prohibiting certain actions as being contrary to virtue.[41]

4. McDowell's Account and the Problem of External Goods

How do external goods fit with Aristotle's conception of eudaimonia on McDowell's account? What goes missing on McDowell's austere account of eudaimonia, as he himself emphasizes, is a conception of the happy life and of happiness conceived of as a good life that a person would desire independently of their attachment to Aristotle's substantive conception of ethical virtue. McDowell's Aristotle does not provide a sketch of the good life for a human being that people accept or would accept once they adequately understood what their real nature consists in, which could then be seen to be brought about by virtuous activity. This explicitly rejects a grounding for virtue in the way envisaged by the Eudaimonist Hope.[42] According to McDowell, Aristotle identifies eudaimonia with the token instances of virtuous activity rather than with something beyond those: for example, as on inclusivist or comprehensivist accounts, a complete lifetime of such virtuous activity, along with a suitable amount of external goods.[43]

---

[41] In Chapter 5, I will consider Meyer's view in relation to Aristotle's conception of eudaimonia as *theoria*. In Chapter 2, we saw that Socrates says nothing about how to decide what to do in cases where, as I put it, virtue is not at issue, subject to the ubiquitous presence of virtue as a limiting condition; one can decide to do what one wants, in any way one wants, as far as SV is concerned, so long as one's action is not required by or contrary to virtue. I argued that this was a way of having Socrates's commitment to SV be operating, in the sense of being a limiting condition, in absolutely all actions. This will be important to the interpretation of Stoicism in Chapter 7, where there is considerable debate about whether there are actions of some significance that are neither required nor forbidden by virtue. I argue there that this plays an important role in the development of the Stoic theory of "indifferents."

[42] See Chapter 1; also Broadie (1994), 42; Irwin (2007–2009) believes that Aristotle is a realist in some sense about the content of virtue and the fine. Thus, although Irwin is one of the strongest defenders of eudaimonism, the eudaimonism he ascribes to Aristotle (and Plato) does not adopt the Eudaimonist Hope. He does, as we discussed in Chapter 1, believe that eudaimonism, and Aristotle's version of it, supplies a naturalist foundation and justification for virtue in the good life, while nevertheless rejecting the idea that this naturalist account provides the *content* of virtue. On some other interpretations of eudaimonism, by contrast, as we have seen, supplying this content is one of the primary points of eudaimonism; see Chapter 2 for scholars who attribute the Eudaimonist Hope to Socrates, such as Bobonich (2010) and Reshotko (2006). This issue will arise again in connection with Epicurus in Chapter 6 and Cicero in the Epilogue.

[43] As McDowell's opponents object, however, this is what Aristotle actually *says*. In the following chapter we will see that it is not, after all, precisely what Aristotle *does* say.

Let's begin with the well-attested point that happiness in some way involves "a complete life" (1098a18, 1100a5, 1101a16, 1177b25, 1178b26). Continuing to leave the details of the text aside for the moment, we can appreciate that once the highest good, conceived of as a Superseding Practical Principle, is "virtuous activity in a complete life" rather than simply "virtuous activity," a situation in which acting according to virtue is going to cut one's life short becomes particularly problematic.[44] If Aristotle believes, as he certainly does, that such situations can arise, then how can his conception of eudaimonia as "virtuous activity in a complete life" continue to function as a Superseding Practical Principle? An agent cannot rationally sacrifice their eudaimonia—for no end could trump the superseding aim of action—and yet they must, if eudaimonia is virtuous activity in a complete life, since *ex hypothesi* they will not have a complete life when they engage in this virtuous activity.

Thus there is no conceptual room, really, on an account like McDowell's for the idea that having a "complete life" *could* be a component of eudaimonia; on his account that would be to let in a factor that would be external to the pursuit of virtuous activity for its own sake, which exhausts the content of eudaimonia.[45] McDowell all but concedes this explicitly when he tries to take the "complete life" requirement on board:

> From NE 1098a18–20, it is clear that Aristotle conceives *eudaimonia* as, primarily, an attribute of a whole life. This can encourage the idea that the point an agent sees in an action undertaken for the sake of *eudaimonia* must be derivative from the independent attractiveness of a life lived according to a certain blueprint. But this idea [sc. the idea of eudaimonia's being the attribute of a whole life] is anyway hard to make cohere with the thesis that character-revealing action [. . .] is undertaken for its own sake. That seems to rule out taking the point of such action for the agent to lie outside itself, in the independent attractiveness of a life into which, if all goes well, it will fit. Suppose all does not go well, and one's life does not achieve the projected shape; does that mean that this particular action, say one of

---

[44] Throughout the rest of the chapter, I am considering eudaimonia as morally virtuous activity, not as theoretical activity, as proposed in *NE* X.7–8; I shall examine that in the following chapter.

[45] So this might be seen as a second problem for inclusivists or comprehensivists as well; we saw earlier that including other things besides virtuous activity (whether moral or intellectual) as components of eudaimonia seemed to be a category mistake. Of course, comprehensivists, like most interpreters of Aristotle, view eudaimonia as a Comprehensive Practical Principle, not a Superseding Practical Principle; and, they would point to this issue as one advantage of their interpretation.

standing one's ground in battle, did not after all have the point it seemed to? Surely not. Of course this does not rule out the possibility that if one's life as a whole goes badly enough, in respect of modes of desirability that are intelligible independently of the worthwhileness of virtuous behaviour, one can lose one's grip on the distinctive point of virtuous behaviour.[46]

McDowell's criticism shifts from what he takes to be a criticism of *interpretations* of Aristotle—what encourages the mistaken "blueprint" model of eudaimonia—to criticism of *Aristotle himself* ("this idea is anyway hard to make cohere"). It is difficult to see that "this idea" does not really refer to the "blueprint" model but to what is Aristotle's *own* demand that eudaimonia—in some way or other—involve a complete life. The point, however, is that McDowell ends up essentially criticizing Aristotle for not adequately distinguishing the special distinctive role of eudaimonia as virtuous activity from eudaimonia conceived of as an ordinarily attractive life. The problem centers on the role of eudaimonia as a practical principle: if it is a Superseding Practical Principle (as one would expect it to be, since the activity that eudaimonia is is virtuous activity), then it is difficult to see how something like "having a complete life" or, indeed, having any external goods can factor into deliberation as ends without that undercutting the commitment to virtuous action that may, in unfortunate but all-too-common circumstances, involve the sacrifice of those very things.[47] Overall, then, the "complete life" requirement explicitly raises the tension between eudaimonia's role as a Superseding Practical Principle and its being a conception of a desirable life.

---

[46] (1998a/1998b), 43–44. See also his (1995/2009), 206: "We can make the difficulty vivid by considering cases of virtuous behaviour that seriously threaten the agent's prospects of achieving an optimal combination of independent goods, on any plausible interpretation of that idea. [Suppose genuinely courageous behaviour risks life and limb.] Surely that should not even seem to reveal that the point a courageous person thought he saw in the action was illusory. But how can we prevent it from seeming to have that effect, if we conceive the point of cultivating virtue as derivative from the attractiveness of a life conceived in terms of procuring those independent goods? [. . .] How can that not have the effect of making the action's value at least open to question?"

[47] But could we not say that eudaimonia is still the best good, which one must unfortunately miss out on in a situation where virtue requires, say, one's premature death? In such a case, a courageous person, while she is to be praised for doing the virtuous action, was unfortunate in that she lost the opportunity for happiness (since she failed to have a complete life). (Sarah Broadie and Hendrik Lorenz have pressed this objection in conversation.) This response is adequate, so far as it goes, but what is critical is that it shows that whatever principle this person was acting on in deeming that an action required that she sacrifice her life, it could not have been *happiness, conceived of as including a complete life*; thus, it implies that there must be *some other* practical principle that supersedes happiness. On this interpretation happiness would be *neither* a Superseding Practical Principle *nor* a Comprehensive Practical Principle, but a mere Prudential Practical Principle. We have seen in Chapter 1 that this is Sarah Broadie's (2005) account of the ancient *summum bonum*.

Turning from the requirement of a complete life to the role of external goods, McDowell unsurprisingly again finds a very similar tension in Aristotle's own position:

> If we take seriously Aristotle's contention that a person's eudaimonia is his own doing, not conferred by fate or other people, but also try to make room *for his common-sense inclination* to say (e.g., 1099a31–b8) that external goods *make a life more satisfactory*, we are in any case required to distinguish, *on his behalf*, two measures of desirability or satisfactoriness: one according to which a life of exercises of excellence, being—as eudaimonia is—self-sufficient (1097b6–21), can contain no ground for regret in spite of great ill fortune; and one according to which such a life would have been better if the fates had been kinder. The derivative employment of the "prudential" notions[48] yields the former measure; and *the strains in Aristotle's treatment of the relation between eudaimonia and external goods* can be plausibly explained in terms of an intelligible tendency to slide between the derivative employment and a more ordinary conception of prudence. ("Role," 18, my emphases)

Here McDowell explicitly attributes the tension to Aristotle's own conception of eudaimonia. The role of external goods is limited to making a life "more satisfactory" in a common-sense way—according to "ordinary prudential reasons," as he puts it above. On McDowell's account, however, such external goods can have no direct impact on the worthwhileness (the happiness) of a life according to virtue; they merely add to the attractiveness of such a life considered from other—"ordinary"—perspectives.[49] There is a general reluctance by McDowell to claim that a loss of external goods can derail virtuous activity. Thinking about his interpretation, even

---

[48] This is McDowell's idea, discussed above, that a special dimension of worthwhileness indicated by *eudaimonia* yields a special employment of ordinary prudential terms, such as harm and benefit, such that the loss, say, of a certain pleasure in a circumstance where having that pleasure would be contrary to virtue (temperance) counts as no genuine loss or harm at all. Hursthouse (1999), 182–187, argues that such things *are* genuine losses and criticizes McDowell (and Aristotle) for denying it.

[49] This is a point to which McDowell repeatedly returns, e.g., (1995/2009, 32): "Factors outside an agent's control can make it impossible to live the life of a virtuous person (*even if they leave isolated bits of virtuous behaviour still feasible*), as perhaps in cases like that of Priam (1100a5–9). But chance goods can surely make a life more desirable, in some obvious sense, otherwise than through their effect on what is possible for the agent to achieve by his own efforts, and the ranking of lives as more or less desirable that is operative here ought not to be relevant to their assessment in terms of eudaimonia."

if we ultimately disagree with it, we can appreciate why he defends it. If one considers the virtuous action to be done as a function of the circumstances in which one finds oneself—and this account may certainly be encouraged by the Doctrine of the Mean (II.6) and I.10 (1100b30–1101a6) —then barring a state in which *no* activity is possible (e.g., being in a coma), some virtuous action, even severely impeded, will remain possible. Given McDowell's *identification* of virtuous activity undertaken for its own sake with happiness, the point at which loss of external goods will prevent engagement in virtuous activity at all will be fairly extreme. McDowell must deny, then, that dropping below what might be an otherwise desirable amount of external goods (along, as he would put it, some alternative dimension of worthwhileness) interferes with one's happiness.[50] An obvious objection to McDowell's interpretation is that this seems unsatisfactory in its own right and seems implausible as an interpretation of Aristotle, who in fact spends considerable time discussing goods of fortune and what they add to a human life.

In the next chapter we will look closely at Aristotle's text to see how well McDowell's claims fit and find that there is in fact a way of preserving McDowell's understanding of the role of eudaimonia as a practical principle, while accommodating Aristotle's repeated remarks about the role of a complete life and external goods. Before doing so, we should note, however, the relevance of the aiming/determining distinction we utilized to understand Plato to Aristotle's conception of eudaimonia. It is one thing to deliberate about the place of external goods in one's conception of eudaimonia, as we have been concerned with in this chapter: are they a component of eudaimonia, necessary for eudaimonia, neither, and so on? It is another matter to consider the role of external goods in determining what the virtuous action *is*.[51] One might think that McDowell's understanding of Aristotle is like the traditional understanding of Socrates: one should care *only* about virtue and never consider things like life, death, pleasure, money,

---

[50] Nevertheless eudaimonia, as an activity, can certainly be more or less *impeded*; thus this is still notably different from the Stoic view, as it is usually understood; if activity is prevented, so is eudaimonia. Since activity can certainly be prevented by a drastic enough lack of external goods, we can adhere to Aristotle's claim that to call the virtuous man on the rack happy is simply to defend a philosophical thesis (I.5, 1095b31–1096a2; VII.13, 1153b19–21). See Chapter 5.

[51] I have argued that missing this distinction makes a mess of understanding Socrates's commitment to virtue as supreme and the nature of Socratic deliberation; see Chapter 2 and, for more details, Vasiliou (2008), chs. 1–2.

and so on. But this is the wrong view of Socrates as well as the wrong view of Aristotle.[52] Both reject consideration of external goods as *ends* that rival virtuous action as an end, but they both accept that the presence or absence of such goods are considerations in determining deliberations about what *constitutes* the virtuous action in some circumstance.

---

[52] And, as we shall see in Chapter 7, the wrong view of the Stoics and their views on "indifferents."

5
Aristotle on Happiness, Being Happy, and External Goods

This chapter argues that Aristotle has distinct criteria aimed at distinguishing (a) what it is for a person to be happy (*eudaimōn*), and (b) what it is for a person "to possess" (i.e., to engage in) happiness (*eudaimonia*); and, at least in the *Nicomachean Ethics* and *Politics*, he seeks to preserve this conceptual distinction terminologically in his use of the words εὐδαίμων and εὐδαιμονία.[1] Although it may initially sound paradoxical, Aristotle does not believe that it is necessary that happiness implies a happy person or a happy life. Before dismissing such a view outright, we might note the following remark by Philippa Foot: "But there is a third interpretation of the word happiness: the one in which we must understand someone who in sacrificing his life for the sake of justice would not have said that he is sacrificing his *happiness*, but rather that *the happy life* had turned out not to be possible for him. We cannot ignore this interpretation of the concept if we identify happiness with the human good."[2] I shall argue that this is precisely Aristotle's view.

This distinction between happiness and the happy life or happy person neatly resolves, in one fell swoop, much of the debate between "exclusivist" or "monistic" and "inclusivist" interpretations, which we canvassed in the

---

[1] For a comparative discussion of the three ethics—the *Nicomachean Ethics*, *Eudemian Ethics*, and *Magna Moralia*—on theses related to happiness, see Irwin (2003). There Irwin leaves open the possibility that the *MM* rejects eudaimonism, 96–97, since 1212b18–20 seems to argue that virtuous person is lover of the good, not a lover of the self, for he only loves himself insofar as he is good. So, I suppose, the view is that if I put something above my own well-being, then I am not a eudaimonist. Irwin also concludes, tentatively, that the *NE* is the most philosophically sophisticated of the three works, and Irwin would "find it difficult to suppose" that the writer of the *MM* had access to the *EE* and *NE* or that the *EE* was a revision of the *NE*, rather than vice versa (107–108).

[2] Foot (2001), 97 (my emphases). The first two conceptions of happiness Foot canvases are happiness as subjective contentment and a conception of happiness according to which a fortunate (in one sense!) evil person might be said to be happy.

previous chapter. On Aristotle's own account, eudaimonia, "doing well" (1095a19), is the same as virtuous activity undertaken for its own sake.[3] But what it is to be a happy person (*eudaimōn*) is not simply "to possess" (i.e., to engage in) eudaimonia. Rather, to be happy one has to engage in eudaimonia *and* to be supplied sufficiently with external goods, including living a complete life (1101a14-17).[4] Succinctly, on Aristotle's view, it is not necessary in order to possess *eudaimonia* that one be *eudaimōn*; it is, however, necessary but not sufficient for being *eudaimōn* that one possesses *eudaimonia*. Thus, external goods are *not* components of happiness itself but *are* components of the happy life.

Furthermore, we shall see that recognizing Aristotle's distinction between happiness and the happy person provides strong evidence that contrary to almost all interpretations he does not conceive of happiness as a Comprehensive Practical Principle.[5] Rather, when Aristotle considers happiness as consisting in what we have been calling morally virtuous activity (as he does until X.7), happiness functions as a Superseding Practical Principle. This will enable a new interpretation of the problem of how to understand Aristotle's claim in X.7–8 that the best eudaimonia is theoretical study. The most significant obstacle to a coherent solution is the idea that eudaimonia must always be operating as a Comprehensive Practical Principle, thereby requiring that, somehow, morally virtuous activity must be for the sake of contemplation. We shall see that conceiving of eudaimonia as contemplation is not only not meant comprehensively, but it is not meant as a *practical* principle at all, and so does not conflict in any way with Aristotle's earlier position that eudaimonia as morally virtuous action is a Superseding Practical Principle.

---

[3] As exclusivists and its sympathizers would have it: Kraut (1989), Lear (2004), Brown (2005). Broadie (1991) takes eudaimonia identified with virtuous activity to be the "central" or core aspect of the concept. We have seen too that McDowell takes an especially hard line here: eudaimonia is identical to virtuous activity, so that engaging in virtuous activity just is engaging in happiness-activity, not promoting it or even a component of it.

[4] As inclusivists, beginning with Ackrill (1980) and including Irwin (1985) (2012a), Cooper (1985), and Roche (2014), among many others, would have it. If comprehensive means all types of goods are included in happiness, as Irwin says (2012b), 164, then I deny that even Aristotle's account of being *eudaimōn* is comprehensive, but I do agree that it is *inclusive*, that is, that it has components—virtuous activity, complete life, and external goods. I also maintain that certain goods in themselves, like harmless pleasures, fall outside the scope even of the happy life; they are simply irrelevant to whether one's life is happy or not.

[5] Charles (2014) is an exception; see also his (1999) and (2017).

1. The *Eudaimōn/Eudaimonia* Distinction (EED)

I know of no English translation that is consistently careful to distinguish when Aristotle ascribes something to the happy person, and when to happiness, since as far as I know only two scholars, C. D. C. Reeve and David Charles, have thought the distinction significant. The conceptual distinction is explicitly in Reeve's 1992 book *The Practices of Reason* (118): "*eudaimonia* is not sufficient to make someone *eudaimōn*."[6] While Reeve published this over twenty-five years ago, as far as I can see it has made no impact on the literature.[7] Reeve himself does not argue one way or the other that Aristotle preserves the distinction in his linguistic usage, reserving εὐδαιμονία in his substantive sense for virtuous activity. Nor does he set up the distinction between the happy person/life and happiness as driven by what I have described above as the dual needs of a conception of eudaimonia: to serve as a Superseding Practical Principle and to serve as an account of the good life. Thus, Reeve himself does not explore the implications of this distinction for the understanding of Aristotle's eudaimonism.[8]

Charles, who does not cite Reeve, explicitly rejects the identification of eudaimonia and the happy life as part of his defense of his paradigm account.[9] Much of his argument is congenial to and supports mine. What

---

[6] See also 159ff. At 166, n. 36: "[Irwin's] account [of the role of external goods] confuses *eudaimonia*, which is an activity, with a *eudaimōn* biographical life, which is not. Virtuous activity is sufficient for *eudaimonia*, since it just is *eudaimonia*. But it is not sufficient to make a biographical life *eudaimōn*."

[7] The book is not even cited in Roche (2014), where the distinction would be most relevant; see below.

[8] In Reeve's (2014) translation and commentary on the *Nicomachean Ethics*, as far as I can tell, he ignores the distinction completely, not mentioning it either in the Introduction or in the notes to the translation; moreover, he does not follow it in the translation itself (see particular notes below). The index entry, 396, is labeled "Happiness, happy (*eudaimonia*)"; what follows is a list of passages indiscriminately about either *eudaimonia* or being a happy person with no indication that they ought to be distinguished, as he himself did in his (1992).

[9] Charles (2014). Furthermore, Charles defends a quite broad view of which activities can count as "doing well" and so as sufficiently resembling the central case of theoria: "In the human case, several distinct activities, such as theoretical activity, virtuous action, and being healthy can all be cases of doing well. They are instances of the type of activity which makes a life worth living and lacking in nothing" (132). Although I cannot argue this here, I part ways with the range of activities (defended on the basis of texts from the *Rhetoric*, see 126) that "make a life worth living" and believe that they are instead constituted by either morally virtuous activity or, better yet, theoretical activity. I agree that given that we are human beings and political animals, we will inevitably have to engage in ordinary virtuous activity; I will argue further that the knowledge that theoretical activity is the best sort of activity is critical to our deliberating well practically in deciding what to pursue. I think we can take Aristotle at his word that theoretical activity is best and morally virtuous activity "secondary eudaimonia" without this generating a conflict once we have been disabused of the idea that eudaimonia is operating in Aristotle as a Comprehensive Practical Principle and appreciated the *eudaimōn/eudaimonia* distinction. And, furthermore, the news that theoretical activity is the best activity in no way alters the virtuous person's commitment to acting morally virtuously as their

follows below, however, adds a philological or terminological argument in addition to the philosophical one; I argue that when Aristotle is discussing his own view of eudaimonia as an activity he is careful to distinguish it from what constitutes either a happy person or a happy life (being *eudaimōn*).

There are 114 instances of eud*[10] in the *Nicomachean Ethics*—55 occurrences of εὐδαιμονία[11] and 36 of εὐδαίμων, together accounting for 91 of the 114. The first ten occurrences are general uses in I.1–7 (–1097b22, i.e., the start of the Function argument), prior to Aristotle's own view being on the table; they concern reputable beliefs about eudaimonia, and other virtual platitudes such as that eudaimonia is living well or doing well.[12] After this, there are four sections of the text where we find significant, clustered uses of eud*: (1) in Book I from the end of the Function Argument to the beginning of I.13 (1098b23–1102a17), where various *endoxa* about eudaimonia are considered, particularly as related to the role of external goods and fortune; (2) in VII.13, where many of the same themes from the Book I passages are rehearsed; (3) in IX.9, in the course of describing the role of friendship as the greatest of external goods; and (4) in X.6-8, when Aristotle reveals that the best type of eudaimonia is contemplation (*theōria*).

The terminological and conceptual thesis is as follows. Whenever Aristotle is discussing *his own* substantive views about happiness in the *Nicomachean Ethics* and *Politics*, he is careful to reserve εὐδαιμονία for the activity of virtue—that is, engaging in genuinely virtuous actions, doing the right thing at the right time for the right reasons.[13] Like any activity, eudaimonia will need certain external goods if it is not to be impeded. Possessing an adequate amount of these external goods in a complete life by a person engaged in virtuous activity for its own sake just is what it is *to be happy*. εὐδαίμων, εὐδαιμονίζω, and εὐδαιμονέω (as well as μακάριος and μακαρίζω) all

---

Superseding Practical Principle, for theoretical activity is not, in fact, any kind of *praxis* at all; as we will see Aristotle makes explicit, it is, crucially, an activity that is *not* a praxis, which is part of why it is divine.

[10] I shall use eud* to indicate any of the following words: εὐδαίμων, εὐδαιμονία, εὐδαιμονικός, εὐδαιμονίζω, εὐδαιμονέω.
[11] I shall use Greek in the main text to indicate when I am talking about the word εὐδαιμονία, εὐδαίμων, and so on.
[12] 1095a18, 1095a20, 1095b15, 1096a2, 1097a34, 1097b4, 1097b6, 1097b16, 1097b20, 1097b22.
[13] Of course, in other works (e.g., *Rhetoric* 1360b15–30) Aristotle is not relying on his own conception of eudaimonia, and so εὐδαιμονία is not restricted to an activity. This happens as well in the *NE* itself, when, for example, he considers various reputable beliefs about happiness in I.4. In *Politics*, however, he does adhere to this distinction: the only two instances of ἐνέργεια (1328a37–38 and 1332a9) are in the context of discussing eudaimonia as the "perfect activity and use of virtue."

indicate a person's being or being called happy.[14] I label this "The Εὐδαίμων/ Εὐδαιμονία Distinction," or EED for short. In the sections that follow, I will show that EED is present in the *Nicomachean Ethics* and *Politics* and how it neatly resolves long-standing interpretative disputes about the nature and role of Aristotle's conception of *eudaimonia*, including his notorious claim that the best eudaimonia consists in the activity of study or contemplation.[15]

2. EED in I.7–13 and VII.13: Happiness and External Goods

At the end of I.10 Aristotle asks, apparently rhetorically: "Therefore what prevents one from saying that the happy man (εὐδαίμονα) is one who acts in accordance with complete virtue and is sufficiently (ἱκανῶς) supplied with external goods, not over any chance time, but for a complete life (τέλειον βίον)?" (1101a14–17). Scholars frequently take this as a revision of the account of happiness first offered after the Function Argument in I.7.[16] There, on most accounts, Aristotle has defined *eudaimonia* as rational activity in accordance with virtue in a complete life. In the passage above Aristotle's revised account now includes a requirement that there be adequate external goods. But, as EED would predict, the passage is explicitly an account of a

---

[14] Brown (2005), 72, 77, claims that Aristotle invokes "blessedness" when "happiness as it is ordinarily conceived" is being discussed. For Brown, while external goods are part of blessedness (which itself sums up all our wishes, but not our choices), they are not part of Aristotle's own conception of happiness. EED enables a similar point more easily, with much broader implications. See also Broadie (1991), for some sympathy with a distinction between being *makarios* and being *eudaimōn*. Karamanolis (2006), 75–76, expresses a similar view of Aristotle, in the course of arguing about Antiochus's Peripatetic position.

[15] While I will not venture to say anything about the chronological order or authenticity of the three Aristotelian ethics, it seems that one remarkable feature of the *NE*, in contrast with both the *EE* and *MM*, is its distinctive focus on the concept of *energeia*: it is presented in the very first lines of the first chapter of the *NE*, which makes the point that sometimes an activity can be its own end. While both the *MM* and *EE* also say that eudaimonia is an activity (*energeia*), this is more often than not connected with "use" (χρῆσις), and together opposed to *hexis* (state). In the *NE*, the author uses χρῆσις only eight times and never pairs it with ἐνέργεια; ἐνέργεια, by contrast, is ubiquitous (119 times), compared with 39 occurrences in *MM* and (26, or 39 with the common books) in the *EE*. Given this, my speculative hypothesis is that in the *NE* Aristotle has thought hard and in detail about the ramifications of his claim that eudaimonia is an *energeia* (perhaps as a result of his theoretical work on *energeia* in *Metaphysics* Z and H and the *De Anima*). In particular, he focuses on the effect the identification of eudaimonia with an *energeia* has on whether external goods, including friends and duration of life, can coherently be a part or component of an activity, which they cannot. The *EE* and *MM*, in their frequent conjunction of use and activity, simply oppose this conception of eudaimonia to one in which it is a state or even compatible with inactivity, without considering the theoretical ramifications of its being an *energeia*.

[16] Cooper (1985), 173–174; Roche (2014), 35, endorses this, describing 1101a14–17 as Aristotle's apparent "revised statement of his earlier sketch of *eudaimonia*."

happy *person, not* of *eudaimonia*; *eudaimonia* is the activity described in the first conjunct, as Aristotle says explicitly many times. See, for example, the opening sentence of I.13, which is presented as a summation of what has come previously and as an introduction to what will follow: "Since *eudaimonia* is some activity of soul according to complete virtue (ψυχῆς ἐνέργειά τις κατ' ἀρετὴν τελείαν), we must investigate virtue" (1102a5–6). Again, a few lines later: "and we say that *eudaimonia* is an activity of soul (ψυχῆς ἐνέργειαν)" (1102a17–18).[17]

Next consider the infamous "in a complete life" added at the end of the Function Argument (1098a18). It too describes not a further condition for *eudaimonia*, but rather what must be *added to eudaimonia* to yield a happy and blessed person. Recall the specific language of the passage: "For one swallow does not make a spring, nor does one day, so too one day or a short time does not *make a man blessed and happy* (μακάριον καὶ εὐδαίμονα)" (1098a18–20). Aristotle does not say here that *eudaimonia* requires a complete life; rather, he says that a complete life is required in order for a *person* to be blessed and happy.

Two points about the additional requirement of "a complete life." First, immediately after the complete life requirement, Aristotle says: "Let the good be outlined in this way (περιγεγράφθω μὲν οὖν τἀγαθὸν ταύτῃ)" (1098a20–21). The good or best life will be the happy life. So, thus far, Aristotle has the happy life consist in virtuous activity undertaken for its own sake (i.e., *eudaimonia* strictly) in a complete life.

Second, at 1101a14–17 (quoted above), the idea that the happy person must have a complete life is mentioned separately from his need for having a suitable amount of external goods. The notion of being complete or perfect, *teleion*, is a complex one in the *Nicomachean Ethics*. The need for a complete life is mentioned three more times in the *NE*. It is clear, at least, that having a complete life is a function of duration. As scholars have noticed, this is not any set duration, but some significant amount of time in which a person may engage in virtuous activity. At the beginning of the following chapter (I.8), Aristotle emphasizes that on his account *eudaimonia* consists in activities and actions of the soul (1098b15–16). External goods, health, wealth, being well-born, beauty—that is, goods of the body, possessions, and

---

[17] Similar remarks are in Book X: Happiness is "in activities according to virtue (ἐν ταῖς κατ' ἀρετὴν ἐνεργείαις)" (1177a10); "activity according to virtue" (1177a12). Broadie (1991) interprets these passages as instances of synecdoche to avoid reading them as identities; Kraut (1993) criticizes this move as textually unsupported.

good luck—are important in two ways, both recognized in the literature. They may be useful as instruments or facilitators of the virtuous activity that is one's eudaimonia, and they may also add their own value to the overall quality of life; an otherwise happy life is marred if one's children have died, and so on (1099b2–8). As EED holds, however, the positive effect of external goods is on a person's having *a happy life*, not engaging in *happiness*—except, as we shall discuss further, in an extreme case where lack of external goods makes action impossible—for example, if one is in a coma.[18]

Despite the fact that completeness of life is mentioned separately from other external goods, it is not in fact different in kind. For one thing, it certainly depends on luck; it is only partly up to one whether one has a complete life. It is reasonably singled out, however, because it has a special status with respect to the happy life. As everyone recognizes, eudaimonia, virtuous activity, is the central element in a happy life. While the possession or loss of ordinary external goods can positively or negatively affect engagement in virtuous activity, and so affect, in an extreme case, whether one has a happy life, it is clear that Aristotle thinks that a person can continue to engage in eudaimonia-activity and so continue to be happy, or at least as we shall see not be miserable, despite quite unfavorable external goods. Having a complete life, however, is different: if one does not have a complete life, whatever duration that consists in exactly, then one loses a happy life: no one would call such a person happy, despite having engaged in eudaimonia-activity for the shorter time. The upshot is that while loss of ordinary external goods is compatible with remaining engaged in eudaimonia-activity and so remaining, to a considerable extent, happy, the loss of a complete life is not.

Near the end of I.8 Aristotle is pointing out that the best activities will also be both the most noble and the most pleasant; and further the best *energeiai*, or the one best of all, will in fact be eudaimonia. Here we have an example of Aristotle's very frequent insistence that eudaimonia is an activity. The next sentence reads as follows: "Yet it is also apparent that it needs in addition the external goods (τῶν ἐκτὸς ἀγαθῶν προσδεομένη), just as we have said; for it is impossible, or it is not easy, to do fine things while being without resources" (1099a31–33). The subject for "needs" is not explicit. The feminine participle, *prosdeomenē*, however, must be understood to agree with εὐδαιμονία from the preceding sentence. This is the only place I have found in the *NE*

---

[18] In the very beginning of the *Ethics*, Aristotle says that no one would call someone happy (εὐδαιμονίζω) who suffered the greatest misfortunes "unless he were maintaining a thesis" (1096a1–2); a very similar thought is expressed at VII.13, 1153b19–25.

where Aristotle says that *eudaimonia itself* needs external goods.[19] As we shall see, in every other case the explicit or implicit subject is "the happy person." While, as Aristotle usually says, it is the would-be happy *person* who needs external goods with which to carry out the activity of *eudaimonia*, it is natural to slide into saying that the activity itself needs these. For to engage in the activity of eudaimonia does require health, strength, and other resources, if it is not to be impeded. Consider the language in two other passages that are clearly making the same point. In the first, Aristotle is in the middle of discussing the role of fortune in the good life. He says that since eudaimonia is something we take to be firm and not easily changed, we cannot simply equate changes in fortune with a movement from being happy to being wretched (*athlios*). If we did, a person's life would be changing all the time and have the character "of a chameleon." "For it is not in these things [changing fortunes] that [we are said to do] well or badly, but rather a human life needs these things [goods of fortune] in addition (προσδεῖται), just as we said; and activities according to excellence are determinative of (κύριαι) of happiness, and contrary [activities] of the contrary" (1100b8–11).

Here what "needs goods of fortune in addition" is not eudaimonia, but rather "a human life," a *good* or *happy* human life.[20] Activities according to excellence, however, are determinative of eudaimonia. It is in line with EED and the rest of Aristotle's remarks to read *kuriai* strongly, as not just what is most important to eudaimonia but as what makes the activity one is engaging in eudaimonia or not, for eudaimonia *just is* the activity. It is a separate matter to see that how unimpeded those activities are is what determines whether a human life is happy or not.[21]

Another passage from VII.13, where some of issues raised in I.8–12 are revisited, makes a similar point in similar language: "Thus, the happy person

---

[19] This passage also has a couple of oddities. (1) It does not explicitly employ *eudaimonia* but it must be supplied for the feminine participle; (2) it contains the phrase "just as we said," but scholars agree that there is no reference to this having been said; and (3) the passage immediately preceding quoting Theognis mirrors the opening of the *EE*. If this passage was originally part of the *EE* (which opens with a discussion of external goods), which is now transplanted here (perhaps also accounting for the absence of a reference for "just as we said"), that would be another reason why eudaimonia might be said to itself need external goods, for the *EE* and *MM* do not always adhere to EED. At 1208a28, the author of the *MM* says they define happiness as "activity of virtue in a complete life"; EED would make this part of the definition of a happy life or happy person, but not happiness. At 1219a38–39, the argument concludes that "eudaimonia would be activity according to complete virtue through a whole life (ἡ εὐδαιμονία ζωῆς τελείας ἐνέργεια κατ' ἀρετὴν τελείαν)."

[20] See too *Politics* 1328b35–36 and 1329a22–23, where the discussion concerns what it is for a city to be happy (*eudaimōn*).

[21] As we shall see later, it also determines whether we have "perfect happiness" (*teleia eudaimonia*).

needs in addition (διὸ προσδεῖται ὁ εὐδαίμων) the goods of the body and external goods and fortune, so that he will not be impeded in these ways" (1153b16–9). The happy person needs external goods with which to perform the activities that constitute eudaimonia. Here we have the same verb, *prosdeomai*, "need in addition," that we have in the above passages. The subject of this verb is, again, the happy person or happy life, and not eudaimonia.

In other passages in the *NE* eudaimonia is limited to a particular kind of activity: doing the right thing in a particular time and place, while "being happy" or a "happy life" is used to signify a lifetime of (relatively) unimpeded exercise of *eudaimonia*. Consider the following from I.9:

> Reasonably, then, we call neither an ox nor a horse nor any other of the animals happy (εὔδαιμον); for none of these is able to participate in [the proper] sort of activity. And for this reason neither is a child happy (εὐδαίμων); for he is not a doer of such things at his age and those who say they are blessed (μακαρίζονται) do so on account of the hope [that they will be]. For [the happy person] requires (δεῖ γὰρ), as we said, not only complete excellence but also a complete life, since many changes and all kinds of turns of fortune occur in life and it is possible that, while being most prosperous to fall upon great disasters in old age, just as is told about Priam in the Trojan cycle; and no one considers someone to be happy (οὐδεὶς εὐδαιμονίζει) who has been through such fortune and has died miserably (ἀθλίως). (1099b32–1100a9)

The first part of this passage indicates that children and animals cannot be happy because they are not able to participate in the most essential and necessary part of being happy: virtuous activity. Irwin, Rowe, and Crisp all translate "for [the happy person] requires" as "happiness requires," but there is no occurrence of εὐδαιμονία in this passage.[22] Aristotle is talking about the necessary and sufficient conditions for being happy, not for happiness. The phrase "for there is required (*dei gar*)" picks up on what is necessary *to call someone happy*: it requires both complete virtue *and* a complete life. Thus, the discussion of Priam's *happiness* is *not* at issue in the

---

[22] Even Reeve (2014) translates, "since for happiness there must be." As I understand it, this translation mars the EED distinction, which, as I said above, Reeve takes to be important in his (1992); as I also mentioned, however, he never tries to defend, as I am, EED as a distinction that Aristotle himself preserves in his usage of εὐδαιμονία and εὐδαίμων. Reeve (2012) ignores the distinction as well, see, e.g., 120–122, 239.

passage; rather the question is whether one would call him *happy*. His previous lifetime of virtuous activity, let's assume, is as excellent as it ever was; but Aristotle's point is that no one, given his horrible fate, would consider him a happy man.

While being happy is a matter of the unimpeded exercise of eudaimonia, being wretched is the condition of "not doing the right thing" or "doing the shameful thing." As others have argued,[23] there is a middle ground between these two: namely doing the right thing under impeded circumstances. Engaging in eudaimonia-activity ensures that you will do the right thing, regardless of how wretched your situation: "If activities are what control (κύριαι) <the character> of life, just as we said [a reference to 1100b8ff., quoted above] no blessed man would become wretched (ἀθλίως); for he will never do hateful and base things (τὰ μισητὰ καὶ τὰ φαῦλα)" (1100b33–35). Therefore, the happy man will never be wretched, since he will always do the right thing and never do base actions, and activities are what control whether a life is happy or not. The middle ground that I am drawing attention to claims that one can fail to be happy, while still engaging in eudaimonia. This arises when one is doing the right thing under the circumstances, but the circumstances are so horrible and impeded that no one would call such a person happy.

Aristotle says that a truly wise and good person will always do the best action in the circumstances, even when the circumstances are (far) less than optimal, just as a general or a shoemaker will do the best he can with the situation he is handed (1101a1–5). Then, in his second mention of Priam, Aristotle continues, again adhering to EED:

> If [such a person will always act best given the circumstances, no matter how terrible], then the happy man (ὁ εὐδαίμων) will never become wretched (ἀθλίως), though neither will he be blessed (μακάριος) if he meets with fortunes like Priam's.[24] Nor indeed will he be variable (ποικίλος) or easily changeable (εὐμετάβολος); for he will not be moved from happiness easily (ἐκ τῆς εὐδαιμονίας κινηθήσεται ῥᾳδίως),[25] nor by any chance misfortune,

---

[23] For example, Broadie (1991), ch. 1, and Roche (2014).

[24] Broadie (2002) suggests that Aristotle may here be drawing a distinction between being happy and being blessed, although she agrees that Aristotle generally treats them synonymously; either way, the point does not affect EED.

[25] Rowe: "he will not be easily dislodged from his happy state"; this translation misses the force of EED. The particular point Aristotle is making here is that he will not be moved from his commitment to a certain type of *activity*: *eudaimonia*.

but [only] by great and many (ὑπὸ μεγάλων καὶ πολλῶν), and from such things he would not become happy again[26] (οὐκ ἂν γένοιτο πάλιν εὐδαίμων) in a short time, but, if at all, in some great and complete [time] in which he has achieved great and fine things. (1101a6–13)

Paying attention to EED, the idea that someone who has been afflicted by great and repeated misfortunes may then be "moved from *eudaimonia*" suggests that a person might lose his commitment to engaging in virtuous activity for its own sake above all.[27] Having lost this, he will not be able to recover "being a happy person" again easily or in a short time. This adds to the evidence that "a complete life" is attached to being a happy person and not to eudaimonia itself; for the passage explicitly says that a "complete" time will be needed not to re-engage with eudaimonia-activity, but to once again become a happy person.

Moreover, attention to EED enables us to better understand the flow of the argument here in 1.10: Aristotle has *already* explained that a good person may be impeded by misfortune from doing virtuous actions but that the *kalon* will still "shine through" and that the good person would still do the best actions possible in these bad circumstances (1100b30–1101a6). In the passage above, Aristotle turns to consider the additional possibility that a person who suffered huge misfortunes *could* (although unlikely and not easily, given the steadiness of virtue and the permanence of its activities, as Aristotle has also just emphasized, 1100b12ff.) be dislodged *from virtuous activity itself*, which means, moreover, that he would not quickly or easily become a happy person again. Appreciating EED shows that the passage is making a new point and not simply repeating what has already been said. Even if one were to get back on track, so to speak, with eudaimonia-activity the misfortunes one suffered would be so great as to take a long time before one could be called "happy"—indeed, whatever length of time constitutes a "complete life." Thus, we see that a person may be engaged in eudaimonia-activity without being happy, just as EED claims.

---

[26] Rowe's translation, "he will not recover his happiness," again gets what I take to be Aristotle's point backward: now Aristotle *is* talking about what it takes to be a happy person *not* about happiness. Irwin too has: "a return to happiness."

[27] McDowell suggests that this can happen (1998a), 43–44; Cooper (1985), 299, n.13, rejects such an interpretation, but does not consider the present passage.

3. EED in IX.9: Friendship

It is not my concern here to explain how all of the intricate and complex arguments in this chapter fit together. I intend only to show that EED is carefully maintained in Aristotle's discussion of the place of friendship in the happy life. Aristotle claims that having friends is the "greatest of the external goods" (1169b10). If EED is correct, we would then expect that friendship would be described as something that belongs to a happy person or happy life, but not strictly speaking to *eudaimonia* itself, which is precisely what we do find.[28]

IX.9 opens with a puzzle about whether the happy person will need friends or not. One might think the answer is "no," since what it is to be a happy person is to have all the goods, and therefore to be self-sufficient and in need of nothing in addition. Aristotle claims, by contrast, that the happy person needs friends for several reasons, including the fact that a friend is the greatest of external goods (1169b10), friends are needed to be the recipients of our noble actions (1169b10-16), and a happy person is not a solitary person and so his companions ought to be his friends (1169b16-22). In all of these passages, only εὐδαίμων and μακάριος are used.

At 1169b22-27, Aristotle raises the question again of what people could mean by saying that the happy person needs no friends. Since the life of the happy person has all the goods, he will not need friends for their usefulness, and since the happy person's life is already pleasant, he will not need friends for pleasure. Ruling out the need for friendships of utility and pleasure, the many, who do not understand Aristotle's account of true friendship where the friend is another self, mistakenly believe that the happy person needs no friends.

The only instance of εὐδαιμονία in the chapter occurs in Aristotle's response to this argument. It is not true that the happy person needs no friends: "for it was said in the beginning that *eudaimonia* is some activity (ἐνέργειά τις) and it is clear that an activity comes into being (γίνεται) and does not belong [to someone] like some possession (οὐχ ὑπάρχει ὥσπερ κτῆμά τι)" (1169b28-30). Here Aristotle speaks about what is true of

---

[28] There are two instances of μακάριος in VIII: in VIII.5, 1169b30, and VIII.6, 1170b18. Both passages argue that although the blessed person needs nothing, he will want good friends since the blessed person will want a pleasant life and one that is not solitary (and good friends contribute to both these ends). The only instances of eud* in books VIII and IX are in IX.9, where eud* occurs sixteen times. Strikingly, εὐδαιμονία appears only once (1169b29), while εὐδαίμων and μακάριος together occur thirteen times, which is what we would expect according to EED.

eudaimonia itself—it is an *activity* not a *possession*. The latter point is critical: *eudaimonia* is not something that belongs to someone. This is an explicit contrast with friends, which, like all goods, are said over and over in this chapter to belong (ὑπάρχει) to the happy person: 1169b5, b19, b25; 1170b2, b17. The happy person will *have* friends, but will *engage in* happiness. The happy person is someone who has all the goods (1169b5, b25), but *eudaimonia* is not one of the goods to be had, it is a distinctive type of activity.

The argument continues: "If being happy is in living and being active (εἰ δὲ τὸ εὐδαιμονεῖν ἐστὶν ἐν τῷ ζῆν καὶ ἐνεργεῖν), and the activity of the good person is excellent and pleasant in itself (σπουδαία καὶ ἡδεῖα καθ' αὑτήν)." (1169b30–32). Note the careful language: being happy is not being active or the activity, that is *eudaimonia*. Being happy consists rather *in* living and being active because *eudaimonia* is the *activity* of the happy person. But the happy person, as this chapter is concerned to argue, does more than simply act virtuously, he has all (or enough of) the valuable good things. The conclusion of this section of argument is that since virtuous activity (*eudaimonia*) is pleasant in itself to the virtuous person and since observing the activities of another is easier than observing one's own, the virtuous person will find observing the activities of his virtuous friend pleasant in itself. What is truly pleasant in itself is what is pleasant by nature. Since the happy person will have all good things (as well, of course, as being engaged in *eudaimonia*), he will need friends (1169b33–1170a4).

The short supplementary argument that follows, while not using the word εὐδαιμονία, continues to contrast the possession of friends and the pleasure that belongs to the happy person with the activity that constitutes happiness. Aristotle again begins with the point that the happy person lives pleasantly (1170a4), taking pleasure as we know from his virtuous activities. But living alone is harsh (χαλεπός), for: "it is not easy to engage in activity continuously by oneself (καθ' αὑτὸν ἐνεργεῖν συνεχῶς), but it is easier with others and toward others. Therefore the activity [with others] will be more continuous and will be pleasant in itself, which must be the case for the blessed person (ὃ δεῖ περὶ τὸν μακάριον εἶναι)" (1170a5–8).

Again, the value of friends is that they add to the in-itself pleasure of the happy person. For a good person, activity according to virtue continues to occur as long as she is capable of activity, but it is easier, more continuous, and less impeded with friends. A life of more continuous virtuous activity is a more pleasurable life. This is what must be the case, not for happiness, but for a happy or blessed person. Without going through the final, complex section of the chapter, I shall just note that the final line fits with EED: "Thus anyone who is to be happy person will need good friends (δεήσει ἄρα τῷ εὐδαιμονήσοντι φίλων σπουδαίων)" (1170b18–19).

We see, then, that overall IX.9 preserves EED perfectly. It is not surprising that εὐδαιμονία occurs only once (and that simply as a repeated reference to the claim that it is an activity), and εὐδαίμων and μακάριος occur frequently, since friends, as the greatest of external goods, are things that belong to the happy person, not to *eudaimonia*.

4. Eudaimonia and the Completeness of Activities: The Case of Pleasure

In the discussions of pleasure in Books VII and X, Aristotle makes important comparisons between pleasure and eudaimonia. In X.3 (1173a29–1173b7) and again in X.4 Aristotle argues that pleasure is neither a process (*kinēsis*) nor a becoming (*genesis*). Building a house, by contrast, is a process in that the form is only complete at the end of the process (1174a28). Processes are things that can be done slowly or quickly, while it does not make sense to claim that one experiences pleasure slowly or quickly. One can become pleased quickly, but he cannot quickly do the activity of pleasure (1173a32–b7). Pleasure is something whose form is complete at each and every time (1174b5–6). At least some pleasures are activities (*energeiai*) and an end (1153a10), or, in the terminology preferred by Book X, pleasure is what completes the activity (X.4 passim). From the fact that both pleasure and eudaimonia are *energeiai*, it follows that they can both be impeded. My pleasure from watching an enjoyable film may be impeded by having a stomach-ache or by the annoying person chattering in the row behind me. Similarly, my virtuous activity may be impeded by my lacking some crucial external good in a specific instance (for example, money with which to be generous). In both cases, of course, the unimpeded condition is more choiceworthy (1153b10ff). We can conclude then that like pleasure, eudaimonia is neither a process nor a becoming, but rather complete in form at every time. It thereby supports EED. It can make no sense to say that the stipulation "in a complete life" (1098a18) applies to *eudaimonia* itself because it is essential to that concept that it is an *activity*, and not a process or becoming, to be complete in form at every moment, as pleasure is. Simply put, it would be a category mistake to claim that a component of an *activity* is possession of something, like wealth or health. This positions us well to consider EED in X.7–8.

5. EED in X.7–8: Two Kinds of Eudaimonia

EED is preserved throughout these two chapters. There is emphasis on identifying eudaimonia with "activity according to virtue (κατ' ἀρετὴν ἐνέργεια)" (1177a10) and "according to the most superior [virtue] (κατὰ τὴν κρατίστην)," which is of course theoretical virtue (1177a17–18). The conclusion is that "perfect happiness (τελεία εὐδαιμονία)" is the activity of theoretical virtue or *theoria*. The phrase *teleia eudaimonia* occurs only three times in the *NE*, all in X.7–8 (1177a17, 1177b24–5, and 1178b7). Aristotle argues for the superiority of theoretical virtue based on its power (1177a19–20), continuousness (1177a21), superior pleasure in its exercise (1177a22–27), and self-sufficiency (1177a27–1177b1). A very similar point is made in the third passage referring to "perfect happiness" in X.8 (1178b7), where Aristotle again identifies eudaimonia with theoretical study, without any qualification. The second occurrence of the phrase, however, might be thought to raise a problem for EED, since Aristotle once again raises the issue of a "complete life": "Perfect happiness for a human being, then, would be this activity, getting a complete length of life; for nothing incomplete belongs to the things of happiness (ἡ τελεία δὴ εὐδαιμονία αὕτη ἂν εἴη ἀνθρώπου, λαβοῦσα μῆκος βίου τέλειον· οὐδὲν γὰρ ἀτελές ἐστι τῶν τῆς εὐδαιμονίας)" (1177b24–26).

Immediately preceding these lines, Aristotle has just summed up the advantages of theoretical study as a candidate for eudaimonia: it is desirable only for itself, leisurely, self-sufficient, unwearying, involves a distinctive and superior pleasure, and "however many other things would be applied to a blessed person (καὶ ὅσα ἄλλα τῷ μακαρίῳ ἀπονέμεται)" (1177b22–23). So, Aristotle is in the midst of discussing the happy or blessed *person* (and, is about to discuss the happy *life*) when he makes the remarks above describing complete happiness. We need not read them therefore as attributing a complete length of life to eudaimonia itself, but rather to the sort of engagement in the activity that is eudaimonia, which would make a person blessed and happy. For part of how Aristotle is arguing for the appropriateness of theoria as eudaimonia is via appeal to the happy life it generates. Note the grammatical detail of the end of the passage: Aristotle does not say that nothing incomplete belongs to happiness, but to "the things of happiness (τῶν τῆς εὐδαιμονίας)," in contrast with both 1177a17 and 1178b7, where eudaimonia is identified solely with the activity. EED would lead us to understand that the same identification is operative here, but that the context of discussion of the happy person and happy *bios* leads Aristotle to emphasize that a complete life is also part of "the things" of happiness. Note that the very next line (1177b26–27) raises an objection that *such a life* (τοιοῦτος βίος) may be thought to be "superior (κρείττων)" to the life appropriate for a human being; again, with the emphasis being on the role of eudaimonia as theoria *in a happy life*. Chapter 7 of course concludes that the life of activity of nous is in fact *eudaimonestatos* (1178a8).[29]

EED is preserved in X.8 as well. Without going through the chapter line by line, we can note that, roughly, the first two-thirds of the chapter argues further for the appropriateness of eudaimonia as morally virtuous activity to count as a sort of "human" happiness, while continuing to argue that eudaimonia as theoria is superior.[30] This is why the gods are most of all (μάλιστα)[31] happy and blessed (1178b8–9), while animals, being deprived of any participation in this activity, correspondingly do not have any share of happiness (1178b24–28). Thus, to the extent that the activity that is theoria constitutes a life, to that extent it is a happy one. As so often, Aristotle concludes by explicitly identifying eudaimonia with the activity: "so that eudaimonia would be a sort of contemplation (ὥστ᾽ εἴη ἂν ἡ εὐδαιμονία θεωρία τις)" (1178b32). What's striking is that in the remaining third of the chapter (1178b33–1179a32), the focus is on the role of external goods for the human being engaged in theoria as well as the one engaging in "secondary" eudaimonia. The key point at present is that the text does not use εὐδαιμονία at all in this section, but instead discusses the role of external goods in making a person or life εὐδαίμων or μακάριος (cf. 1179a1–2, 1179a2–3, 1179a9, 1179a10, 1179a14, 1179a31, 1179a32).

So, we see that EED is preserved in Book X's account of happiness as theoria.

---

[29] See also 1178a21–22, where, after considering a life of virtuous action as specifically human, he sums up by *distinguishing* bios and eudaimonia, as EED would expect: "But the excellences of the compound are human ones; so too, then, is the life in accordance with these, and the happiness (καὶ ὁ βίος δὴ ὁ κατὰ ταύτας καὶ ἡ εὐδαιμονία)" (1178a21–22).

[30] I shall turn to the proper interpretation of this in the following section.

[31] Scott argues persuasively that in these sorts of contexts something being *malista* X means that it is paradigmatically or strictly speaking X; see Scott (1999), 228.

6. Eudaimonia as Contemplation

With EED, together with the rejection of the idea that eudaimonia functions as a Comprehensive Practical Principle, I shall argue that a simple solution emerges to the puzzle that Aristotle's conception of eudaimonia as theoretical contemplation (*theōria*) poses. Throughout the *Ethics*, Aristotle has argued for his novel conception of eudaimonia as an *activity*. This activity is central to a person's having a happy life. This activity is desirable for its own sake and never for the sake of anything further and by itself is sufficient to make a life worth living. As we have seen, like any activity, it needs some external goods in order not to be impeded. Aristotle acknowledges, however, that a person may lead a life of morally virtuous activity, and yet suffer such bad fortune in terms of external goods, that no one would count this person happy.

As we have mentioned, once Aristotle introduces eudaimonia as theoretically virtuous activity (*theōria*) and claims that it is the best or highest eudaimonia (since it is the best activity a human being is capable of), scholarly difficulties arise. Exclusivist and inclusivist interpretations run into problems with the role of eudaimonia as a practical principle, in particular with the idea that morally virtuous action would be undertaken for the sake of contemplation. It seems highly implausible that adhering to the demands of moral virtue would promote or optimize theoretical contemplation; indeed, the contrary seems far more likely. One's own theoretical contemplation (and thus one's own happiness) would often seem to be enhanced by shirking or ignoring, to some extent anyway, one's moral duties. Alternatively, inclusivists or exclusivists could understand the identification of happiness with theoretical contemplation as an example of the fulfillment of the Eudaimonist Hope, using the account of the good to give *content* to our concept of virtue.[32] So, once we have a new conception of the good on the table, we have a new conception of virtue as well. For good reason, however, many scholars claim that virtue is the central concept for Aristotle, around which he bends his notion of eudaimonia.[33] It seems quite implausible to think that Aristotle countenances, say, revising his conception of what is shameful and now considers a previously shameful action *kalon* because it helps in

---

[32] At the end of Charles (1999), 222, he puts forward a putative advantage of his paradigm-type account. He suggests that the value of the "nonethical" good (contemplation) can be taken as a "starting point" for accepting the value of the ethical life, constituted by the activity of practical reason. This is not the Eudaimonist Hope, as I have defined it, since it is the *value* of the practical life, not its *content*, that is being rationally supported by our understanding of the best sort of activity.

[33] Annas (1993), Broadie (1991), McDowell (1980), (1998a), Louden (2015), 16.

some way to promote contemplation. Thus legions of commentators have attempted somehow to "reconcile" the conception of eudaimonia as contemplation in X.7–8 with the conception of it as morally virtuous activity in what precedes. One datum to keep in mind is that Aristotle himself betrays no hint of worry about the possible "moral problem" that scholars have thought so glaring. The only concern that is actually in the text, as we have briefly mentioned, is the idea that the life of contemplation, being divine, is "too high" a life for a human being. He never so much as considers the thought that someone might, say, act contrary to courage, so that they could run away to gain more contemplation, and so more happiness.

Moreover, despite the various aspects of McDowell's position on eudaimonia that I have endorsed and defended, his brief remarks on eudaimonia as contemplation are not satisfactory, and turn out to be partly illustrative of the difficulties we face. He writes:

> If we suppose a conception of *eudaimonia* is meant to embrace all potential reasons for acting, and yield a procedure for resolving conflicts between them, this singling out of contemplation is extraordinarily difficult to swallow. We have to take it that all other activity is to be evaluated in terms of conduciveness to contemplation [. . .] But if we exorcize the idea that a conception of *eudaimonia* is a general conception of practical rationality, we can take the introduction of the contemplative life in our stride. We can see how Aristotle might want to single out [. . .] the worthwhileness of exercises of our highest excellence. His identification of what that is does in a way disparage the worthwhileness of ordinary civic ("merely human") virtue. But the worthwhileness of civic virtue can still be genuine (though second-grade), and intrinsic, not derivative from a higher end to which its acts are supposedly conducive. [. . .] we can [thus] avoid letting it [eudaimonia as contemplation] disrupt our appreciation of the main body of the *NE*, which we naturally find more congenial.[34]

I have argued that McDowell is right in his main claim that we should not see eudaimonia as a "general conception of practical rationality"—that is, as functioning as a Comprehensive Practical Principle. This is a necessary but not sufficient step toward resolving the tension between eudaimonia as moral virtuous activity and eudaimonia as contemplative activity. By

---

[34] McDowell, (1998a), 45–46.

rejecting eudaimonia as a Comprehensive Practical Principle, it is true that McDowell is not saddled with the implausible idea that morally virtuous activity must be for the sake of one's contemplation. But even if we agree, as I have been arguing, that eudaimonia as morally virtuous activity functions as a Superseding Practical Principle, eudaimonia as contemplative activity cannot simply do the same without leading to the worry that one might do actions contrary to moral virtue in a situation where one might think that contemplation superseded the morally virtuous action. The mere fact that morally virtuous action remains a non-derivative and intrinsic good is not sufficient to explain why one would ever choose it *over* contemplation, if the latter were primary or perfect happiness.[35] If this is right, then we cannot simply let eudaimonia as contemplation sit comfortably next to the view of eudaimonia that, as McDowell says, we "naturally find more congenial." The weakness of McDowell's interpretation on this issue is what I had argued in the previous chapter was one of its strengths: the focus on eudaimonia as a practical principle. As I shall now argue, however, in X.7–8 Aristotle is *not* discussing eudaimonia as a practical principle *at all*: he is discussing eudaimonia as the activity that is central to the best and happiest life. Once we appreciate that Aristotle is no longer discussing action (*praxis*), and so, *a fortiori*, he is not discussion acting well (*eupraxia*), literally speaking, we can see that eudaimonia as theoria is not providing us with an alternative Superseding Practical Principle—Supremacy of Theoria rather than our familiar Supremacy of Virtue—that could be in conflict with acting for the sake of the fine or, what is the same, engaging in morally virtuous actions for their own sakes.

Turning to the text we find that in X.7–8, Aristotle never says that we should do everything for the sake of theoria.[36] He does provide a new account of eudaimonia as part of the best, happiest, and most perfect life,

---

[35] As we saw in the previous chapter, the same weakness exists for "paradigmatic accounts," such as Charles (1999), endorsed by Scott (1999) (see too Charles [2015]). On Charles's account even though theoria is the best activity, still morally virtuous action is an activity of *part* of our essence. This may be the case, but how does one determine when (and why) one would engage in the activity of the avowedly *inferior* part of one's essence at the expense of the *superior* part? It is helpful to learn that in engaging in morally virtuous activity instead of theoria one is still activating part of one's essence, but this nevertheless remains a consolation prize. Lear (2004), 88–90, has similar doubts about the effectiveness of Charles's and Scott's solution, but I think that her own account is susceptible to similar worries. Acting morally may teleologically approximate contemplation insofar as the former seeks practical truth while the latter seeks theoretical truth, but it too is still explicitly second best and so it is unclear why one would choose it over contemplation if one could avoid it. See Vasiliou (2007b) for some further discussion.

[36] Noted by Natali (2001), 174–175; cited by Meyer (2011), 59.

which consists, as before, centrally of an activity (*energeia*), but while earlier the activity consisted of virtuous actions (*praxeis*), now it consists of theoria. The best, happiest life is an unimpeded engagement in the activity of theoria, over a complete life, with a suitable quantity of external goods. But the difference is not only in the *content* of eudaimonia (as theoria rather than morally virtuous action) but in the *role* that eudaimonia is playing. Eudaimonia is *not* functioning here as a practical principle *of any type*. A Superseding Practical Principle is, of course, a matter of *praxis*, not merely activity (in Aristotle's technical sense). The practical end that supersedes any other remains the same as always: acting for the sake of the *kalon*. In the realm of *praxis* commitment to eudaimonia as the highest good still functions as a Superseding Practical Principle. But in considering what constitutes the best, happiest life, it would be one which consists of the *best* activity under the *best* conditions, which turns out to be uninterrupted theoria, or at least as uninterrupted as human theoria can be. But this, as Aristotle says, is to return to the question of what happiness *is*, not to considering its role as a practical principle. The latter, as always, is undertaken, ideally under the guidance of practical wisdom (*phronēsis*), for the sake of the fine (*kalon*). So, eudaimonia as contemplation does not supply us with a new account of a practical principle, only a revision of the account of what constitutes the very best activity one can engage in.[37]

What leads to this revision, or, perhaps better, addition to Aristotle's position? The basic account of the best life remains, simply, engagement in the best sort of activity in the best (i.e., least impeded, most continuous) way, which would consist in having sufficient external goods and a complete life in order to conduct the activity in question. What Aristotle highlights in X.7–8 is his discovery, of which he is rightfully proud, of the idea that one can be *active* without engaging in *actions*. To put the point in Aristotle's Greek, there is a way of engaging in an *energeia*, which is not also a *praxis*. Contemplation is just such an activity.[38] Supreme practical commitment to the *kalon* in the realm of *praxis* is different from a judgment about what the best *energeia* is, engagement in which constitutes (the best) eudaimonia and which is the central component in the most happy life.

---

[37] See Walker (2018) for a different account of how contemplation guides practical reason.

[38] This is also a partial explanation of why Aristotle is so concerned with pleasure as a candidate for eudaimonia: as an *energeia* it is of the right ontological type to be a serious contender for the claim to be eudaimonia (see brief discussion above).

To support this interpretation, recall that *theōria* is something pursued "in leisure"; "contemplating" is explicitly contrasted with practical matters (*ta praktika*, 1177b3–4). Likewise, Aristotle says, political and warlike actions "lack leisure" and are contrasted with the "activity of understanding (ἡ δὲ τοῦ νοῦ ἐνέργεια)" (1177b17–19). It is clear throughout X.7–8 that while morally virtuous activity counts as a kind of *energeia*, the *energeia* of theoria is *not* a kind of *praxis*. What Aristotle contrasts in the second half of X.8 are the external goods that virtuous actions (*praxeis*) require in comparison with those required by contemplative activity. He goes on to add, as a *reductio*, the ridiculousness of supposing that the gods engage in morally virtuous activity by doing just actions, and so on. His category of *energeia* allows humans (at their best) and the gods to be *active*, and so not asleep (as he worried about in I.5 and here again at 1178b20–21), and yet not engaged in actions undertaken for their own sakes (another kind of *energeia*). Indeed, the gods are deprived of *all* acting: "If, then, living has practical doing (τοῦ πράττειν) taken away from it, and (still more) producing (τοῦ ποιεῖν), what is left except contemplation (θεωρία)?" (Rowe trans., modified) (1178b20–21). We thus miss the point of these chapters if we think that Aristotle is now providing a new practical principle as eudaimonia. Happiness as contemplation presents *no rival whatsoever* to acting for the sake of the *kalon*, which remains the Superseding Practical Principle.

At the same time, X.6–8 still adheres to the idea that knowledge of what happiness and the happy life are would be helpful in attaining them. Learning that the best human activity, an activity in which a human being may participate in the divine, is contemplation is certainly of *practical* significance: this information will affect an intelligent person's life and how they organize it. In our terms, this would be a Prudential Practical Principle, which, as I argued in the Introduction and Chapter 1, reflects the relatively mundane fact that any rational agent ought to be affected in their deliberations and decisions by a true account of the human good. That said, the Superseding Practical Principle to which they adhere—acting for the sake of the *kalon*, which is the same as engaging in virtuous action for its own sake—remains just as it has for the first nine books. Adherence to SV prevents running people over to get to the library faster not because this is part of our nature,[39] but because this violates the *kalon*, to which we ought, as always, to have supreme practical

---

[39] As Charles (1999) and Irwin (2012a), 524, maintain.

commitment. This explains why Aristotle never so much as entertained such an objection; the "moral problem" with contemplation is a red herring.

Moreover, in the *best* life, there is no tension between the political and contemplative life. In this case, analogizing with our[40] contemporary situation is misleading. In our world, one might ask: should I continue my theoretical research on Greek philosophy or try to make an incredibly unjust world a better place? If I begin work on the latter project, I may well never get to the former. But without discussing Aristotle's political philosophy in any detail, if we are in a well-ordered polis already, there will not be any large-scale injustice to rectify. Our polis, anyway, will be harmonious and just (whatever that consists in), if we have proper statesmen and they are doing their jobs, and we citizens will live committed as always to the *kalon* with its ubiquitous and constant effect on our actions via its role as a limiting condition. Sometimes it will make actual demands on us for particular actions, such as service in the government or war, and so on. But otherwise, in the leisure one can expect it to afford under relatively propitious circumstances, one can lead the happiest life by engaging in the best activity: *theoria*.

In the world we actually inhabit it would arguably be difficult by Aristotle's lights to justify engagement in activities like the writing of this book: there are too many injustices around one, too many demands of the *kalon*, to allow one to engage in the best activity of contemplation. On my view, we do not have an ultimate *practical* commitment to theoria—our ultimate practical commitment is, as always, to the *kalon*, and so we will engage in theoria whenever it is not contrary to the fine (*kalon*). There is no conflict between this ultimate practical commitment and the recognition that, in fact, theoria is the most valuable activity in which a human being can engage and so, in that sense, it is our highest or best good.[41] On my account, whether we *are* in fact within what we saw Meyers call the "space of permissions" to engage in *theoria* is a substantive question for the *phronimos* to determine; this is what it means for our commitment to morally virtuous activity (i.e., our commitment to the *kalon*) to be our Superseding Practical Principle and so operate

---

[40] As always, the extension of "our" is the potential (and hoped for) readers of this book.

[41] My position ends up somewhat similar to Meyer's (2011), 62–65. Although she does not put the point this way, Meyer is, as I see it, attempting to break what has been an assumed connection between the highest and best good and the ultimate practical principle.

always as a limiting condition on all of our decisions, including our decisions about when and whether to engage in *theoria*.[42]

7. Conclusion

It is crucial, finally, that the highest practical good—the supreme aim of our actions—is eudaimonia, not being *eudaimōn*. The features that make a life *eudaimōn*, such as one's life being complete, having a suitable amount of external goods, or even engaging in the most excellent activity of contemplation—are not to be considered in what I have called an aiming deliberation. Aristotle, like Socrates, is committed to the Supremacy of Virtue. One may pursue the happy life, so long as it is not contrary to virtue. Whether one is going to be killed (and so fail to have a complete life, and so fail to have a happy life) is certainly going to be relevant in an Aristotelian deliberation, a deliberation that seeks to determine (epistemologically) what the right thing to do is here and now, namely which token action is in fact *kalon*: is the action genuinely courageous and required by courage or is it, rather, rash? As in Socratic deliberation, whether one lives or dies, or whether one's children live or die, and so on, while not relevant in a deliberation about what one's superseding aim ought to be—that is always to do the virtuous thing—they *are* of paramount importance in the deliberation about what the virtuous thing to do in fact *is* in particular circumstances.[43] If having a happy life were one's superseding practical aim, then questions about living and dying, gaining or losing external goods, would end up pitted against the goal of acting virtuously.

Thus too, the main obstacle to McDowell's view was the assumption (even by him) that Aristotle clearly thinks that a complete life and external goods are attributes, in some sense or other, of happiness, the best life. EED separates the contribution that eudaimonia as Superseding Practical Principle makes from conceiving of eudaimonia as the best and happiest life, by showing that the latter is what Aristotle relegates to the idea of being *eudaimōn*, whereas only the former functions as the Superseding Practical Principle. In this way he adheres unwaveringly to a version of Socrates's Supremacy of Virtue, as

---

[42] Note the opening lines of the final chapter of the *NE* (X.9, 1179a33–35), where Aristotle asks whether we should think that we have adequately followed through with our "*decision (prohairesis)*" to have examined the virtues, friendship, pleasure, and so on.

[43] See Chapter 2 and Vasiliou (2008), introduction and ch. 1.

I have said, but also still respects the *endoxa* concerning what it is to have a good and happy life. Aristotle believes that sometimes one must act in ways contrary to what will lead to or constitute one's happiest life, but he nevertheless denies that acting according to virtue could ever be *sacrificing* eudaimonia.[44] Thus too certain aspects of McDowell's view—such as that a loss as ordinarily conceived could never count as a loss from the perspective of the virtuous person—is accommodated but also mitigated to some degree.[45] Aristotle does not hold the view that one simply acts virtuously *in opposition to* one's happiness; rather one engages in eudaimonia-activity, ignoring whether it promotes *a happy life*.

---

[44] See, again, the quote from Foot that opened this chapter.
[45] Thus EED helps to avoid McDowell's less attractive "rigorism," as Wiggins (1995) has dubbed it. See also Foot (2001), 97–98, and Hursthouse (1999), 182–183. We saw in Chapter 4 that McDowell's view has difficulty with what Aristotle says about external goods and, in this chapter, with his interpretation of eudaimonia as *theoria*.

6
Epicurus, Pleasure, and Happiness

We have seen that neither Socrates, Plato, nor Aristotle holds that eudaimonia operates as a Comprehensive Practical Principle. Furthermore, none of these philosophers, with the exception of Socrates in the *Protagoras*, so much as entertains the Eudaimonist Hope. Instead, each maintains that virtue and the fine have their own objective natures, which the virtuous and fine person grasps and follows in their actions, justified in this not by the effect of such actions on their lives but by the fact that the actions are indeed virtuous and fine. While all three philosophers hold that being virtuous and acting virtuously are necessary for the happy life; most plausibly none of these takes it to be sufficient, and Aristotle explicitly does not. Nevertheless, they all believe that acting virtuously is a Superseding Practical Principle, and the highest end achievable in *praxis*. Plato and Aristotle also praise the happiest life as being one of theoretical contemplation and understanding. As we have seen, Aristotle goes further in making it explicit that contemplation is a type of *activity* that is nevertheless not a *praxis*. Finally, while appeal to eudaimonia does not, as just mentioned, justify virtuous or fine actions, it may provide an account, and therefore some rational motivation, for pursuing such a life.

I propose to read Epicurus (in this chapter) and the early Stoics (in Chapter 7) in light of the interpretation of Socrates, Plato, and Aristotle on eudaimonia defended above, rather than, as is typically done, against the background of the "Ciceronian" framework of so many of our later sources. I shall argue that in fact on critical questions, such as the role of eudaimonia as a practical principle and whether the conception of eudaimonia in fact supplies the content and/or grounds our conception of virtue, the positions of Epicurus and the early Stoics are in fact closer to Plato and Aristotle than to their late second- and first-century followers.

1. Epicurus

Epicurus calls the highest good "living blessedly (τὸ μακαρίως ζῆν)" and identifies it as tranquility or freedom from disturbance (ἀταραξία), which he takes to be equivalent to freedom from pain, both physical and psychological (*Letter to Menoeceus* [*Men.*], 128).[1] As we shall examine in greater detail, Epicurus holds that once one examines the issue properly, one will realize that the state of freedom from pain is not only pleasure but also, in fact, the greatest pleasure (*Principle Doctrines* [*Kuriai Doxai, KD*]), (*KD*) 3). Thus, his conception of pleasure is opposed, on the one hand, to Plato's, who in the *Philebus* explicitly rejects as a blatant confusion the idea that pleasure could be equated with the neutral state, freedom from pain, and on the other, to Aristotle's, who in *Nicomachean Ethics* argues that pleasure should not only not be conceived of as a state, but not even as change or motion (κίνησις) but rather as an activity (ἐνέργεια).[2] So, while it is correct to say that Epicurus is a hedonist and so pleasure is central to his account, his conception of pleasure is unique. Indeed, he himself is already complaining in his own letters that his actual position has been slandered and misunderstood (*Men.* 131): "So when we say that pleasure is the goal (ἡδονὴν τέλος ὑπάρχειν) we do not mean the pleasures of the profligate or the pleasures of consumption, as some believe, either from ignorance and disagreement or from deliberate misinterpretation, but rather lack of pain in the body and lack of disturbance in the soul."

Since Epicurus identifies living blessedly with the state of the absence of pain, his conception of eudaimonia is also striking since it explicitly does not contain or make reference to virtue. As the passage just cited shows, even though the conception of pleasure that constitutes the highest good may be uncommon and not include many activities and pursuits that are typically deemed pleasant, nevertheless pleasure is still the end and Epicureanism is unquestionably a hedonist theory. In the discussion of the Hedonist Argument in the *Protagoras* in Chapter 2, we saw that monistic hedonism and its calculus lends itself to a full-blown version of eudaimonism, wherein

---

[1] Epicurus rarely uses the word εὐδαιμονία, and I shall usually refer to his conception of the highest good as "living blessedly"; see Mitsis (2024a) for discussion. That said, I have been using "eudaimonia" throughout this book for the generic concept of well-being or the highest good for a human being. So, I will sometimes continue to speak about Epicurus's conception of eudaimonia, having noted the significance of his not generally using that term for the concept.

[2] See brief discussion in Chapter 5, §4. Epicurus of course also acknowledges "kinetic pleasures," which play an important role in his theory; see below.

the conception of eudaimonia plays the role of a Comprehensive Practical Principle, supplies the content of virtue or right action and, therefore, also supplies the ground and justification for our attachment to virtue. If one believes that the conception of eudaimonia provides the content of virtue, it also supplies the motivation, justification, and ground for its pursuit, since these are already contained in the concept of eudaimonia as a concept of well-being.

The discussion of Epicurean ethics that follows has two aims. The first is to understand what sort of practical principle eudaimonia is for Epicurus, which will involve exploring his conception of living blessedly in some detail. The second is to examine Epicurus's conception of virtue and determine how it relates to living blessedly. As the earlier discussion of the *Protagoras* also makes clear, the roles of virtue and happiness in action are not as separable in a hedonist theory as they are in the ethical positions of Socrates, Plato, Aristotle, and, as we shall see, the Stoics. The latter theories maintain that virtue and virtuous action have an objective content that is independent of eudaimonia while they are nevertheless integral constituents of it. If the Epicureans, by contrast, adopt the Eudaimonist Hope and therefore reject the idea that genuine virtue has any content apart from what leads to or constitutes eudaimonia, then it can seem a forgone conclusion that eudaimonia must be operating as a Comprehensive Practical Principle. But we should not be too hasty; we have already seen an instance in which this is not so. For, as in the case of Aristotle, one might conceive of actions undertaken for the sake of eudaimonia as a distinct subset of all rational actions in general, so that there are still actions, albeit relatively unimportant ones, that might be undertaken for reasons that are not connected with eudaimonia. It will turn out, perhaps surprisingly given Epicurus's hedonism, that this will be the case for Epicurus too. In fact, one of the features of Epicurean philosophy, which I will argue it shares with Stoicism, is to engage in significant theorizing about how one should act precisely when achieving or maintaining the highest good is *not* at issue.

I adopt a particular approach to reconstructing Epicurus's position. I shall eschew Cicero, at least initially, and focus on the two primary texts on ethics that we have from Epicurus: the *Principle Doctrines* (*KD*) and the *Letter to Menoeceus* (*Men.*).[3] The former not only presents both familiar and less familiar parts of Epicurean philosophy, but also indicates connections among

---

[3] Contrast the approach of Striker (1996/1993) and also Wolfsdorf (2013), ch. 7.

topics that contemporary scholars sometimes ignore. In particular, I shall argue that appreciating the tight connection between living blessedly and not fearing death is essential for properly understanding the conception of living blessedly itself.

The *Letter to Menoeceus* and the central *Principal Doctrines* on which I focus are uniformly taken by scholars to be Epicurus's own. I shall begin with crucial texts from the latter and then propose to read critical parts of the *Letter to Menoeceus* in light of them. The latter has been thought to be an example of protreptic, although some scholars have disputed that.[4] Regardless, the letter is clearly an overview of Epicurean ethics aimed at being accessible to a general reader. There is nevertheless no reason that it might read one way to the Epicurean neophyte and differently to those more experienced with the philosophy. I shall read the letter as consistent with the more technical details we find in *KD*, with particular attention to what many but not all scholars believe to be the absolutely critical distinction between katastematic and kinetic pleasure, despite the fact that the letter itself does not dive into such technical matters with the associated technical vocabulary. Kinetic ("moving") pleasures are ordinary pleasures gained from activities like drinking while thirsty, eating when hungry, and so on; katastematic pleasure refers to the state of the absence of all pain, which critics, both ancient and modern, famously doubt should count as a pleasure at all, rather than a state between pleasure and pain.[5]

Moreover, some readers of the *Letter to Menoeceus*, like Cicero (e.g., *Fin.* I.33), have seen some sort of ordinary hedonic calculus at work, according to which one forgoes a present pleasure or endures a present pain for the sake of greater pleasure in the future, which is essentially the view we saw in the *Protagoras*. Such a reading goes hand-in-hand with ignoring the centrality of katastematic pleasure and focusing on ordinary kinetic pleasures (again, as the Ciceronian account given by Torquatus in *Fin* I does). I shall argue that this is deeply mistaken for two important reasons. First, it destroys Epicurus's originality and the radicalness of his understanding of pleasure; not only is the alternative view familiar from the *Protagoras*, but it is (minus the philosophical apparatus) the stuff of ordinary reasoning we offer to children all the time: the pleasure of jumping off this high wall will be outweighed by the

---

[4] For the standard position, which leads her to focus on Cicero's account to reconstruct Epicurus conception of pleasure, see Striker (1996/1993). See too Woolf (2004), 314.

[5] See further discussion below. Wolfsdorf (2013), 158–163, argues for a very a different understanding according to which kinetic pleasure depends upon katastematic pleasure.

pain of hurting one's leg, the pleasure of a fourth cookie will be outweighed by the stomach ache to follow, and so on. More importantly, however, we shall see that displacing katastematic pleasure from its identification with living blessedly would undermine one of Epicurus's most central and well-attested aims, which is essential for the removal of mental pain and so for living blessedly: to eliminate fear of death.[6]

2. Eudaimonia as a Practical Principle in Epicurus

The most radical aspect of Epicurus's account of pleasure is the claim that it is a *state*, the state of the freedom from all pain. On the interpretation I favor the distinction between katastematic pleasure and kinetic pleasure is absolutely fundamental to Epicurus's account.[7] Consider the following from Diogenes Laertius:

> [Epicurus] disagrees with the Cyrenaics on the question of pleasure. For they do not admit katastematic pleasure, but only kinetic pleasure, and he admits both types in both the body and the soul, as he says in *On Choice and Avoidance* and in *On the Goal* and in Book I of *On Ways of Life* and in the *Letter to his Friends in Mytilene*. Similarly Diogenes too in book seventeen of his *Selections* and Metrodorus in his *Timocrates* take the same position: both kinetic and katastematic pleasures are conceived of as pleasure. And Epicurus, in his *On Choices*, says this: "for freedom from disturbance and freedom from suffering are katastematic pleasures; and joy and delight are viewed as kinetic and active." (DL 10.136, Inwood/Gerson [1998], trans.)

Not only does Diogenes here present the katastematic/kinetic distinction as central to Epicurean philosophy, he presents the recognition of katastematic pleasure as the distinctive mark of Epicurean hedonism, noting this as the central point of disagreement with the Cyrenaics. According to most accounts of Epicurus, beginning with Cicero's, the katastematic/kinetic distinction is mentioned but fits at best uncomfortably with the role of the

---

[6] There are, of course, many features of Epicurus's ethics about which I will have nothing original or nothing at all to say. In particular, I will not have anything new to say about the specific natures of katastematic versus kinetic pleasures or about the divisions of desires. For some discussion of the latter, see Mitsis (2024a).

[7] Contrast, for example, Nikolsky (2001), who denies that the distinction is genuinely Epicurean; there is no mention of how to square this position with the eradication of the fear of death. See below.

more familiar kinetic pleasure and the hedonic calculus associated with it.[8] The standard contrast between the Epicureans and Cyrenaics is that whereas the Cyrenaics pursue a "presentist" sort of hedonism, where one ought to pursue the pleasure of the moment, the Epicureans apply rational calculation to the pursuit of pleasure and so are willing to forgo a smaller immediate pleasure (or endure a present pain) for the sake of greater pleasure in the future.[9] But, we should note at the start, this is not at all how Diogenes presents matters. The most crucial distinction between the schools is not a matter of calculating versus non-calculating hedonism, but between the recognition of katastematic pleasure as a *distinct species* of pleasure.

Let's turn to the *Principle Doctrines*. The first three concern a central Epicurean trio: gods, death, and pleasure.[10] Before we get into details, let me make a couple of more general remarks. The two most prominent psychological fears or anxieties concern, reasonably enough, the gods and death. The prospective Epicurean must learn to eradicate these fears if they are going to achieve freedom from (psychological) pain. I shall not say anything about Epicurean theology, except that the upshot is that the gods ought to be thought of as exemplars of Epicurean blessed living, being eternally and absolutely free from any pain whatsoever. They do not care about us (for this would cause them disturbance), and we need not worry about them; we should just take pleasure in our contemplation of their perfection and try to emulate it so far as possible (*KD* 1, *Men.* 123–124).[11] Of course, as atomists, there is no such thing as life after death for the Epicureans, and so a fortiori no possibility of punishment or reward from any divinities in an afterlife. All experience is sense-experience, and sense-experience ends at death. Thus, the well-known slogan: death is nothing to us (*KD* 2, *Men.* 124).

---

[8] We see this at its most extreme in Nikolsky (2001), who references Gosling and Taylor (1982) as one of the first to question the authenticity of the distinction. But it is also present in more mainstream interpretations, like Sedley (2017), who do not dismiss the distinction, but, in my view, diminish its centrality.

[9] See brief discussion of Cyrenaics in the Introduction. The Cyrenaics are brought up most frequently as the "exception that proves the rule" that the Greeks are eudaimonists. Since the Cyrenaics are supposed not to be interested in formulating a conception of eudaimonia, they can hardly be eudaimonists. In the Introduction I speculated that this is part of what has misled some scholars into thinking that if one *does* provide a conception of eudaimonia that is sufficient for being a eudaimonist. As I mentioned, scholars have also tried to defend the inclusion of Cyrenaics within the eudaimonist fold; see Tsouna-McKirahan (2002) and Tsouna (2020).

[10] The same three, in the same order, also open the *Letter to Menoeceus*.

[11] As we shall see below, Epicurus claims at the end of *Men.* (135) that following Epicureanism will make one "like a god among human beings (ὡς θεὸς ἐν ἀνθρώποις)."

The Epicurean account of death, however, is intimately connected with their accounts of pleasure.[12] To appreciate this, we need to separate what I call the arguments about the "metaphysics of death" from the arguments about "duration of life." The metaphysics of death arguments, which I will not discuss here, centrally engage with Epicurean atomism and appeal to the cessation of sense-experience and the absence of any afterlife. Even if some of the arguments are less than persuasive, the position about death that emerges is one that many contemporary secular philosophers and intellectuals might be fully in agreement with, namely, the conclusion that death is not an event that we shall experience, but the cessation of any experience after which, for us as individuals, there is nothing more. It is obvious that for the Epicurean this must be *part* of removing one's worries about death; for if one harbored the suspicion that one would be judged or punished in the afterlife for one's actions while alive or that an afterlife might itself be pleasant or painful, that might well generate lots of worry.[13] But what is less often recognized is that these arguments, even if entirely persuasive, are hardly sufficient.

Let's suppose one is utterly in agreement with Epicurus's conclusions about the metaphysics of death, as, perhaps, many readers of this book are. Does this eliminate one's fear of death? Epicurus (along with everyone else) acknowledges kinetic pleasures: the pleasures of eating, drinking, and sex, but also (some) conversations, sitting in the sun on a beautiful day, the joy of looking at beautiful scenery, and so on. Once these obvious pleasures are acknowledged, the duration of one's life for experiencing such pleasures becomes an issue; and once duration becomes an issue, fear of death arises. So long as there is a reasonable expectation of more kinetic pleasure to be

---

[12] Many discussions take little notice of this. For example, Nikolsky (2001) makes no mention of death at all in his argument that the katastematic/kinetic distinction is not genuinely Epicurean. Woolf (2004), 315, discusses eliminating the fear of death as an Epicurean view, but does not connect this with katastematic pleasure. As we shall see, without katastematic pleasure the argument against fearing death collapses entirely. Mitsis (1988), (2022), and (2024) appreciates the crucial significance of the way the arguments about pleasure and death are intertwined. Here too we see the problem, despite how reasonable it is from one perspective, with dividing areas into topics as Long and Sedley (1987) do; they quote *KD* 19–21 in the "Death" section, whereas *KD* 3, 10, 18 fall under "Pleasure." What is easily lost, then, is the intimate connection among all these remarks. The same goes for discussions of Epicurus focused on Cicero's *De Finibus*, which devotes little attention to the importance of the eradication of the fear of death for Epicurus's views about happiness; see I.49, where there is no discussion about the duration of life, but simply the claim that the Epicurean will not fear death.

[13] This is to ignore a central question about the "metaphysics of death" arguments: is the non-existence of oneself something that one does not find worrying or upsetting? Some claim (perhaps Socrates in the *Apology* [40c]) that non-existence is no worry at all; others find it upsetting and so are impervious to "asymmetry" arguments, such as Epicurus's about the time before one was born and the time after one has died.

had—or if we want to be slightly more sophisticated about it, so long as there is a reasonable expectation of more pleasure than pain to be had—surely a longer life is better than a shorter one and death is something to be avoided no matter how old one is or how much pleasure one has already experienced. One may be entirely unconcerned about what happens when and after one dies (namely, nothing), having been convinced by Epicurean-like arguments, but still be petrified of death because of the prospect of losing out on all of life's enjoyments and pleasures. And surely such a worry is a paradigm of psychological disturbance and leaves us far from living as "gods among humans."

In order to make the finitude of life a matter of contentment and to be free from any worry about its duration, the metaphysics of *pleasure* (and not just of death) needs to be deeply explored and the duration of life must be rendered utterly unimportant for living blessedly.[14] In fact, this is just what we find in Epicurus's texts and his focus on the distinction between katastematic and kinetic pleasure, which, as we have seen, Diogenes took to be the defining aspect of his position. Furthermore, if one seeks to eliminate all worry about the duration of one's life, we can already appreciate that appeal to an ordinary hedonic calculus—where one looks to future pleasures and pains in order to maximize pleasure—would be unsatisfactory in almost all cases.

3. The Evidence of the *Principle Doctrines*

Let's look in more detail at the evidence from the *Principal Doctrines*, beginning with 3: "The limit of the magnitude (ὅρος τοῦ μεγέθους) of pleasures is the removal of all pain. Wherever being in pleasure (τὸ ἡδόμενον) is present, as long as it is there, there is no being in pain (τὸ ἀλγοῦν) or being in distress (τὸ λυπούμενον) or their combination (τὸ συναμφότερον)."[15] Here

---

[14] Thus, this reading runs counter not only to most readings of Epicurus, but in particular to Sedley's (2017), which assimilates Epicurus's position to an Aristotelian account of a "happy life," where that includes having a "complete life." For detailed critique of Sedley's position, see Mitsis (2024b). See also Miller (1976) and Lesses (2002).

[15] Note the subtlety of the language in *KD* 3: the repetition of the article with the passive participle—τὸ ἡδόμενον, and so on—puts the emphasis on the *state*. While the reference to pleasures in the plural (here and throughout Epicurus) is undoubtedly a reference to kinetic pleasures, *to hēdomenon* refers to the katastematic state. Long and Sedley (1987) translate simply "pleasure" for τὸ ἡδόμενον misleadingly suggesting that the text is ἡ ἡδονή. Inwood and Gerson (1998) capture the difference in phrase with "a pleasurable feeling" and "feeling of pain" and "feeling of distress." While I commiserate about finding a suitable translation, "feeling" risks being phenomenological in a way

is the infamous claim that the removal of all pain is not just pleasure, but the "limit of the magnitude of pleasure." The notorious objection is that katastematic pleasure is really not pleasure at all, but some sort of neutral state, which is neither pleasant nor painful. It is important to emphasize, however, that *ataraxia* is not simply the freedom from disturbance that its etymology suggests. It is a state of calm and confidence and implies excellent functioning of body and mind.[16] In being free from all pain (physical but more importantly mental), Epicurus is describing a healthy and so, we might say, positive state—not some sort of neutral numbness. The argument over the nature of the katastematic state is frequently conducted over conflicting intuitions about *phenomenology*: does being in a state of complete absence of physical pain and discomfort—being neither hungry nor cold nor thirsty nor hot, and so on—itself *feel* like anything? The criticism, since ancient times, is tied to answering this question negatively. My focus, however, moves us away from worries about phenomenology. As we shall see, the texts repeatedly stress that the appreciation of katastematic pleasure, its status as in fact the *greatest* pleasure—greater than and superior to any amount of kinetic pleasure—and, therefore, its constituting what living blessedly is, are all conclusions reached *via reasoning and argument*. Epicurus is well aware that katastematic pleasure is neither what an ordinary person thinks of when they think of pleasure nor is its claim to be pleasure, let alone the greatest pleasure, intuitive or common-sensical. Rather, it is a hard-won philosophical conclusion, reached only after sustained and intense philosophical reflection as well as, most probably, something akin to cognitive behaviorist practice.[17]

How is such a conclusion reached? Let us turn to *KD* 10 and 11:

> If the things which produce the pleasures of profligate men dissolved the intellect's fears about the phenomena of the heavens and death and pains and, moreover, *if they taught us the limit of our desires* (ἔτι τε τὸ πέρας τῶν ἐπιθυμιῶν ἐδίδασκεν), then we would not have reason to criticize them [...]
>
> If our suspicions about heavenly phenomena and about death did not trouble us at all and were never anything to us, and, moreover, *if not*

I think Epicurus is trying to avoid. What are being contrasted here are *states*. Surely, they may come with "feelings," but that is not what is primarily important; it is rather the state of being in pleasure or pain, regardless of what it does or does not feel like. See discussion above.

[16] See Miller (1976) on Epicurus's relationship in this regard to Aristotle.
[17] See, e.g., Nussbaum (1994), ch. 4.

understanding the limits of pains and desires did not trouble us (ἔτι τε τὸ μὴ κατανοεῖν τοὺς ὅρους τῶν ἀλγηδόνων καὶ τῶν ἐπιθυμιῶν), then we would have no need of natural science (φυσιολογίας). (Inwood/Gerson [1998] trans., modified)

Note first the triplet we identified in *KD* 3: gods, death, pain/pleasure. Both passages emphasize the crucial importance of philosophical inquiry and study for the aim of coming to an understanding (*katanoein*) of the limits of pain and desire. This is as significant as learning the truth about the gods and about death: the third item is learning about the limits of desires, for which natural science (*phusiologia*) is required. As above, I emphasize that Epicurus is telling us that his conclusion about the state of the absence of all pain is neither obvious nor intuitive, but something that requires intense study and thought, a crucial component of which will be its role in eliminating the fear of death. Finally, we should note here—a point I will return to—that the things that generate the "pleasures of the profligate," such as food, drink, and sex, are certainly things that the Epicurean Sage[18] will engage in. The problem with them is not that such kinetic pleasures are bad in themselves, but simply engaging in such pleasures will never teach one "the limit of our desires." What does this mean? As we shall now see, it does not mean that such pleasures do not, by themselves, teach you lessons about how much one can pleasurably eat or drink: they manifestly do. At some point, one reaches one's "limit" and additional food or drink is no longer pleasurable but becomes, rather quickly, painful. This, however, is not the "limit of our desires" that reason and philosophy teach us about, as the following passages make plain.

KD 18: The pleasure in the flesh does not increase when once the pain of need has been removed, but it is only varied. And the limit of pleasure in the mind (τῆς δὲ διανοίας τὸ πέρας τὸ κατὰ τὴν ἡδονὴν) is produced by a reasoning out (ἐκλόγισις) of those very things [pleasures of the flesh]

---

[18] I use this phrase simply as shorthand for the Epicurean who has achieved complete *ataraxia*—the ideal Epicurean. This person will indeed be "wise," so the phrase is apposite in that sense. Of course, "the Sage" is explicitly used by the Stoics for their ideal person, who figures centrally in their philosophy and their critics' attack of it. We should note therefore an important difference. The Stoic Sage is an extremely rare human being, who is born perhaps once every couple of centuries (or even "as rare as the Phoenix"). The ideal Epicurean life, by contrast, seems to be available to any human being—young or old—who has the discipline to practice and study the doctrine (see *Men.* 122). That is not to say it is an easy achievement, but it is a significant difference from the Stoic conception.

and their congeners, which used to present to the mind the greatest fears (μεγίστους φόβους).

KD 19: Unlimited time and limited time contain equal pleasure, if one measures its limits by reasoning (τῷ λογισμῷ).

These closely connected *Doctrines* (along with 20 below) need to be unpacked one at a time to appreciate their cumulative argumentative force. In 18 we return to the idea of the "limits" of pleasures, that is, kinetic pleasures, which reach their limit in the complete absence of pain. After this, one can only "vary" the pleasure; more on this below. Note two things here, however. First, the limit of pleasure is understood via an intellectual activity, a "reasoning out (*eklogisis*) of those very things," namely, the pleasures of the flesh.[19] Secondly, and more obscurely, the pleasures of the flesh and their congeners, about which one is "reasoning out" the limits, "used to present *to the mind (dianoia)* the greatest fears." Why would reasoning about the pleasures of eating and drinking, and, relatedly, pleasurable food and drink help to alleviate fears in the mind? What does the mind fear without understanding the limits of pleasure and desire? The answer is that it fears losing out on future kinetic pleasures. So, the fear referred to in 18 is ultimately simply a part of the fear of death, not in the metaphysical sense, but in the sense of the limit of duration of life. Thus, 18 clearly sets the theme for 19 and 20 to follow. 19 refers now to the katastematic pleasure, which is a state whose pleasure is absolutely unaffected by duration, *if one measures its limits by reasoning (logismos).*[20] When Epicurus says, as he frequently does (e.g., *Men.* 130–131; *KD* 3, 18, 19), that the simple satisfaction of hunger with bread contains "equal pleasure" to the satisfaction of hunger with a gourmet meal, he is not suggesting that our ordinary sensory experiences of these things are false or confused. Rather, he is saying that the experiential differences, the differences in kinetic pleasures, play absolutely no role with respect to our living blessedly one way or the other. This is why Epicurus emphasizes the role of *reasoning* (*KD*, 18, 19, 20: ἐκλόγισις, λογισμός, ἐπιλογισμός; cf. *Men.* 131, νήφων λογισμός) in such assessments: it is by reasoning that we learn the limits of desire and that living blessedly is

---

[19] Note the *ek* as suggesting it is a matter of uncovering or extracting something; see also *exereunōn* at *Men.* 131, discussed below.
[20] See Lesses (2002), 64.

constituted entirely by the katastematic state and not by any kinetic pleasure or pain that may be associated with it. So, again, we have reasoning and philosophy revealing to us a truth that we can understand with our minds—not with our flesh or our feelings—that katastematic pleasure is in fact the greatest pleasure not only "in magnitude" (*KD* 3) but also as is now made clear in its imperviousness to duration. As we shall see, two things follow from this: (1) if my state of pleasure is impervious to duration, I have no reason to worry about how long my life will last; and, (2), kinetic pleasures, which *are* obviously increased by both qualitative intensity and duration, cannot be any part of living blessedly whatsoever. Let us see how this is articulated in *KD* 20:

> The flesh took the limits of pleasure to be unlimited and [only] an unlimited time would have provided it. But the intellect (ἡ δὲ διάνοια), grasping the reasoning (λαβοῦσα τὸν ἐπιλογισμὸν) of the goal and limit of the flesh and dissolving the fears of eternity, provided us with the perfect way of life and had no further need of unlimited time. But it [the intellect] did not flee pleasure, and even when circumstances cause an exit from life it did not die as though it were lacking anything (ὡς ἐλλείπουσά τι) of the best life. (Inwood/Gerson [1998] trans., slightly modified)

In this passage we explicitly hear from the perspective of "the flesh": it takes the limits of pleasure to be unlimited and so only an unlimited time will suffice. Here we have additional evidence for our interpretation of "limits" above. The flesh does not take it that one can engage in any episode of eating or drinking for an unlimited time. As above, the flesh will feel and thus grasp when it has reached its limit; and so, the point made here is not the one in stories about the person who wishes for a throat the length of a stork to prolong the pleasure of eating and drinking. The point is that no matter how careful one is in engaging in a hedonic calculus concerning the kinetic pleasures so as to maximize them on any particular occasion, the opportunities for them will go on ad infinitum. So, being careful to stop eating and drinking today once eating and drinking cease providing me with pleasure, my *mind* worries about whether I will survive to do this again tomorrow, and the day after, and so on; for if I do not, think of all the pleasure—all of the delicious meals and wines—that I will be missing out on. Thus, an ordinary hedonic calculus is no part of living blessedly for the Epicurean; rather it consists in hard-won understanding via philosophical reasoning that the greatest, most genuine pleasure consists entirely in the katastematic state of the absence of pain.[21]

From the *Principle Doctrines* alone, we have now extracted the core Epicurean views concerning pleasure, duration of life, and living blessedly. Furthermore, I suggest that living blessedly functions as a Superseding Practical Principle. One deliberates about kinetic pleasures and pains with a view to the goal: achieving the complete absence of physical and psychological pain. Once this achieved, one may follow nature by engaging in an ordinary hedonic calculus, avoiding larger pains and seeking greater kinetic pleasure, but *always subject to the katastematic state as a limiting condition.* Thus, one should never do or believe anything that would disturb the katastematic state; subject to that condition, one may pursue various kinetic pleasures as variations in the maintenance of that state. We shall see this view repeated, supported, and elaborated in the *Letter to Menoeceus*.

4. The *Letter to Menoeceus*

Although the *Letter to Menoeceus* does not make the katastematic/kinetic distinction explicitly, I will argue that it is carefully written so as to respect it. Furthermore, the evidence that scholars from Cicero onward have found in it for the idea that the Epicurean engages in an ordinary hedonic calculus is in fact mistaken and such a calculus, as argued above, is relegated to deliberations about "variations" once the katastematic state has been achieved.

The letter opens recalling the order of the first three *Principle Doctrines*, urging us to get rid of false beliefs about (1) the gods, (2) death, and (3) desires. After the division of desires, Epicurus writes the following:[22]

> [128] Fixed contemplation of these things [desires, their types and limits] knows how to lead back every choice and avoidance to the health of the

---

[21] Cf. too *KD* 25 and *Sententiae Vaticanae* 59. Recall also the remarks above that this should not be thought of as a negative, phenomenological absence, but as a positive, healthy state of calm, confidence, and proper functioning.

[22] As I said, I shall not explore the division of desires into types, which would lead me too far afield. It is clear that part of the exercise of reason that the Epicurean engages in explores not only the limits of desire (with the resulting limit expressed by the absence of physical and psychological pain)—my focus above—but also the nature of different *kinds* of desires with a view to ridding oneself of those that are merely empty and vain and therefore generate disturbance for the soul and body (cf. *Men.* 127, *KD* 26, 29, 30). For recent discussion, see Mitsis (2024a), with references.

body and to the mind's absence of perturbation, since this is the goal of living blessedly; for we do everything [make every effort] for the sake of this, so that we might not suffer pain or be afraid (τούτων γὰρ ἀπλανὴς θεωρία πᾶσαν αἵρεσιν καὶ φυγὴν ἐπανάγειν οἶδεν ἐπὶ τὴν τοῦ σώματος ὑγίειαν καὶ τὴν τῆς ψυχῆς ἀταραξίαν, ἐπεὶ τοῦτο τοῦ μακαρίως ζῆν ἐστι τέλος. τούτου γὰρ χάριν πάντα πράττομεν, ὅπως μήτε ἀλγῶμεν μήτε ταρβῶμεν).

Epicurus here states that health of the body and absence of perturbation in the mind are what living blessedly consists in. We see too that living blessedly as the "highest good" is that for the sake of which we do everything or make every effort. As I have discussed throughout, this idiomatic phrase ought to be read so as not to already beg the question against the idea that there are deliberate, significant, and non-acratic actions that we engage in that fall outside the scope of this phrase. I argue that Epicurus too understands the phrase with some restriction, namely pertaining only to those actions undertaken with a view to living blessedly (or with a view to not ruining the blessed state of *ataraxia*). Our primary, Superseding Practical Principle demands that every choice and avoidance be considered from the perspective of complete *ataraxia*: we must do (or refrain from doing) anything in order to achieve it, after which we must not do anything that would reintroduce disturbance. For once the state is achieved, the Epicurean does not literally cease to act, but his actions (provided they are not prohibited as actions that would disturb that state) will no longer be governed by living blessedly as an end, except as a limiting condition.[23] Indeed, we will see how such actions ought to be conducted according to Epicurus. So, as a principle of action, it seems that Epicurus is providing a Superseding Practical Principle, similar in form to Socrates's Supremacy of Virtue. Like the latter, Epicurus's Superseding Practical Principle insists that we act so as to eliminate bodily pain and disturbance in the soul and to refrain from acting in ways that generate bodily pain and mental disturbance, parallel to the way that the Supremacy of Virtue requires that acting virtuously trumps any other end in action and, as a limiting condition, requires that one never act contrary to virtue. Once these demands are met, however, I argued that the Supremacy

---

[23] Recall how a Superseding Practical Principle captures the idea of what I called "ubiquity"—the idea that our conception of happiness is always everywhere operative in our lives—without it therefore needing to be a Comprehensive Practical Principle; see Introduction.

of Virtue offers no guidance in the choice among actions that are neither required by virtue nor contrary to it. Similarly with Epicurus, so long as pain is alleviated, the selection of what to do or what to contemplate is left as an open question so far as Epicurus's primary practical principle is concerned; we will see, however, that Epicurus (and his contemporaries the Stoics) offer guidance about our choices outside of those that affect our happiness.

> [128, cont] When all of a sudden we achieve this [state] every storm in the soul is dispelled (ὅταν δὲ ἅπαξ τοῦτο περὶ ἡμᾶς γένηται, λύεται πᾶς ὁ τῆς ψυχῆς χειμών), since a living creature is not having to go off on foot because of some lack and to search for another thing by which the good of the mind and the body might be completed (οὐκ ἔχοντος τοῦ ζῴου βαδίζειν ὡς πρὸς ἐνδέον τι καὶ ζητεῖν ἕτερον ᾧ τὸ τῆς ψυχῆς καὶ τοῦ σώματος ἀγαθὸν συμπληρώσεται). For at that time we have need of pleasure, whenever from pleasure not being present we suffer pain (τότε γὰρ ἡδονῆς χρείαν ἔχομεν, ὅταν ἐκ τοῦ μὴ παρεῖναι τὴν ἡδονὴν ἀλγῶμεν) and <when we are not in pain>, we no longer need pleasure (<ὅταν δὲ μηδὲν ἀλγῶμεν>, οὐκέτι τῆς ἡδονῆς δεόμεθα).[24]

Here Epicurus expands on the achievement of the highest good and its effects. When we "all of a sudden (*hapax*)" achieve *ataraxia*, we have achieved a complete and self-sufficient good. Unlike other living creatures (including fellow non-Epicurean human beings), we Epicureans have what we need for living blessedly and do not have to spend our lives in a constant search, thinking that one more meal, a slightly larger house, or better food over the hill is somehow needed to complete our happiness. Of course, this does not mean that the Epicurean Sage does not get hungry or sprain their ankle. But throughout this discussion we should remember that physical pain or discomfort, especially ordinary discomfort like the hunger experienced from a missed meal, is only the simplest example and analogy for the disturbance that would dislodge a blessed state, such as fear of death. It would be ludicrous to think the Epicurean Sage loses his blessed *ataraxia* whenever lunchtime rolls around and temporarily ceases to be a like a "god

---

[24] This last sentence is corrupt and a bit awkward. However we interpret it (and the standard interpolation cited above is fine, provided it is not misunderstood), I understand "at that time" as at the time before katastematic pleasure has been achieved; at that point, we are still in physical and psychological pain and need to eliminate it. Then (assuming the interpolation is correct), "we no longer need pleasure" must refer to kinetic pleasure used as a means for eliminating pain; it cannot, of course, mean we no longer need katastematic pleasure, since that just is the highest good.

among humans." Rather, the serenity generated by the freedom from mental disturbance because they have no fear of the gods, death, or anxiety about the duration of their life (the last because of their understanding of the limits of desire, as we have seen above) is a stable, well-functioning state.

The letter continues, emphasizing the practical role of living blessedly:

> [129] And this is why we say that pleasure is the starting point and goal of living blessedly (καὶ διὰ τοῦτο τὴν ἡδονὴν ἀρχὴν καὶ τέλος λέγομεν εἶναι τοῦ μακαρίως ζῆν). For we understand that this [katastematic pleasure] is the primary and congenital good, and that from it we begin every choice and avoidance, and return to it while judging every good by [this] *pathos* as a criterion (ταύτην γὰρ ἀγαθὸν πρῶτον καὶ συγγενικὸν ἔγνωμεν, καὶ ἀπὸ ταύτης καταρχόμεθα πάσης αἱρέσεως καὶ φυγῆς, καὶ ἐπὶ ταύτην καταντῶμεν ὡς κανόνι τῷ πάθει πᾶν ἀγαθὸν κρίνοντες).

It is the *pathos* of the state of katastematic pleasure that functions as the ultimate criterion of action: we "begin" from it in our quest to active *ataraxia*, and then, having achieved it, we "return" to it as a limiting condition to make sure we do not act in a way (or, as is more likely, acquire false beliefs) that would disturb it.[25] We should note too that katastematic's pleasure being the "primary and congenital good" is something *we Epicureans*, who have studied and reasoned and practiced, now "understand" or "recognize" (*egnōmen*); it is not intuitive and immediate, like the appeal of kinetic pleasure or the undesirability of pain.[26]

The next step in the argument turns to kinetic pleasure and pain, having established that the highest good is *ataraxia*. Readers from Cicero on have too quickly taken the point here to be an example of an ordinary hedonic calculus:

> [129, cont] And although the primary and innate good is this [the state of *ataraxia*, i.e., katastematic pleasure], we do not even choose every pleasure on account of this, but it is the case that sometimes we pass up many [sc. kinetic] pleasures when we get more of what is disagreeable from them [which could be either a disturbance of *ataraxia* or pains that are irrelevant to *ataraxia*] (καὶ ἐπεί[27] πρῶτον ἀγαθὸν τοῦτο καὶ σύμφυτον, διὰ τοῦτο καὶ οὐ

---

[25] Calling the katastematic state a *pathos* does not, I think, necessarily imply that it has a distinctive phenomenology, although it does not preclude that either. Presumably, I might be suffering something and in a particular state, which I may know about (e.g., via a diagnosis from a doctor) and yet which has no phenomenological feel because there are no perceptible symptoms.

[26] This claim disagrees with Woolf (2004), who argues that in general the "we" in *Men.* refers to "we humans" and not "we Epicureans".

[27] See Smyth-Messing (1984), §2244, for ἐπεὶ having the "force of although."

πᾶσαν ἡδονὴν αἱρούμεθα, ἀλλ᾽ ἔστιν ὅτε πολλὰς ἡδονὰς ὑπερβαίνομεν, ὅταν πλεῖον ἡμῖν τὸ δυσχερὲς ἐκ τούτων ἕπηται). And we believe many pains to be superior to pleasures, when a greater [kinetic] pleasure follows for a long time, having endured the pains (καὶ πολλὰς ἀλγηδόνας ἡδονῶν κρείττους νομίζομεν, ἐπειδὰν μείζων ἡμῖν ἡδονὴ παρακαλουθῇ πολὺν χρόνον ὑπομείνασι τὰς ἀλγηδόνας). Therefore, every pleasure is good because it has an appropriate nature, however not every [pleasure] is to be chosen (πᾶσα οὖν ἡδονὴ διὰ τὸ φύσιν ἔχειν οἰκείαν ἀγαθόν, οὐ πᾶσα μέντοι <γ᾽> αἱρετή); likewise, each of the pains is also bad, but not every pain is in its nature always to be avoided (οὐ πᾶσα δὲ ἀεὶ φευκτὴ πεφυκυῖα). [130] It is appropriate, however, to judge all these things by measuring and looking at the advantages and disadvantages [which could include both ordinary hedonic calculations irrelevant to living blessedly and "eudaimonic" calculations about how to reach and not disturb one's *ataraxia*]. For sometimes we use the good as bad on the one hand, and again the bad as good on the other.

Now Epicurus moves from discussion of the katastematic state that constitutes living blessedly to the role of kinetic pleasures and pains not only in achieving and maintaining that state but also once that state has been achieved. Even though the "primary and innate good" is the *ataraxia* that is katastematic pleasure, that does not mean that the Epicurean chooses every *kinetic* pleasure or avoids every pain. All pleasures, meaning all kinetic pleasures, are in themselves and because of their nature good, and all pains are correspondingly bad. Faced with choices among them, an Epicurean, like anyone else, would seek to maximize pleasure and minimize pain. That said, however, it is the criterion of the state of living blessedly that is always acting as a limiting condition on the kinetic pleasures and pains to avoid or pursue. So, while kinetic pleasures are always good by nature and pains always bad, "sometimes we use the good as the bad and again the bad as the good." This, of course, makes no sense in reference to katastematic pleasure, but involves the shuffling of kinetic pleasures and pains in the achievement and maintenance of the katastematic state and in decisions about variations in kinetic pleasure and pain where living blessedly is not at issue. As an example of the view being proffered here, imagine a prospective Epicurean who has been brought up on an intellectual diet of the *Phaedo*, *Phaedrus*, and *Republic* and is immensely worried about the fate of his incorporeal soul. Part of the necessary antidote to these flights of Platonic metaphysics are intensive courses in atomist physics in order to grasp and fully appreciate the truth that all there is is atoms and void; an incorporeal substance that can act or be acted upon is absurd. I take it that for many people, the study required may be quite painful—it is not nearly as fun as reading the myth at the end of the *Phaedo*. The prospective Epicurean, however, would forgo such kinetic pleasures and embrace the pain of hard study for the sake of achieving *ataraxia*. I think such examples are worth reflecting on, because what afflicts most people most of the time is mental disturbance more than physical pain. Of course, there are exceptions: horrible diseases (like that apparently suffered by Epicurus himself at the end of his life), famine and starvation, and so on. But, given moderately propitious circumstances where one can get *something* (edible) to eat and *something* (potable) to drink, physical pain is not the intense constant affliction that mental pain and anxiety, such as worry about death, may be.

This passage is followed by a further, well-known discussion of the advantages of simple, not extravagant pleasures, when one keeps in mind that what counts is *not* the greater or lesser kinetic pleasure but the elimination of pain. Such training makes a person self-sufficient, having been disabused of the notion that a gourmet meal affords more pleasure than barley-cakes and water. What I have argued is the way to understand such remarks is not to deny that Epicurus thinks that the former is more kinetically pleasurable than the latter—it surely is—but the mistake is to think (as the flesh falsely believes) that that greater kinetic pleasure in any way adds to one's blessedness. As I have insisted and shall insist below, kinetic pleasure adds absolutely nothing to living blessedly, for if it did (or, crucially, even if we *believed* it did) we would then falsely think that we would have a happier life by having a longer life, since it contains more kinetic pleasure. And then, of course, we would worry about our life coming to an end and so have anxiety about death.

Epicurus returns to the relationship between kinetic pleasure and the state that genuinely constitutes our highest good:

[131] So, when we say that pleasure is the goal, we do not mean the pleasures of the profligate or the pleasures of consumption (ὅταν οὖν λέγωμεν ἡδονὴν τέλος ὑπάρχειν, οὐ τὰς τῶν ἀσώτων ἡδονὰς καὶ τὰς ἐν ἀπολαύσει κειμένας λέγομεν) [as our opponents claim] but rather lack of pain in the body and lack of disturbance in the soul (τὸ μήτε ἀλγεῖν κατὰ σῶμα μήτε ταράττεσθαι κατὰ ψυχήν). [132] [For it is not partying, etc....] that generates the pleasant life, but sober reasoning when one examines

every choice and avoidance and drives out [false] opinions from which the greatest turmoil seizes souls (τὸν ἡδὺν γεννᾷ βίον, ἀλλὰ νήφων λογισμὸς καὶ τὰς αἰτίας ἐξερευνῶν πάσης αἱρέσεως καὶ φυγῆς καὶ τὰς δόξας ἐξελαύνων, ἐξ ὧν πλεῖστος τὰς ψυχὰς καταλαμβάνει θόρυβος).

Here we have the key elements I have emphasized: lack of pain in the body and lack of disturbance in the soul is what we Epicureans mean by pleasure, namely katastematic pleasure. This is not appreciated by the flesh but by "sober reasoning (*nēphōn logismos*)." What has blocked an appreciation of the argumentative progression here, I think, is Epicurus's denial at the beginning that when he is speaking of pleasure he is speaking about the "pleasures of the profligate" or "the pleasures of consumption." Readers who have in mind the ordinary hedonic calculus hear this as Epicurus being against excess, accusing non-Epicureans of having weighed pleasure and pain incorrectly. But I hope this analysis shows what is mistaken about such a reading. The pleasures of the profligate or of consumption—food, drink, and sex—are not in themselves bad things; all pleasures are by nature good.[28] They are bad all and only insofar as they disturb the state (primarily a mental state) of *ataraxia*. It is only as excessive engagement in kinetic pleasure erodes or prevents one's understanding that living blessedly has nothing to do with kinetic pleasure, except incidentally in the course of instrumentally removing one's pain, that it is bad. And anyone who engages in such pleasures, without the "sober reasoning" of Epicurean philosophy, is bound to believe that such pleasure at least adds to the happiness of life, which leads them to fear death, to be disturbed, and so on. So, Epicurus is not simply condemning *excessive* kinetic pleasures; he is saying that such pleasures do not constitute the pleasure that is the highest good *at all*; for they are entirely the wrong *kind* of pleasure.

Thus too the natural goodness of kinetic pleasure is *not* a goodness derived from the "highest good," freedom from pain, but just a natural fact about it; release from pain may frequently be kinetically pleasurable, but unsurprisingly the kinetic pleasure may wane considerably.[29] Contrast the view of

---

[28] Thus Cicero and others think Epicurus is being inconsistent: he admits that kinetic pleasures as such are good, and has no other candidate for the good than pleasure, but then condemns some as excessive.

[29] See Mitsis's (1988), 45–51, example of the fifteenth day in a row of eating brown bread for dinner. Or one could imagine that the only food available, which keeps one alive and also alleviates the pain of hunger, is in fact quite bad tasting, so that, despite being hungry, it is actually not kinetically pleasurable at all to eat. In such a situation, the Epicurean Sage's living blessedly would not be affected.

Long and Sedley: "Hence Epicurus firmly subordinates kinetic to static [i.e., katastematic] pleasure, treating the former either as a stage on the way to the ultimate goal of absence of pain, or as a variation of that condition when achieved."[30] This makes it sound as though kinetic pleasure is a good, as it were, of the same kind as katastematic pleasure, but inferior or subordinate. By contrast, I have argued that kinetic pleasure as such has *no role to play* in achieving the highest good.[31] As we have seen, for the Epicurean the person who eats brown bread for dinner the thirtieth night in a row may derive little kinetic pleasure from the meal, but is nevertheless no less happy than the person who has had thirty distinct wonderfully prepared meals. The idea that the latter is a better, more pleasurable scenario is the result of a mistaken view, curable through the careful employment of reason (KD 18, 19, 20). Kinetic pleasures are not just subordinated to katastematic pleasure, they are of a different kind, which at best are instrumental means to katastematic pleasure. But even when kinetically pleasurable activities *are* a means to the katastematic state, their being kinetically pleasurable is not what is important about them; painful actions that led to the katastematic state would be just as good as far as blessedness is concerned. While Epicurus is happy to acknowledge that one would naturally prefer the former scenario to the latter, this has no effect on one's living blessedly, and so what explains the respect in which the former is preferable lies *outside the reasons* connected with happiness. The katastematic state is not improved no matter how many more kinetic pleasures one may add to it.

Such a view, then, raises issues very similar to those we will see in the Stoic conception of indifferents. For Epicurus seems to appeal, in the scenario above, to something like the idea of simply following nature. But just as for the Stoics, one would not choose a "preferred" or "promoted" indifferent in a situation where it would be contrary to virtue to do so, so too for Epicurus one would not choose the carefully prepared meals under a variety

---

[30] Long and Sedley (1987), 123.
[31] Long and Sedley (1987), 124, reject such a view and cite a variety of passages from different Epicurean sources over the centuries to indicate that the Epicurean must, in the end, accord a subordinate but similar value to kinetic pleasures. For example, they write: "the principal Epicurean means of counteracting bodily pain is the recollection and anticipation of pleasures, and in order to provide a sufficient variety for the purpose these would have to be kinetic." The two passages cited in support both come from Cicero's *Tusculan Disputations*, but he is not only generally hostile to Epicureanism but specifically hostile to the idea that one can make good sense of the distinction between katastematic/static and kinetic pleasures in the first place. Given that, the fact that passages from Cicero are the evidence that Epicurus *must* acknowledge the significance of kinetic pleasures for the achievement and maintenance of the highest good are suspect.

of circumstances that might put one's *ataraxia* in jeopardy. For example, perhaps such meals begin to generate an attachment to luxury and a weakening of the belief that what matters in eating is simply the satisfaction of a natural and necessary desire, and the subsequent removal of pain, which in turn might generate psychological anxiety about whether such meals would continue, which in turn might lead to worry about obtaining what was necessary to procure such a meal, like money or a particular chef, and so on.

Finally, sticking with our example, *how* hunger is alleviated has no effect whatsoever on our happiness. Does it follow, therefore, that we have "no rational ground for preference" between, say, a gourmet meal and plain bread?[32] It depends on whether we think that eudaimonia must embrace *all* reasons for acting whatsoever. But why should we think this? Rather, as I have argued we have seen at least for Aristotle, eudaimonia is a practical principle that singles out a particular dimension for acting, a particular type of supremely important reasons, without needing to claim that it therefore exhausts absolutely all reasons for acting.

If we interpret the practical role of living blessedly as a Superseding Practical Principle, then we can choose among available food on any basis we like, provided we understand that the choice is not one that affects our happiness, without having to say that there is no rational ground whatsoever for our preference. This dovetails nicely with various remarks Epicurus makes about those needing extravagance least enjoying it most (*Ad Men.*, 130). The enjoyment of extravagance referred to here is genuine enjoyment, a kinetic pleasure, and its kinetic pleasure, we might think, is a reason, other things being equal, for choosing it. The crucial point, however, is that we do not understand this choice as being undertaken for the sake of living blessedly since it is utterly irrelevant to that end.

5. Pleasure and Living Blessedly

I have tried to mount a strong defense of Epicurus's view of pleasure and living blessedly, but I do not mean to suggest that it is unassailable or wholly persuasive. Let's consider two objections. If I am correct that Epicurus wholly identifies living blessedly with the katastematic state, and thus it makes the duration of the Sage's life irrelevant so far as their happiness is concerned,

---

[32] As Mitsis (1988), 47, once contended.

why does the Sage not simply kill himself? For, the objection continues, if longevity does not make life any *better*, why continue? Here I think the answer is straightforward. As Epicurus boasts, he has found the *perfect* way of life and lives as a god among humans. So, why would someone who is living the best life, absolutely free from pain or worry, kill themselves? As we will see in a different context with the Stoics in the following chapter, suicide under certain circumstances would presumably be advisable, if one could no longer live without extreme physical pain. But here too we should remember the superiority in kind of mental freedom from disturbance compared with physical pain, especially when, as is the case for the Epicurean Sage, physical pain, even severe pain, is not accompanied with any fear of death.

A second objection might be more conciliatory. While it is agreed that the katastematic state is sufficient for living blessedly, Epicurus nevertheless also considers kinetic pleasures good. Given this, the objection continues, a life of katastematic pleasure combined with a (significant) period of kinetic pleasures—lovely food and wine, stimulating conversation with friends—is surely a *better* life than one with the katastematic pleasure alone for a very short period of time.[33] I think that Epicurus, as I interpret him, has a solid reply here as well. Kinetic pleasures *are* surely pleasurable and their pleasure is natural, and so the more and longer one experiences them, the more kinetic pleasure one achieves. While the Epicurean Sage will agree with this much, she will not agree about what is alleged to follow, namely, that a longer life is therefore a better, more blessed life. For it is *this very belief*—that a longer life is a better life—that would constitute a most significant disturbance to the Sage's mental tranquility. So, while the Epicurean Sage will continue to enjoy whatever kinetic pleasures come their way, they will do so without being seduced into the false belief that this makes their lives in any way more blessed, for that belief itself would ruin their blessedness.

I do think that, despite objections, Epicurus's position is stronger when it is understood that living blessedly consists entirely in the katastematic state and that kinetic pleasures add nothing at all to state of living blessedly, except for mere "variation." That is, they offer reasons for acting that lie outside of eudaimonic reasons, a way of "following nature," akin as we shall see in the following chapter to the role of Stoic indifferents.

---

[33] As mentioned above, for the defense of such a position as actually Epicurean, see Sedley (2017) and criticism in Mitsis (2024b).

6. Epicurus on Virtue and Happiness

So far, no reference has been made to virtue. It is difficult to develop a definitive interpretation of Epicurus's account of virtue and its role in happiness, but it is instructive to consider why. In the terms of this book, we might expect that Epicurus would be an advocate of the Eudaimonist Hope. As a hedonist, katastematic pleasure appears to provide a clear standard of right and wrong: right action is what constitutes or leads to katastematic pleasure, that is, absence of pain; wrong action is what constitutes or leads to the disturbance of that state. Indeed, my interpretation of katastematic pleasure as a Superseding Practical Principle might seem to support this: for I have argued that what makes an action to be done (or a belief to be held) is its relationship to that state and not even, despite his hedonism, the action's kinetic pleasure or pain. We would not expect, then, that Epicurus would value conventional or ordinary moral virtue, unless it happened to bear the right relationship to the highest good; indeed, if he holds the Eudaimonist Hope, only by reference to that good can genuine virtue get its content.

Julia Annas rejects the idea that Epicurus adopts such a radical stance toward the content of virtue.[34] The difficultly in assessing this claim stems, unsurprisingly, from the oddity of katastematic pleasure and its relationship to the standard virtues as they are conventionally understood. For one thing, as we have seen, Epicurus believes that such a conception of pleasure is sufficient to show that the length of one's life is irrelevant to one's happiness. Obviously, if a cogent argument can be made that length of life is irrelevant to the happiness of a life, so long as one has achieved *ataraxia*, then this will have significant impact on one's overall deliberation and planning (recall the positive aspects of *ataraxia*). Combined with Epicurus's other arguments against fear of death, the clear upshot of the position is, as he says in *Men.* 125: "there is nothing fearful in life for one who has grasped that there is nothing fearful in the absence of life." So, at first blush, we have someone who could presumably meet what is typically thought of as the most difficult aspect of courage: overcoming fear of death. This is not to say that they will be courageous in the sense of not being rash, but they will certainly avoid the defect of cowardice.

Combine this with other ramifications of the Epicurean view. One will not be overly desirous of money, for one will have rejected all desires that are

---

[34] For example, Annas (1993), 340–342.

for things that are neither natural nor necessary. Given the idea that what is natural and necessary is "easy to achieve," where that means that if all one needs is *something* edible to eat, *something* potable to drink, and so on, these are, except in rare circumstances, relatively easy to come by. There will be no desire to be unjust, then, since there is no belief that acquiring some object will increase one's happiness. Similarly, conventional understandings of temperance would be easy and natural, so to speak, for the Epicurean to meet; as a matter of prudence, the Epicurean would hardly grow large and extravagant appetites. Without prolonging examples, if the Epicurean has no fear of death and no desire for any more than a minimal amount of money, there would be every expectation that she would act in accordance with the ordinary moral virtues. And, indeed, several passages in Epicurus make just this point (*KD* 15, 16, 17, 26, 29, 30).

But note what Epicurus says about the significance of *phronēsis*:

> Prudence (φρόνησις) is the principle of all these things [what searches out reasons for every choice and avoidance and drives out beliefs that cause disturbance in the soul] and is the greatest good (τούτων δὲ πάντων ἀρχὴ καὶ τὸ μέγιστον ἀγαθὸω φρόνησις). That is why prudence, from which all the other virtues naturally arise (πεφύκασιν), is a more valuable thing than philosophy, teaching that it is impossible to live pleasantly without living prudently, honorably, and justly, and impossible to live prudently, honestly, and justly, without living pleasantly. For the virtues naturally grow together with (συμπεφύκασιν) living pleasantly and living pleasantly is inseparable from them. (*Men.* 132)

The natural source from which the other virtues arise is prudence. Prudence, of course, crucially includes the understanding of the nature of the best pleasure as a katastematic state and searches out the reasons for all choices based on it. What seems equally clear is that the *justification* for adhering to the conventional virtues, so far as one does, is *because* of their contribution to happiness, which represents a significant departure from Plato and Aristotle. For Aristotle, virtuous action aims at the fine (*kalon*), which is valuable in its own right; virtuous actions must be chosen for their own sakes (*NE* II.4) and so on. Furthermore, the idea that the virtues are means or intermediates between excess and defect also seems a poor fit for Epicurus: Aristotle's courageous person does not shrink from death, but fears danger in the right way, to the right extent, in the right circumstances.

By contrast, for Epicurus it seems that virtuous action does not have value in its own right, independently of its leading to or constituting freedom from pain: "And in his *On the Goal* he again [says]: 'One must honour the noble, and the virtues and things like that, *if* they produce pleasure. But if they do not, one must bid them goodbye'" (Athenaeus *Deipnosophists* 12, 546f, Inwood/Gerson [1998], trans.).

While this fragment is not much to rely on, the pleasure referred to must be katastematic pleasure. And so, it seems that this sort of statement implies the Eudaimonist Hope. Even more significantly, there is little question that the central virtue of justice is for Epicurus an entirely conventional construct, developed for its usefulness:

> [33] Justice was not a thing in its own right, but [exists] in mutual dealings in whatever places there [is] a pact about neither harming one another nor being harmed. [34] Injustice was not a bad thing in its own right, but [only] because of the fear produced by the suspicion that one will not escape the notice of those assigned to punish such actions. [35] It is impossible for someone who secretly does something which men agreed [not to do] [. . .] to be confident that he will escape detection, even if in current circumstances he escapes detection ten thousand times. For until his death it will be uncertain whether he will continue to escape detection. (*KD*, 33–35, Inwood/Gerson 151 [1998] trans. and insertions)

The reasons for the Epicurean to refrain from injustice as conventionally understood, then, are multiple: there is (almost always) nothing to be gained from injustice, for what good could be obtained by it that would increase one's katastematic pleasure? If one is caught and punished, that would consist in pain and disturbance of *ataraxia*. And even if one escapes detection, one will always *worry* about being caught and punished, which will itself ruin one's tranquility. And, returning to the first point, what good would be worth acquiring for the Epicurean, who is completely unafraid of death?

The upshot then is that, try as some scholars might, Epicurus does not value the virtues as such, but neither, as we saw in our discussion of the *Protagoras*, does he engage in the radical revision of our conceptions of the virtues that one might expect for someone who is a hedonist and buys into the Eudaimonist Hope. In a monistic hedonism of the Protagorean sort, the goal is to maximize pleasure; and the craft of measurement is the knowledge that ensures that one measures correctly. That said, as we saw in Chapter 2, any action, regardless of its intrinsic nature, may be the virtuous one, if it truly leads to the most pleasure; the possibilities for actions that run counter to the conventional virtues are easy to imagine. By contrast, Epicurus's more conservative, non-revisionist stance with respect to the virtues is driven, as we have seen, by his radical conception of the pleasure that counts as the final good. At the end of the day, he holds that the "rightness" of virtuous action, is ultimately grounded (metaphysically) in the conception of happiness as is the case for someone who also buys into the idea of the Eudaimonist Hope; if an action ruined one's *ataraxia* (which, as we have seen, is not necessarily the same as an action that is painful), then it would not be genuinely virtuous, meaning it would not be truly right action. There is no independent value, like Aristotle's conception of the noble, that makes virtuous actions right. These aspects of Epicurus's view, however, are sometimes less than apparent since his unique conception of pleasure makes it the case that acting in accordance with the conventional virtues turns out to be largely correct.

7
Virtue and Happiness in Early Stoicism

1. Introduction

Even more than Epicurean ethics, the contemporary study of the Stoics is deeply affected by assumptions about eudaimonism. In particular, the assumption that they allegedly share with Aristotle the ideas that eudaimonia must be the source of anything that has value in itself and that absolutely all of our rational actions are aimed at eudaimonia.[1] The prevalence of this reasoning is widespread, and, indeed, where much scholarship begins when addressing controversy over the Stoic conception of indifferents. That is, it begins where Cicero begins, but not, as I shall argue, where the actual ethical philosophy begins. Chapters 4 and 5 worked to undermine such a reading of Aristotle, arguing that for him eudaimonia is not a Comprehensive Practical Principle. Further, we saw that although Aristotle has an inclusivist conception of a *happy life*, he holds that *happiness* is always, in its primary and secondary forms, constituted by a particular activity (*energeia*), either morally virtuous action or theoretical contemplation. When it comes to the sort of practical principle furnished by the inclusivist conception of a happy life—that is, virtuous activity (eudaimonia), in a complete life, with a suitable amount of external goods—it is simply a Prudential Practical Principle: one that tells us what our good consists in, and therefore what we ought to pursue, so long as the Superseding Practical Principle of action, acting in accordance with the fine (i.e., doing morally virtuous action for its own sake) does not intrude. Thus, it was argued, that Aristotle, like Socrates and Plato before him, adhered to the Supremacy of Virtue and its associated claim that it is never right to do wrong, and that this practical principle operated as a Superseding Practical Principle not a Comprehensive one.

---

[1] Consider, e.g., Nussbaum (1994), 361: "But the Stoics, like Aristotle, also hold that eudaimonia is, by definition, inclusive of everything that has intrinsic value, everything that is choiceworthy for its own sake." Such a view is similar to Vlastos's (1991) position; see Introduction. Klein (2012) and (2015), 228 n. 4, says he accepts Glenn Lesses's (1989) reasons for supposing that, quoting Lesses (98–99), "the Stoic conception of happiness satisfies Aristotle's basic constraints on an adequate notion of happiness." See also Annas (1993), Inwood (1999a), 684.

Freed from the traditional interpretation of Aristotelian eudaimonism, we need to look with fresh eyes at whether in fact there is independent evidence that the Stoics hold that (1) all rational actions aim at eudaimonia; and (2) eudaimonia is, by definition, inclusive of everything that is worth choosing in itself. If the Stoics hold these two views, according to the account defended here, it would mark a break with their predecessors, and not, as the scholarly tradition would have it, a continuation.

Terence Irwin occupies an interesting position here.[2] On his view, the Stoics break with traditional Greek eudaimonism in rejecting the idea that, in my terms, happiness is a Comprehensive Practical Principle. While for Irwin (as we have seen) rational eudaimonism is defined as a view maintaining that all deliberate, non-acratic actions are undertaken for the sake of eudaimonia, the Stoics break with the tradition by adopting an axiological dualism. There are particular values, good and bad, which apply to two particular conditions, virtue and vice, and it is these that are the sole determinants of happiness. Most other so-called goods and evils, such as life/death, honor/dishonor, and wealth/poverty, are indifferent as far as happiness goes, but do have a distinct kind of value or disvalue that provides an agent with reasons to pursue or avoid one or the other, but these reasons are disconnected from happiness. We will consider this in what follows, but we should note up front how the historical account defended here differs from Irwin's. Whereas he understands the Stoics as breaking with the earlier tradition because of its rejection of the idea that eudaimonia embraces all reasons for action, I see the Stoic view as a continuation and elaboration of a tradition that never thought of eudaimonia in this way in the first place. As some of Irwin's critics remark, if he is right, then the Stoics mark a sudden unprecedented difference in their adoption of axiological dualism (or pluralism); this leads those critics, such as Jacob Klein, to figure out how to bring the Stoics back into the rational eudaimonist fold.[3] But if the account defended in this book is correct, then there is no fold to return to and no need to posit such a drastic rupture.

As in the treatment of Epicurus, we need to be careful to try, so far as is possible, to reconstruct early Stoicism on these questions. For, as I suggest in the Epilogue, a robust eudaimonism *is* front and center in Cicero, while

---

[2] See Irwin (1986) and (2007), ch. 13. My reading of the Stoics will agree with Irwin's insofar as it maintains that the Stoics do not think acting for the sake of virtue exhausts all rational reasons for action; Irwin (1986)'s description of the differences between Aristotle and the Stoics, however, is significantly different in emphasis, given the interpretation of Aristotle argued for in Chapters 4 and 5.
[3] See Klein (2012), (2015).

our concern is to examine carefully where the elements of such a view first emerge. We have seen that there is no evidence Epicurus intends his conception of eudaimonia to function as a Comprehensive Practical Principle, for the "variations" of ways of relieving pain are not supposed to be "irrational" or "non-rational," and yet they also make no difference one way or the other toward one's blessedness or *ataraxia*. I shall argue that the Stoics hold a similar position, although of course not connected to hedonism. The Stoic view is complex, particularly because of the controversial and confusing role of Stoic indifferents. So, I shall start there and work my way out to larger issues about Stoic eudaimonism.

2. Stoics on Indifferents: An Overview

All Stoics believe that virtue is the sole good and vice the sole bad. External goods are not in fact goods at all but really utterly indifferent when it comes to a person's happiness, which consists solely in the possession of virtue. The list of indifferents varies in different sources, but certainly includes such things as life, health, wealth, beauty, pleasure, strength, and their contraries. The notorious and ubiquitous Stoic claim, and the sense in which the contemporary use of the word "Stoic" contains some historical accuracy, is that gain or loss of indifferents has absolutely no effect on one's happiness. For the virtuous person, whatever happens to them cannot diminish (or augment) their happiness.[4]

As the word "indifferent" suggests, one common gloss on its meaning is that it refers to something that does not "stimulate impulse one way or the other" (DL 7.104). Something truly indifferent does not move a person either to pursue or avoid it or to believe or disbelieve it. Obviously, the Stoic view that life, health, and so on are "indifferent" sounds extreme, especially when compared to what are eventually distinguished as "absolute" indifferents, such as whether one has an odd or even number of hairs on one's head or whether the number of stars is odd or even. One motivation, then, for dividing indifferents into classes is to avoid the extreme implausibility that an ideal Stoic, the Sage, would care as little about their life as they do about the number of hairs on their head. A second motivation, which will be more important for our purposes and which I will turn to below, concerns the role of

---

[4] See the passages collected in Long and Sedley (1987), §§58, 60, 61, and 63. Henceforth, texts from this collection will simply be cited as LS58A and so on.

indifferents in action; this will be particularly important since the Stoics believe that the happy life and the virtuous life are the same.

For these two reasons, perhaps among others, Zeno, the founder of Stoicism, divides indifferents into two classes. The first includes those, as above, designated "absolute" indifferents, while the second class, although remaining strictly speaking indifferent, concerns those that do stimulate a natural impulse for or against (LS58B). Thus, this second group itself is divided into those designated as "promoted" and "according to nature" (e.g., life, health, wealth), and are to be selected when permissible, while others, the "demoted" or those "contrary to nature" (e.g., death, illness, poverty) are to be avoided when permissible. The permissibility in question must be when virtue does not require that a promoted indifferent be avoided or a demoted indifferent be selected (LS58F). The reason that one selects the promoted indifferents and avoids the demoted ones is that they have some value (*axia*) or disvalue (*anaxia*), respectively, although they are not either good or bad, which belong exclusively to virtue or vice (LS58D–E).

One of the fundamental issues about Stoicism, both among the ancients and today, then, concerns how one can make sense of this other type of value, which makes something (sometimes) to-be-selected (or to-be-avoided). As Cicero notoriously argues, the objection quickly arises that the Stoics are trying to have it both ways: on the one hand, possession or lack of promoted indifferents are irrelevant to happiness; on the other hand, they do have some value, only value of a different sort. Thus, in *De Finibus* IV the character Cicero claims that the Stoic position of promoted and demoted indifferents is unstable and inconsistent. Either the Stoics should align themselves with their renegade member, Aristo, and declare that all indifferents are, simply, indifferent or, if they hold that some indifferents really do have some value, they ought, like other Academics and Peripatetics, simply to admit that they are also goods, even if not as important as virtue. While I shall argue that Cicero's critique warps the positions in early Stoicism in several respects, it is important to note it up front because it centers on what is for our purposes the interesting philosophical question: how do indifferents relate to the agent's actions? We have already developed the conceptual structure to make a few initial moves quite quickly.

The Stoics, like Socrates, Plato, and Aristotle, and unlike Epicurus, hold the Supremacy of Virtue; that is, again, they think that doing the virtuous action trumps any other end one might have in acting. Indeed, they would seem to hold an extreme version of this, since, depending on how we understand indifferents, they may hold that virtue is the *only* end one should have in acting. SV has operated in Socrates, Plato, and Aristotle as a Superseding Practical Principle. We contrasted this with, on the one hand, a Comprehensive Practical Principle, according to which eudaimonia is the end of all (rational) actions, and, on the other, a Prudential Practical Principle, which guides all actions aiming at our happiness, but without exhausting all reasons for action whatsoever. The Stoics occupy an interesting position here. If they take virtue or living virtuously[5] to be the sole constituent of happiness, and they take everything else to be utterly indifferent, then, the distinction between eudaimonia operating as a Superseding Practical Principle and a Comprehensive Practical Principle would seem to collapse, since virtue becomes the sole aim of all actions. Contrast this with our understanding of Socrates's position. We argued that Socrates holds SV, but that SV was not a guide to action at all in cases where virtue was not at issue. I argued in Chapter 2[6] that when Socrates says that acting virtuously trumps any other end one may have in action, it ought not to be understood as making every action a matter of virtue—as though a person had to walk virtuously, select red or white wine virtuously, and so on. Rather, the Socratic position is that SV operates in all situations as a limiting condition: one must never act contrary to virtue.[7] But in cases where virtue is not at issue one way or the other, Socrates gives no guidance at all as to how to act. In particular, he does not tie every one of our actions to the end of eudaimonia, in the way that eudaimonist interpreters claim. A common understanding of the Stoics is that they make virtue, as the sole component of eudaimonia, the *only* end of *every* action. In other words, the Stoics hold the view that I argued we ought *not* to attribute to Socrates: namely that he cares *only* about virtue in the sense that he thinks that *every deliberate action* is either a requirement of virtue or contrary to virtue; in colloquial language, this makes everything a "moral issue." Perhaps, though, this *is* the Stoic position?

Such a view would prima facie seem to be, like other elements of Stoic philosophy, implausible and unattractive. But the discussion of indifferents is complicated by inadequately distinguishing between two roles that

---

[5] I shall not attempt to understand the different Stoic formulations of the end and how they could possibly be equivalent; see Barney (2003), 304–309, for a list of the formulations and their connection to the topic at hand.

[6] And in Vasiliou (2008).

[7] See Introduction and Chapter 1 for how the Kantian—and I have argued Socratic—idea of a limiting condition captures the sense of "ubiquity," that is, of virtue always and everywhere being relevant to one's actions.

indifferents might play. The first concerns the role of indifferents in situations where virtue is, as I have been putting it, "not at issue." We might think that the Stoic doctrine of indifferents is deployed in this capacity, so that their position ends up being similar to Socrates's on my account of it. There is the rationality at work in virtue, and then, when virtue or its contrary is not at issue, one selects the promoted indifferents and avoids the demoted ones, according to their distinct kind of value, despite their not being goods or evils.[8] The mainstream Stoics,[9] however, *unlike* Socrates, would *also* be providing some rational guidance in these "neutral" situations as well by means of the distinction between promoted and demoted indifferents. This marks a potential similarity with the Epicureans. In the previous chapter, I argued that Epicurus's general claim that kinetic pleasures are good is subject to the limiting condition that the kinetic pleasures do not interfere with the katastematic state of *ataraxia*; so, Epicurus, like the Stoics, is filling a gap in the Socratic account addressing deliberation in cases where virtue and happiness (or, for the Epicureans the state of pleasure that constitutes living blessedly) are not at issue.

But there is a second topic that is not adequately distinguished from this one in the literature. Cicero complains that the Stoics have no clear and adequate way of obtaining *a standard of right and wrong* (*Fin.* IV.46–47, 68–69) since they consider everything besides virtue and vice to be, strictly speaking, indifferent. Now this concerns a *determining question*: in determining what *is* virtuous in the here and now, there is no "matter (*hulē*)" for virtue other than the promoted and demoted indifferents (cf. LS59A). Virtue and vice must consist in some sort of selection and use of these "indifferent" materials. Therefore, if they are simply completely indifferent (as Aristo insists), then there is no way of making any decisions: why not take food from a baby, if food is no more important than the number of hairs on one's head? One ends up in a position with respect to action that parallels the classic challenge to the Pyrrhonean sceptic: if this is no more poison than not poison, why not drink it? Similarly, if death is no more valuable than life, as an even number of hairs is no better than odd number, then why not end one's life? On the other horn of the Ciceronian dilemma, if life *is* more valuable than death, other things being equal (as it seems to be on the view

---

[8] This is in line with Irwin's attribution of axiological dualism to the Stoics; see note above.
[9] For present purposes, "mainstream" Stoics are simply those who, unlike Aristo, divide indifferents into promoted, demoted, and absolute.

of the "promoted indifferents" in mainstream Stoicism), why not just admit that it is a good that contributes to our happiness? The relevant point here, though, is not to resolve the alleged dilemma but to see that the question is *not* about how a person decides *when virtue is not at issue*, but how the Stoics, holding the doctrine of indifferents, determine what the virtuous thing to do is. Cicero does not distinguish clearly between these different circumstances and neither do contemporary scholars, but they sometimes address one, sometimes the other, and sometimes it is unclear which. I shall argue in what follows that the distinction is essential, particularly in considering the plausibility of the view of Aristo and its relationship to the position of the mainstream Stoics.

We have briefly sketched, then, two potential but distinct roles for indifferents: First, promoted and demoted indifferents may provide a guide for selecting things when virtue (or its opposite) is not at issue. Second, indifferents are considered whenever one is trying to determine what the virtuous action is in the here and now or in general (to the extent that the Stoics are concerned with principles and rules).[10] What determines whether an action is virtuous is presumably something about the selection and use of items within the class of "indifferents."[11] Is it just to deprive someone of their property, health, or life? Why is it just to deprive someone of their property in *this* situation, but not in *that* one? As interpreters since at least Cicero have complained, if (as Aristo is accused of) we remove all indifferents from consideration, and look only to virtue, what are we going to consider? Surely, right and wrong action involves physically helping or hurting, giving or taking away property, caring for parents or children, and so on. Thus, as we have seen, determining what virtue is is an entirely different matter from selecting among "indifferents" when virtue is not at issue or from deciding the relative importance of virtue versus indifferents.[12]

---

[10] See the debate between Brad Inwood and Phillip Mitsis, especially Inwood (1986), (1999b/2005), and Mitsis (1993), (1994), and (2003).

[11] Barney (2003) examines complexities in the Stoic position concerning how one ought to select among indifferents.

[12] As so often, the roots of this conceptual distinction are in the Socratic dialogues. In Vasiliou (2008), ch. 2, I argue that this issue infects scholarship on Socratic deliberation, particularly in interpreting the *Crito*. Since Socrates seems to consider the welfare of his children, his age, the benefits or harms of exile, and his agreements and promises all together in his deliberation about whether to escape, many commentators conclude that these cannot be his real reasons for remaining in prison. Why? Because Socrates cares *only* about whether he does what is right and virtuous and this trumps money, pleasure, pain, the welfare of children, and his own life or death; so, it follows that if he relies on any of these "indifferents" (as we call them in the Stoic context), he must not be giving his real reasons. But this is to miss the crucial distinction above: it is one thing to treat indifferents as the *ends* of one's action. In this case one might weigh money or saving one's children *against* doing

Before considering how mainstream Stoics handle these two issues—action when virtue is not at issue and the determination of what the virtuous action is—let me begin with the iconoclast Aristo, since his view will provide a useful and instructive counterpoint. To tip my hand, I shall argue that Aristo is the Stoic who does, in fact, seem to make every token action a matter of virtue in his rejection of any distinction between promoted and demoted indifferents; contrary to the criticism of Cicero and many contemporary interpreters, Aristo does not, however, consider indifferents worthless and so fail to provide any matter with which to determine which actions *are* virtuous.

3. The Iconoclast Aristo

Despite being repeatedly dismissed and even mocked by Cicero as well as some contemporary scholars, Aristo was an immensely popular and major figure in the early to mid-third century. As Gisela Striker notes, Chrysippus, the most dominant figure in the development of Stoicism, nevertheless only becomes the head of the school in 232 BCE, at about fifty, although he must have been an important figure considerably earlier.[13] Furthermore, even though the evidence for Aristo's own views is relatively scant and frequently comes from hostile sources, it is interesting how often he is mentioned by Cicero and even much later sources, like Sextus, Diogenes, Plutarch, and Seneca (if only sometimes to be quickly dismissed), which suggests his importance in the history of the Stoa. The account in Diogenes Laertius relates that he was a very well-known, charismatic, and influential figure.

In the fragments we possess, discussion of Aristo and his divergence from "orthodox" Stoics centers around five claims: (1) his rejection of physics and logic (dialectic) as appropriate parts of philosophy; (2) his rejection of moral rules at least of a fairly specific nature, leading some scholars to think of him as ancient philosophy's first "intuitionist" about morality; the virtuous person's knowledge or wisdom simply enables her to see what virtue requires

---

the virtuous thing. But it is entirely another thing to take into consideration money or one's children's welfare *in a deliberation about what the right thing to do is*. It is the latter sort of deliberation that Socrates is engaging in the argument of the "Laws" in the *Crito* and that I am arguing is at issue above.

[13] See Striker (1996 [1991]), 231.

in any circumstance;[14] (3) the idea that the virtues are, in some sense, one, and simply have different names depending on their relationships to different fields; (4) his idea that the highest goal of a human life, which he agrees with all Stoics, is virtue is *also* "indifference" (*SVF* I.360, 379);[15] and (5) an insistence that everything other than virtue and vice is absolutely indifferent; therefore, he rejects any division of indifferents into "promoted" and "demoted" or according to nature and contrary to nature. My focus will be on (4) and (5). I shall argue that when the evidence on these issues, scant though it is, has been analyzed carefully, we can gain a better understanding of what his distinctive contribution to the structure of ancient eudaimonism is. Let's turn to the details; I will begin with the better-attested (5) and then offer some speculation on the nature of (4).

There are two central texts that provide further information beyond the bare fact that Aristo rejected the promoted/demoted distinction. The most interesting is in Sextus (*Against the Ethicists* 64–67/LS58F):

> [64] Ariston of Chios said that health, and everything like it, is not a promoted indifferent. For to say that it is a promoted indifferent is equivalent to deeming it a good—the difference is almost solely in name. [65] For quite generally, the indifferent things between virtue and vice have nothing to differentiate them, nor are some of them by nature promoted and others demoted, but in keeping with the circumstances, which differ with the times, neither do the things which are said to be promoted turn out to be invariably promoted nor are the things which are said to be demoted necessarily demoted. [66] At any rate, if it were necessary for healthy men to serve a tyrant and for this reason to be executed, whereas sick men were released from service and so also exempted from destruction, the wise man would choose sickness over health on such an occasion (κατὰ τοῦτον τὸν καιρόν). And thus neither is health invariably a thing promoted nor is sickness a thing demoted. [67] As, then, in writing names, we sometimes place some letters first and at other times others, fitting them to their different circumstances (we write D first for Dion's name, the I first for Ion, the O first for Orion); it is not because some letters are given precedence over others by nature, but because the situations require us to do this. In the

---

[14] See Annas (1993), 99–107, endorsed by Inwood (1999b/2005), 105–106; Sedley (1999) disagrees.
[15] *SVF* refers to von Arnim (1903-1924).

same way in things which are between virtue and vice, there is no natural precedence for some one of these over others but, rather, it is [determined] by circumstances (οὕτω κἀν τοῖς μεταξὺ ἀρετῆς καὶ κακίας πράγμασιν οὐ φυσική τις γίνεται ἑτέρων παρ' ἕτερα πρόκρισις, κατὰ περίστασιν δὲ μᾶλλον). (Bett [1997] trans., modified.)

The main claim seems clear: since indifferents are always pursued or avoided depending on what is required, that is, what virtue requires in specific circumstances, they cannot be simply promoted or dispromoted in their own right. The example of the tyrant in [66] is apparently supposed to illustrate and perhaps augment this point, but does it less than perspicuously. We have three elements in the example: (a) being healthy/sick, (b) serving/not serving a tyrant, (c) being dead/alive. There are two different ways of understanding how these operate together, which affects our understanding of how the metaphysics of virtue is being described. One way is to take "serving a tyrant" as an example of an unjust (and so contrary to virtue) action, taking the fact of the person's being a tyrant to imply that he is unjust—in itself a reasonable inference in the context. Since a wise man would never do an injustice (adhering to SV), the wise man chooses sickness (a putative demoted indifferent) over health (a putative promoted indifferent).[16] The problem with this interpretation is that it leaves the third element in the example dangling: serving the tyrant leads to the person's execution, while not serving the tyrant, despite making one ill, actually saves the person's life; and, of course, life and death are also indifferents. So why include reference to execution if it isn't relevant to the proper deliberation?[17]

Gisela Striker offers another reading: "it seems pretty obvious that the wise man who opts for illness rather than health in such an exceptional situation is not preferring illness to health, but rather survival with illness to destruction with health. Which does nothing to show that health is not in general preferable to illness when there is no disadvantage connected with health. So this example is not likely to convince anyone that there is no natural order of preference among external things or bodily states."[18] While this makes clear sense on its own, it too has problems as a reading of Aristo's argument, for it

---

[16] See Mitsis (1994), 4836.
[17] The way Sextus relates it, in any case, does seem to emphasize the importance of the execution, saying "if it were necessary for healthy men to serve a tyrant and *on account of this* (διὰ τοῦτο) be destroyed."
[18] Striker (1996 [1991]), 236.

makes the entire example rest on selection of indifferents rather than what virtue requires. Who wouldn't choose to be (somewhat) ill but remain alive rather than be healthy but be (shortly?) put to death? How does this go any distance at all toward showing people that "indifferents" are all truly indifferent, since it is an example of a person choosing a promoted indifferent, life, over demoted indifferent, death? As Striker complains, not only does this not help Aristo's case ("this example is not likely to convince..."), but it seems to help his opponent's point. Additionally, it makes the reference to a tyrant rather redundant. Neither reading of the example, I think, is satisfactory. That said, the first interpretation at least supports the idea of a person rightly choosing an allegedly "demoted" indifferent to avoid injustice, which is the sort of case Aristo would want to highlight.[19]

In any case, the analogy with spelling that begins in 67 is more illuminating and, I shall argue, straightforward.[20] The analogy is between a virtuous and wise person, who wants to and does act correctly, and a literate person, who wants to and does spell correctly. Spelling a word correctly, then, is going to be analogous to performing the virtuous action. So, the circumstance we are to consider is one in which there is a virtuous action to-be-done or a specific word to-be-spelled. Obviously in the spelling case it is the word to-be-spelled that dictates the letters one must choose. The idea that someone who is literate would think that there is some sort of "natural preference" for one letter over another is ridiculous; it would be like preferring to spell "cat" as "kat" because of some random preference for k's over c's. So, just as one selects different letters depending solely on those that are required for the correct spelling of the word in question, so too does the virtuous person select or reject *whichever* indifferents they must in order to realize the virtuous action in the circumstances.[21] The sole aim of the virtuous person is to do the virtuous

---

[19] See, DeFilippo and Mitsis (1994) and Inwood (1999a), 695–697.

[20] Striker (1996 [1991]) thinks this analogy has serious shortcomings as well: "The analogy of the letters has no force by itself and might indeed be rejected as misleading, since there is usually only one way of spelling a given word, while there may be many different ways of reaching a certain result, even in special situations, and we might well prefer one means of action to another apart from the circumstances." Bett (1997), 95, agrees: "the [mainstream] Stoics would contest this [lesson from the letter analogy]; while agreeing that health is not *invariably* to be valued over sickness, they would still insist that health is by its very nature such as to be usually worth pursuing." This, as with the tyrant example, is plausible in its own right, but I think it significantly underestimates the power of the spelling analogy; see above.

[21] As Striker remarks in the previous note, the analogy does break down insofar as there is only one correct way to spell the word-type "cat" and there may be a multiple distributions of wealth that might count as just, depending on the circumstances. But I take it that Aristo holds that there is one correct, virtuous action to-be-done in concrete circumstances and the point is that the wise person will knowledgably select whichever indifferents correctly constitute the appropriate action in each token situation.

action just as the sole aim of the literate person is to spell the word correctly. Since this is the case, it would be as "wrong" to prefer living over dying, if dying were necessary for doing the virtuous thing, just as it would be for a person to prefer the letter k over the letter c in order to spell "cat."

This has more analogical force and coherence than scholars have granted it. First, aside from the shocking word "indifferent" (more on which in a moment), the resulting view has much in common with Socrates's (who is often explicitly compared to Aristo). Socrates too says shocking things at his trial, such as that he "couldn't care less" about living or dying *compared with doing the right thing* (*Ap.* 32d). Again, as I have emphasized throughout, for Socrates (and now too for Aristo), external "goods" or promoted "indifferents" count for *nothing as ends* when compared with virtue. As people who strive to be happy and virtuous, and so to do virtuous actions, it is whatever the virtuous action is in the circumstances that entirely dictates which indifferents will be selected or rejected, just as the word to-be-spelled dictates which letters are to be chosen.

A second crucial point emerges from this example. The term "indifferent" has suggested both to ancients and to contemporary scholars the idea of being something *valueless*, that is, utterly worthless. Striker writes, "Chrysippus argues that declaring all bodily and external things to be totally indifferent *and valueless* would leave the wise man with no method for making a selection among them."[22] Some examples of indifferents, like the number of hairs on one's head being odd or even, encourage such a thought. But Aristo's spelling analogy suggests no such thing. No literate person thinks individual letters are utterly *worthless*; they may be, by themselves, *meaningless*, but they are also extremely valuable since obviously we could not spell words without them. Indeed, it would be reasonable to call them the "matter" of words, which in turn bear the semantic content that makes language possible (cf. LS59A).[23] Analogously, then, living/dying, health/disease, beauty/ugliness are not worthless in the sense of being ignorable or utterly without value, for, even on Aristo's own view, they are what needs to be properly arranged and handled in order to do virtuous actions.[24] When Aristo declares everything

---

[22] Striker (1996/1991), 236 (my emphasis). She provides no reference for the evidence that Chrysippus said this; I take it that she may have in mind *Fin* IV.68–69. But I think there is reason to be skeptical that this is an accurate description by Cicero of Chrysippus's objection; see note 28 below.

[23] The point is not affected if wants to go up a level to sentences or phrases as the bearers of content.

[24] I take it that this is true for all the Stoics, since indifferents are the "matter" of virtue; all virtuous actions are constituted by a selecting among indifferent things, as scholars have recognized. See, e.g., Inwood (1999a) and Barney (2003).

simply indifferent, he is saying that without consideration of what the virtuous action is, one would have no idea of which among the indifferents to select. But just as I could not spell words *without* letters, I could not perform virtuous actions without indifferents, so indifferents are hardly *worthless*.

A second passage, with another analogy, supports our understanding of the Spelling Analogy: "Aristo of Chios . . . said that the goal was to live in a state of indifference with respect to what is intermediate between virtue and vice (τὸ ἀδιαφόρως ἔχοντα ζῆν πρὸς τὰ μεταξὺ ἀρετῆς καὶ κακίας), acknowledging no distinction whatsoever in them but treating them all alike. For the wise man is like a good actor who plays either role fittingly, whether he takes on the role of Thersites or Agamemnon" (DL 7.160/LS58G, Inwood/Gerson [2008] trans.).

An excellent actor plays the required role excellently, whether the role is that of a member of the rabble or a hero. One role requires one type of language, deportment, costume, and so on; the other, a different set. The excellent actor has no preference for these as such, without reference to the role that they are required to play. Only a bad, ignorant actor would prefer the mannerisms of a hero in themselves and then wrongly apply them to the role of Thersites, like spelling the word "cat" with a k because of preference for k's. Similarly, the truly virtuous person will have a disposition of indifference when, in some circumstance, they are required by virtue to play *their* role by, say, sacrificing life or limb.

A further significant feature of this passage is that it says that the agent should be in a *condition of indifference* toward such things. This is a more perspicuous phrase than calling the things *themselves* "indifferent," which is liable to trigger the misunderstanding concerning worthlessness discussed above. More speculatively, it might also shed light on the few texts (*SVF* I.360, 379) that say that Aristo took the end or goal itself to *be* "indifference (ἀδιαφορία)," rather than simply virtue or living virtuously.[25] As mentioned, Aristo seems to have been a very popular figure in his day and a compelling speaker. Given what we have seen so far to be his position, it should perhaps be less surprising that he came to be known as holding the view that indifference *itself* is the goal. For, his emphasis, much like Socrates's own, must have been on persuading people to treat what had been called "external goods" (and "evils") as entirely irrelevant when it comes to doing the virtuous action. Of course, Aristo realizes that we have natural preferences for pleasure over

---

[25] This is the fourth iconoclastic position I mentioned at the opening of this section. See, again, Striker (1996/1991), 233–235, for a discussion of the difficulties in defending indifference as the end and its compatibility with the end being virtue/wisdom.

pain, life over death, whereas it is preposterous to think we have preferences for k's over c's. Perhaps his position, however, is that what people need, as a matter of their moral education and moral progress, is to cultivate a "state of indifference" in themselves toward such things, which, while essential as the matter of virtue, in themselves have no value. This might lead us to a more positive evaluation of his position.[26]

If these readings of the Spelling and Actor Analogies are correct, then, Aristo has a defensible position: the letters are the "matter" of correctly spelled words just as the indifferents are the matter of virtuous actions and not valuing one letter *as such* over another is not to say that letters *have no value at all*. Thus, certain criticisms of Aristo in Cicero are not only unsympathetic, but arguably miss the mark, such as when he says: "Aristo held that there is no difference between one object and another, and that there is no significant distinction between anything except the distinction between virtues and vices" (*Fin*. IV.47).[27] Given the Actor and Spelling Analogies, this is unfair: of course, there are significant distinctions among indifferents on Aristo's view, just as there are significant distinctions among individual letters and the requirements of individual theatrical roles.[28]

Aristo, then, plausibly holds the view that we will see is attributed to all the Stoics. According to this, every token action is a matter of duty and the failure to act appropriately is to act wrongly and viciously. On Aristo's analogy, one is always in every token action attempting to spell a word correctly. I will argue in the rest of the chapter that the Stoic account of intermediate appropriate actions presents a different view.

---

[26] Cf. Striker, 239: "I suspect, in any case, that Aristo's fame among his contemporaries was due more to his personality and his apparent talent for witty remarks than to his philosophical acumen." Inwood (1999a), 695–697, credits Aristo with a more philosophically important position.

[27] See also *De Fin* II.43: "Aristo and Pyrrho considered all such items valueless, resulting in their claiming that there was absolutely no difference between being in excellent health and being gravely ill. People long ago stopped bothering to argue against this position, and rightly so. It seeks to make virtue the only thing that matters, to such an extent that it is stripped of its power of choice and is given nowhere to start from or rest upon." Here we see the explicit claim that Aristo's positions makes indifferents "valueless"; this is addressed above.

[28] Cicero complains again: "In declaring what is moral to be the only good, you do away with concern for one's health, care of one's household, public service, the conduct of business and the duties of life. Ultimately morality itself, which you regard as everything, must be abandoned. Chrysippus took great pains to make this point against Aristo. [. . .] [69] Wisdom had nowhere to stand once all appropriate action was done away with; and it was done away with when every form of choice and distinction was abolished" (*Fin* IV.68–69; Woolf trans.). Two points about this passage. First it shares with the earlier ones the same unfair characterization of the view, especially in its claim that "every form of choice and distinction was abolished." Secondly, we should note that, as far as I can tell, this is the only reference to Chrysippus criticizing Aristo on this specific point, as opposed to on the question of how distinct the virtues are; see *SVF* III.259, III.264.

4. Stoics on Moral Luck

Before turning to the Stoics on appropriate actions (*kathēkonta*), I need briefly to consider a famous part of Stoic doctrine—their rejection of moral luck—in order to clear away a potential misunderstanding. The Sage's goal or end, in which their happiness consists, is being virtuous and striving to do the virtuous thing; success—described in the archer simile at *Fin*. III.22—is to be "selected but not chosen."[29] One can only choose what is in one's power, which is to aim as best as one can to strike the target, but actually hitting it is not in one's power. This part of the Stoics' view is not particularly important for the argument that follows. But I note that when I say, "the Sage performs the virtuous action," what that has to mean is that the Sage does "everything in their power" (*Fin*. III.22) to achieve the end of the action (which is of course itself indifferent). So, the Sage will do everything in their power to save the drowning person, but actually saving the person is not up to the Sage and not the Sage's goal; the person's being saved will occur or not in accordance with the unfolding of cosmic nature and, moreover, as an indifferent, should not and does not have any effect on the Sage's happiness.[30]

There is one aspect of this part of Stoic doctrine, however, that is relevant to the interpretation I am defending. For obvious reasons, the Stoic rejection of moral luck is connected to Kant's moral philosophy and compared with his claim that the only thing good without qualification is a good will.[31] This comparison risks, however, a serious misunderstanding. When we think of a person "willing" something, we may conceive of that as an entirely internal affair—completely a matter of one's inner disposition. For example, colloquially, we might say that as I lay in bed, wakened by an early alarm and still exhausted, I "summon the will" to get up. Then, once I have adequately gathered my willpower, I get up; that is, I engage in an external action. So, in this example, the summoning of the will is entirely internal and dispositional, and then the external action follows. One might thus conclude (as some scholars of the Stoics and Kant do) that all of the moral goodness lies merely in this internal mental disposition and not at all in any external

---

[29] See LS64 for associated passages, including criticism of the Stoic position.

[30] Moreover, the Sage will not have any (of the usual) emotions or feelings over succeeding or failing to save the person's life. The Sage's happiness will be perfect and invulnerable either way. This is perhaps the most notorious and, to many, repugnant part of Stoicism.

[31] *Groundwork*, 4:394. The interpretation of this is controversial. Several more recent Kant scholars wish to correct older and cruder interpretations of Kant that reject all concern with external actions and "results": see Herman (1993), ch. 5, Uleman (2010), (2016), and Wood (2008).

actions in the world. This would be to get the Stoic view badly wrong. As Phillip Mitsis puts it: "Attention to the inner motivation of an action and indifference to an action's success does not commit the Stoic to the claim that actions themselves are merely dispositions to act. Thus, a sage obeys a moral injunction to act, not merely to get himself into a particular moral mood."[32]

Recall that the Sage does *everything in their power* to, for example, save the person. Unless we imagine bizarre circumstances where the Sage is utterly incapacitated but still aware that a person is drowning (and, we are assuming, the virtuous action is to attempt to save the person), the Sage's grasp of what is to be done will involve a whole series of external actions that constitute attempting to save the person—jumping in the river, calling for help, administering CPR, and so on. These actions will be right, correct, and morally required; to fail to do them would, as we shall see, be a moral error. This is important to keep in mind because I will be arguing against interpretations that understand the moral worth of the Sage as residing entirely in some internal, dispositional state in a way that ends up omitting the importance of the external actions that are performed in the token situation. There is no doubt that the Stoics place a very high value on the state of the agent. Not only does the state of the agent determine whether someone *is* a Sage but it will also affect how actions are classified. We should not think, however, that the Stoics have thereby dispensed with the idea that what is done in the world is also relevant to the classification of action. I emphasize this up front since I suspect that a misreading of the Stoics' rejection of moral luck may be partly to blame for this over-internalizing interpretation of their position. Let us now turn to the topic of appropriate actions (*kathēkonta*).

5. Appropriate Actions: A Hypothesis

Kathēkon is a technical term of art from the time of Zeno and understanding it is a central issue in Stoic scholarship.[33] In major accounts of Stoic ethics,

---

[32] Mitsis (2003), 44. Most of the attention to the debate among Mitsis (1986) (1994), Paul Vander Waerdt (1994a) (1994b), and Brad Inwood (1986) (1999b/2005) has focused on the role of rules in answering, in my terms, determining questions: what role, if any, do rules have in determining what the right thing to do is in token circumstances? But there is a second aspect to the debate, more relevant to my focus, that concerns the extent to which moral value is entirely a matter of an agent's inner disposition—the "internalist" position, defended in Vander Waerdt (1994a) (1994b)—versus whether *what is done* in the world also plays a role—and the "externalist position" defended especially in Mitsis (2003); cf. also Mitsis (1994).

[33] See Visnjic (2021), ch. 1 and appendix 1, for discussion of the term itself and its use prior to Zeno.

such as Diogenes Laertius's (7.107) and Stobaeus's (8), the topic of appropriate actions (*kathēkonta*) reasonably follows discussion of indifferents.[34] Whereas "indifferents" refers to things or states of affairs, such as money or being physically injured (DL 7.104–105), appropriate actions are those *actions* or *activities* that are in accordance with our nature. Thus, they are not something that one can *have* (like money) or a state one can be *in* (like wisdom). Stobaeus says (8/LS59B): "Appropriate action is defined [thus]: 'what is consistent in life (τὸ ἀκόλουθον ἐν ζωῇ), which when done admits of a well-reasoned defense (ὅ πραχθὲν εὔλογον ἀπολογίαν ἔχει).'" What is consistent in life is not necessarily what is by nature promoted but what is consistent with the unfolding of the divine cosmos—that is, the natural law of the universe, the following of which is living virtuously (DL 7.88/LS63C). Thus, it can be consistent with life and an appropriate action to maim oneself in the appropriate circumstances, which, presumably, would then be cited as part of "a well-reasoned defense."[35] The well-reasoned defense may thus sometimes consist in the fact that a certain action, although unattractive in itself, which is to say it traffics in demoted indifferents, is nevertheless what virtue requires in the circumstances.

Even non-rational animals and plants engage in "appropriate actions" when without reason they act in ways that are in accordance with their nature (DL 7.107/LS59C, Stobaeus 8/LS59B). It is the application of the term *kathēkon* to plants and animals that motivates Long and Sedley's translation "proper function" (LS59). Of course, this sounds odd in the context of rational human action, especially when virtue requires pursuing a demoted indifferent "in a situation" (*kata peristasin*), meaning in some emergency situation.[36] To say that maiming oneself or starving oneself is performing a "proper function" strains sense, while to say that it is an "appropriate action"

---

[34] All references to Stobaeus will be from the text in Pomeroy (1999).

[35] Brennan (1996) has influentially argued that the "well-reasoned" defense is well-reasoned not in accordance with ordinary, everyday reasoning but the actions that accord with the perfect reasoning of the Sage.

[36] See Visnjic (2021), 42–44, for some recent discussion and the translation "in an emergency." The thought is captured as well in colloquial English in the expression "we have a situation." The scope of what counts as an "emergency situation" is disputed. One interpretation, defended by Mitsis (2003), 45–48, is that the early Stoics were influenced by the Cynics on these matters and so rejected prohibitions against cannibalism and incest as merely conventional. If this is correct then, perhaps, there need be fewer references to an "emergency situation"; if there is a perfectly good detached foot hanging around, then one could eat it. But even so, examples like maiming oneself, which clearly involves pursuing a demoted indifferent, would still be something to pursue only "in a situation" where virtue requires it; otherwise, one would never simply maim oneself. Vogt (2008), 25–28, and ch. 4, downplays Cynic influence.

in some special circumstance is more readily intelligible.[37] Since my concern is with human actions, I will use the translation "appropriate action" (or else simply *kathēkon*) in what follows. Before proceeding, however, it may be useful to pause to consider potential ramifications of the broadest application of *kathekonta* to plants and animals. A central and philosophically significant aspect of Stoicism is its interest in and account of how the advent of reason and language transforms all aspects of a human being's life. Since for human beings impulse is a matter of assent, and assent is to what is assertible in language, even basic functions such as perception are transformed. When an expert and non-expert look at some domain, the expert sees things the non-expert does not because of her training and more sophisticated conceptual repertoire—for example, a summer tanager and not just a red bird.[38]

There are two ways of thinking about the transformation from performing the proper functions of animals (and of our early childhood selves) to performing the appropriate actions of a fully rational human being. On the interpretation I shall defend, there remains an important difference between proper functions, such as eating when hungry or drinking when thirsty, and appropriate actions, such as risking one's life for one's country or going hungry for the sake of a stranger. While the former actions involve the pursuit of preferred indifferents, the latter are aiming at virtue. On this view, these two sorts of pursuits and two sorts of deliberations retain their distinctness. On an opposing view all token actions that are to-be-done are of a piece, as it were, whether it is eating an apple as a snack or attempting to save someone from drowning; a central part of this standard interpretation, as we shall see, is the idea that every token action performed by a Sage becomes a "right action" (*katorthōma*).[39]

Animals and our earlier animal selves did not, of course, even have virtuous actions in view; virtue becomes possible only with rationality. As is well known, for the Stoics virtue just is the state of perfection of that rationality, which is called wisdom. When virtue becomes possible in a rational human being, a whole new range of actions become not only possible, but

---

[37] *Kathēkon* is translated by Cicero as *officium*, which is then translated into English as "duty." Of course, "duty" has an even more narrow sense and, philosophically, is associated especially with Kant. In a token circumstance it may be *kathēkon* to drink when thirsty, but it would be odd to say it is my *duty* to drink when thirsty (either in general or in a token situation), unless one meant something like it is my duty to drink at some point so that I do not die of thirst.

[38] See Shogry (2021).

[39] *katorthoma* is a technical term of art for the Stoics, described as "perfect appropriate action," and an action performable only by the Sage. See further discussion below.

essential for human happiness; pursuing virtuous actions and the wisdom that constitutes doing that correctly is the human good (see, e.g., DL 7.87-89/LS63C). Nevertheless, we might think that, given the broad range of the proper functions (*kathēkonta*) that provide the seeds for our adult appropriate actions (also, of course, *kathēkonta*), the Stoics would wish to retain a distinction between those actions that our new appreciation (however imperfect) of virtue puts into our view and those actions where virtue is not at issue, but where following nature is still in effect over a range of preferred indifferents albeit in a transformed way.

So, we can maintain that the Stoics believe that we are transformed, head to toe as it were, by the development of reason—even the consumption of food and drink is transformed in human beings into a culturally complex and highly ritualized affair[40]—but nevertheless, we might still maintain that there remains a significant difference, which the Stoics wish to mark, between having a glass of water when thirsty and properly sacrificing oneself for one's country. The difference here is not at the level of objects, which are all indifferent—the pain of thirst, water, country, death—but at the level of actions: drinking when thirsty in ordinary circumstances, I will argue, is an "intermediate *kathēkon*," whereas (rightly, i.e., appropriately) sacrificing oneself for one's country is, we might say, a "proper" *kathēkon*. The performance of a proper *kathēkon* by the Sage constitutes a perfect, complete *kathēkon* and so a *katorthōma* (often translated as "morally correct action"), while the performance of the same *kathēkon* by most of us constitutes an incomplete *kathēkon*, although a *kathēkon* nonetheless. The argument for this position will take most of the rest of the chapter.

The standard interpretation of appropriate actions and their performance by Sages and by the rest of us eliminates the distinction between drinking water when thirsty (in ordinary circumstances) and dying for one's country (when it is virtuous to do so); for it holds, on slim textual evidence as will see, that literally everything that the Sage does is perfect and virtuous.[41] The Sage drinks a glass of water virtuously, and the Sage attempts to save a drowning person virtuously; they are both right actions

---

[40] How the acquisition of reason transforms a human being according to the Stoics is a complex issue; see influential articles by Frede: (1994), (1996), (1999).

[41] Not unrelatedly, a theme of this book has involved pushing back on what I have argued has been an overzealous reading of "all" and "every," such as in the understanding of happiness as a Comprehensive Practical Principle.

(*katorthōmata*). Before we consider the textual evidence, however, we can appreciate that the view is philosophically rather unappealing. Of course, its proponents may acknowledge this and simply add it to the list of paradoxical-sounding, counterintuitive Stoic conclusions: the difference between the appropriateness of drinking a glass of water when thirsty (in ordinary circumstances) and trying to save a drowning person is an illusion; they are both simply what is to-be-done, token appropriate actions in their specific circumstances. Employing the Latin translation of *kathēkon*, *officium*, the position may be seen as a broadening of our duties: *every* action that is to be done is a duty; correspondingly, the failure to perform an appropriate action, no matter how mundane, would constitute a (moral) mistake.[42]

In what follows I shall maintain, in agreement with the standard view, that there are two fundamental types of people: Sages and non-Sages. But against almost all scholars I shall argue that there are three types of actions, which are defined independently of the state of the agent:

(1) (proper) appropriate actions;
(2) intermediate appropriate actions; and
(3) actions that are "contrary to appropriate action," that is, mistakes (*hamartēmata*).

The Sage always acts perfectly and correctly and non-Sages always act imperfectly; Sages are virtuous and happy; non-Sages are vicious and miserable.[43] On the standard view, actions are classified solely in terms of the *state*

---

[42] In keeping with this, Tad Brennan (1996), 329, claims that "there are no competing duties in Stoicism." This conclusion is, however, tendentious in two respects. First, it is based on only one text: *SVF* III.510/LS59I, which we will look at below. Second, its plausibility stems from a well-known history of translation, from *kathēkon* to *officium* to "duty." To deny "competing duties" sounds, in English, like one denies the thesis, controversial but recognizably plausible, that there are no genuine moral dilemmas. But as we have seen *kathēkonta* in Stoicism include all sorts of ordinary actions, some with their origins in our natural proper functioning, that would be at best misdescribed in English as "duties." See too Cooper (1996/1999) and Vogt (2008), esp. 198–202. Below, §8 I call this a "flattening out" view, whereby all appropriate actions are duties.

[43] In the image in Cicero (*Fin.* III.48; see also LS61T/Plutarch, *Comm* 1063a–b), only the virtuous, happy person is above the surface of the water; the rest of us are below the surface (and so non-virtuous and miserable), whether we are one foot below or a thousand feet down. The image of being at different depths illustrates the important Stoic notion of "progress" (*prokopē*); we will see below the importance of "the Progressor," as the person moving toward virtue is called.

of the agent that performs them. Correct actions are performed all and only by the Sage; mistaken actions all and only by non-Sages. Furthermore, it is a universal assumption (as far as I know) that every token action performed by the Sage is a right action (*katorthōma*), while every token action performed by a non-Sage is a mistake (*harmatēma*) (although this latter claim comes with some caveats, as we shall see).

Although the texts are difficult, I will argue that they are clear in positing the three classes of actions listed above and in classifying actions *not only* in terms of the state of the agent performing them, *but also* in terms of what action is done externally. In particular, the class of intermediate actions are those actions, for ordinary persons and for Sages, where virtue is not at issue and the "reasonable defense"—even the perfectly reasonable defense of the Sage—consists solely in an action's being the pursuit of a promoted indifferent or the avoidance of a demoted one. Even when a Sage performs an intermediate appropriate action, it does not thereby become a right action (*katorthōma*). To be sure, it is not an action that is *contrary* to virtue either; it is simply an action where virtue is not at issue one way or the other. There will still be a difference *epistemically and dispositionally* between the Sage's performance of an intermediate appropriate action and the non-Sage's, insofar as, among other things, the Sage will know that the action is of this sort, while we will at best have a true opinion about it; in addition, the Sage will never confuse an intermediate appropriate action with a "proper" appropriate action. Moreover, we ordinary people may, of course, simply be wrong in some cases, falsely thinking that a certain action is an intermediate appropriate action when it is an appropriate action full stop. The Sage would never make a mistake about what is an intermediate *kathēkon* and so would never act in a way that was in fact contrary to virtue (or, as I have been putting it, contrary to a "proper" *kathēkon*). The best the rest of us can do, as above, is to do what the Sage would do, even though, because of our characters, that will not make it a right or virtuous action.

Most importantly, I shall argue that virtue operates for the Stoics as it does for Socrates, as a commitment to the Supremacy of Virtue as a Superseding Practical Principle; moreover, the Sage's perfection consists in their perfect adherence to it. We should thus interpret the Sage's perfection in action in terms of the limiting condition imposed by their absolute commitment to the Supremacy of Virtue: the Sage, unlike the rest of us, never acts contrary to virtue.

6. Appropriate Actions versus Mistakes

Let us consider, first, the evidence for a distinction between appropriate actions and mistakes (*harmatēmata*). This distinction will make it clear that the Stoics allow for discriminating between token actions independently of the state of the agent. "They [the Stoics] say that a right action is an appropriate action which covers all the features or, as we said before [8], a complete/perfect appropriate action. What is done contrary to right reason is a mistake; or an action in which something appropriate has been omitted by a rational animal [is a mistake] (κατόρθωμα δ᾽ εἶναι λέγουσι καθῆκον πάντας ἀπέχον τοὺς ἀριθμούς, ἢ καθάπερ προείπομεν, τέλειον καθῆκον· ἁρμάτημα τε τὸ παρὰ τὸν ὀρθὸν λόγον πραττόμενον, ἢ ἐν ᾧ παραλέλειπταί τι καθῆκον ὑπὸ λογικοῦ ζῴου)" (Stobaeus, 11a, Inwood/Gerson [2008] trans., modified). Here a mistake is specifically described as an action "contrary to right reason"; recall that an appropriate action in general is one that has a "well-reasoned defense." A perfect appropriate action is an appropriate action that is perfect in every way—namely, it is an appropriate action performed by the Sage. A passage from Cicero offers some supplementary detail: "we see something that we call right action (*recte factum*), that is, a complete appropriate action (*perfectum officium*). However,[44] there will also be incomplete (*inchoatum*) appropriate action, so that if returning a deposit justly (*iuste*) is a right action, then returning a deposit will be an appropriate action. For the addition of 'justly' makes it a right action (*recte factum*); in itself, however, the return of the deposit is [merely] appropriate" (*Fin.* III.59, Woolf trans., modified).

Here the account begins with a right action (*recte factum*), which is the same as a *perfectum officium* (i.e., a perfect appropriate action, i.e., a *katorthōma*), which is performable only by the perfect Sage. But it is made explicit that there is also an incomplete or imperfect appropriate action, which would be a *kathēkon* performed by an imperfect agent, a non-Sage. While only the Sage can return a deposit *justly*—for only the Sage is just—the rest of us can return the deposit (as we should) even if we cannot do it perfectly, and so our action will never be a right action (a *katorthōma*).

Thus too if I try to save a drowning person as *ex hypothesi* virtue requires, I still only perform an incomplete appropriate action because of the kind of agent I am (a non-Sage); in the same circumstances when the Sage tries to

---

[44] Retaining *autem*, deleted by Lambinus.

save the drowning person, they perform a right action. If, however, I decide to keep reading the *Phaedo* instead of trying to save the drowning person, I then make a mistake. What *makes* it a mistake is not only something about my character, but something about the fact that in these circumstances trying to save the person is what is genuinely appropriate; continuing to read the *Phaedo* in these circumstances is an action that is "contrary to right reason." Continuing to read certainly says something about me and my character and my moral progress (*prokopē*), but it is not simply my *character* that *makes* my action wrong; I am *doing* the wrong thing. So, while neither my attempting to save the person nor my continuing to read makes me more or less miserable—I am wretched either way—there is an important difference between the actions themselves as registered in the distinction between imperfect appropriate actions and mistakes. Only mistakes are *contrary to right reason*; imperfect appropriate actions are not.[45]

The distinction, then, between appropriate actions and mistakes makes it clear that the Stoics distinguish actions *not only* according to who does them (Sage or non-Sage) *but also* according to what is done. I hope, therefore, to have made plausible the idea that the Stoics might introduce a third class of actions—intermediate *kathēkonta*—that are also distinguished by features of the actions rather than the characters of those who perform them. Such a distinction would not represent a departure from doctrine, for they already do this with the distinction between imperfect *kathēkonta* and mistakes (*harmatēmata*).

Moreover, an additional advantage of my interpretation is how well it fits with what is said about the Sage's perfection in the context of epistemology. Just as non-Sages may perform many appropriate actions but never a right action (*katorthōma*), they will also assent to many cataleptic impressions, without achieving knowledge (*epistēmē*). When a non-Sage assents (correctly) to a cataleptic impression, it does not count as (scientific) knowledge (*epistēmē*), but merely a grasp (*katalēpsis*); one can have the best *katalēpsis*, but if it is not locked into the complete, systematic, dialectically defended perspective of the Sage, it will never count as *epistēmē*. Nevertheless, opining

---

[45] See too Stobaeus, 8a: Every "contrary to appropriate action (παρὰ τὸ καθῆκον)" is a mistake. Appropriate actions, despite being imperfectly performed because of the flawed character of an agent, could not sensibly be considered an action "contrary to appropriate action." I take *para to kathēkon* and *para ton orthon logon* to be equivalent.

correctly is not making a mistake—that is, assenting to a false impression—but achieving a genuine grasp.[46]

On the view I shall defend in the rest of the chapter, even the Sage, whose perfected reason is the criterion for an action's being *kathēkon*,[47] is sometimes not seeking to identify what the virtuous action is, but merely what achieves the value (*axia*) in token circumstances of promoted indifferents.[48] We have developed the conceptual apparatus to explain this more clearly. The Sage adheres, of course, to the Supremacy of Virtue. As we have seen since Plato's early dialogues, SV is ubiquitous in the virtuous person's reasoning insofar as it operates as a limiting condition: of course, the Sage will never act contrary to virtue. But as we have seen with every philosopher and school so far considered, the Stoics too will hold that sometimes there are actions, and not simply "mere behaviors," where virtue is not at issue. For mainstream Stoics, deliberation concerning such actions will take place in the realm of the value (*axia*) and disvalue (*apaxia*) that promoted and demoted indifferents have.[49] The deliberation will seek to pursue as much *axia* as possible not as an ultimate aim, but *within the circumscribed context of unfailing adherence to SV as a limiting condition*. Since the Stoics plainly equate happiness with virtue, these are not deliberations about good and bad—virtue and vice—but only about the secondary category of things that have value (*axia*). So, I shall argue that the Stoics give an account of how to act when virtue and happiness are not on the line by appeal to the value of promoted indifferents. We shall now see that such actions are labeled "intermediate appropriate actions" (*mesa kathēkonta*).

---

[46] One might wonder about how much damage is done to the Stoic view in both the epistemological and ethical contexts because of a (perhaps unjustified) focus on the Sage and the possibility of their being; see Vasiliou (2019), esp. 74–76, for the epistemological context. As Tad Brennan (2005), 176–179, nicely brings out, the "Progressor" toward virtue may not only do just what the Sage does but even have all the same thoughts and motives as the Sage; yet the perfect state of the Sage will still be distinct. Brennan (2014), 65–67, also argues that the Sage and non-Sage are not so far apart in some cases insofar as non-Sages regularly have *katalēpseis* and perform *kathēkonta*.

[47] It is the criterion under an "externalist" not "internalist" interpretation; see Mitsis (2003).

[48] Dentsoras (2018) defends a view with certain similarities to mine. He argues that we ought to distinguish complete appropriate actions (perfect actions) as those that have virtue as their object, while intermediate appropriate actions are those aiming only at securing or avoiding indifferents, without consideration of virtue. Dentsoras, however, does not take account of the division between complete and incomplete *kathēkonta* (both of which may be aiming at virtue), as I described above in the example of attempting to save a drowning person.

[49] See Cooper (1989/1999), 532, and Irwin (1986), (2007) for support of the idea that the Stoics were "axiological dualists"; Klein (2015) argues against this on the basis that it would conflict with the Stoics' rational eudaimonism. See discussion below.

7. Intermediate Appropriate Actions

It is difficult and confusing to distinguish the class of intermediate appropriate actions in part because of the term "intermediate" (*medius*, μέσον). When the term is applied to *things* in Cicero, Plutarch, and others, it is simply a synonym for indifferent (*indifferens* but also *media*). The classification system in play is good (virtue), bad (vice), and intermediate or indifferent (everything else). By contrast when there is talk of intermediate *actions*, the class of intermediate appropriate actions is being referred to. What makes this especially confusing is that, as we have said, *all* appropriate actions traffic in indifferents or, in other words, in intermediate things—things that are in themselves neither good nor bad. So, despite the terminological overlap there is no special connection between intermediate appropriate actions and intermediate or indifferent things. What is distinctive of intermediate appropriate actions is that pursuing (or avoiding) certain intermediate/indifferent things is appropriate and not contrary to virtue, but yet not required by virtue; they are actions where virtue is simply not at issue. Finally, what adds to the confusion is that *kathēkonta* as a term is sometimes used generically to cover both *kathēkonta* that become complete and perfect when performed by a Sage (what I have been calling "proper" *kathēkonta*) and those, I am claiming, that do not, that is, intermediate *kathēkonta*.

All three primary sources for Stoic ethics—Stobaeus, Cicero, and Diogenes Laertius—refer to intermediate actions, which I take to be strong evidence in favor of its being an important part of early Stoic doctrine. The details of the individual accounts are confusing and even conflicting, not only with one another but sometimes even within the same source; I do not pretend that I can harmonize all the details of the three accounts. For our purposes, however, the important point will be simply to establish the category as such and not to read it as a confused, slightly tangential classification as the standard scholarly view has it.

The account in Stobaeus (8) divides actions as follows:

And of appropriate actions (τῶν δὲ καθηκόντων), some are complete [or perfect], and they are called [morally] perfect actions. [Morally] perfect actions are activities in accordance with virtue (τὰ κατ' ἀρετὴν ἐνεργήματα), such as acting prudently[50] and acting justly. Things which are not of this character are not [morally] perfect actions (οὐκ εἶναι δὲ κατορθώματα τὰ μὴ οὕτως ἔχοντα); indeed, they do not call them complete appropriate actions either,

---

[50] Inwood and Gerson have "being prudent" for τὸ φρονεῖν, but this misses the emphasis on the fact that these are actions or doings, ἐνεργήματα, as in the end of the passage, "marrying (τὸ γαμεῖν)," "going on embassy (τὸ πρεσβεύειν)," and so on.

but intermediate ones (μέσα), such as getting married, going on embassy, conversing, and similar things." (8=LS59B, Inwood/Gerson trans., modified)

The passage makes clear that some appropriate actions are perfect or complete (τέλεια) and labels these "right actions (κατορθώματα)." We know that Stoic doctrine is that *katorthōmata* can only be performed by the Sage. Further, as discussed, I agree with most interpreters that part of what *makes* them *katorthōmata* is that they are performed by a Sage, that is, done by an agent with a perfect, virtuous disposition. So far, then, one class of action has been delimited, described synonymously as perfect *kathēkonta*, *katorthōmata*, or as activities in accordance with virtue (τὰ κατ' ἀρετὴν ἐνεργήματα). The final sentence of the passage describes a second class, which are *not katorthōmata*, not in such a condition (presumably, perfect or complete, *teleia*), and so also not called perfect appropriate actions (*teleia kathēkonta*): these are labeled "intermediate" *kathēkonta*. The three examples— marrying, going on embassy, and engaging in dialectic— conspicuously avoid any modifying adverbs. As intermediate *appropriate* actions, these clearly do not fall into the "inappropriate action (παρὰ τὸ καθῆκον)" category, which are referred to in the following passage:

> Every action contrary to the appropriate which occurs in a rational <animal> is a mistake; and an appropriate action when perfected is a right action. The intermediate appropriate action is measured by [reference to] certain indifferent things, which are selected according to or contrary to nature (πᾶν δὲ τὸ παρὰ τὸ καθῆκον ἐν λογικῷ <ζῴῳ> γινόμενον ἁρμάτημα εἶναι· τὸ δὲ καθῆκον τελειωθὲν κατόρθωμα γίνεσθαι. Παραμετρεῖσθαι δὲ τὸ μέσον καθῆκον ἀδιαφόροις τισί, ἐκλεγομένοις δὲ παρὰ φύσιν καὶ κατὰ φύσιν) [...]" (Stobaeus, 8a, Inwood/Gerson [2008] trans., modified).

First, we see that mistakes are identified with acting "contrary to the appropriate παρὰ τὸ καθῆκον)," supporting the view that when a non-Sage performs an appropriate action, it will not be a mistake, but simply an "imperfect appropriate action" (cf. Cicero, *Fin.* III.59, quoted above).

What, then, makes certain appropriate actions intermediate rather than simply appropriate? The passage may suggest, although it does not explicitly say, that the distinction consists partly in the fact that intermediate appropriate actions are not perfectible in the way that ordinary (what I have labeled "proper") appropriate actions are. For these intermediate actions "selection" (*eklogē*) not "choice (*hairesis*)" is what is involved, and the contrast is between selecting indifferents according to nature or against nature—that is, promoted versus demoted indifferents. On the interpretation I am defending, such actions are intermediate because they are to be understood as actions that are performed in a context where they are neither required nor forbidden by virtue: that is, they are meant as examples of acting when, as I have been putting it, virtue is not at issue.[51] On the standard interpretation such intermediate actions would, if performed by the Sage, be transformed into complete appropriate actions (*teleia kathēkonta*), and so perfect actions (*katorthōmata*). On this interpretation, there are no morally neutral actions; there are simply actions that ought to be done.

Here's a third relevant passage from Stobaeus:

> Again, they say that some activities are right actions, some are mistakes, and some are neither (ἔτι δὲ τῶν ἐνεργημάτων φασὶ τὰ μὲν εἶναι κατορθώματα, τὰ δὲ ἁμαρτήματα, τὰ δ᾽ οὐδέτερα) [the examples that follow are virtuous actions for right actions, such as acting justly, acting temperately; actions contrary to virtue for moral mistakes, such as acting unjustly, acting intemperately; and, finally] such things as these are neither right actions nor mistakes (οὔτε δὲ κατορθώματα οὔτε ἁμαρτήματα τὰ τοιαῦτα): speaking (λέγειν), asking (ἐρωτᾶν), answering (ἀποκρίνεσθαι), walking (περιπατεῖν), going out of town (ἀποδημεῖν), and similar things (τὰ τούτοις παραπλήσια). (Stobaeus, 11e/LS59M, Inwood/Gerson [2008] trans., modified)

This passage again clearly divides actions into three categories, those actions that (at least when done by the right sort of agent) are virtuous actions, actions that are contrary to virtue (mistakes), and neither (intermediate actions). Again, on my reading, the view is that simply talking, or questioning and answering ("How are you?" "Fine. What's new?") or going out of town (e.g., leaving the city walls to go for a walk in the country)—these are the sorts of actions that one might pursue in a way that promotes value and avoids disvalue, so long as none of these actions is contrary to virtue. These examples are not about some odd circumstance, in which simply taking a walk might be contrary to virtue; in that case, of course, it would be mistake (*harmatēma*). Thus too, I propose, even when a Sage simply takes a walk, we should not think of that token action as a "perfect action" rather than as an intermediate action, in the absence of special circumstances.

Let's look at the other sources before arguing the point further. Here is the relevant passage from Diogenes:

---

[51] See, again, Dentsoras (2018) for a similar view.

VIRTUE AND HAPPINESS IN EARLY STOICISM   195

For of actions performed according to impulse [i.e., voluntarily], some are appropriate, some inappropriate, and <some are neither appropriate nor inappropriate>. Appropriate [actions] are those which reason constrains [us] to do, such as honoring our parents, brothers, [and] fatherland and spending time with friends (καθήκοντα μὲν οὖν εἶναι ὅσα λόγος αἱρεῖ ποιεῖν, ὡς ἔχει τὸ γονεῖς τιμᾶν, ἀδελφούς, πατρίδα, συμπεριφέρεσθαι φίλοις). Inappropriate are those which reason constrains [us] not to do, such as things like this: neglecting our parents, ignoring our brothers, being out of sympathy with our friends, overlooking [the interests of] our fatherland, and such things (παρὰ τὸ καθῆκον δὲ, ὅσα μὴ αἱρεῖ λόγος, ὡς ἔχει τὰ τοιαῦτα, γονέων ἀμελεῖν, ἀδελφῶν ἀφροντιστεῖν, φίλοις μὴ συνδιατίθεσθαι, πατρίδα ὑπεροᾶν καὶ τὰ παραπλήσια). [109] Neither inappropriate nor appropriate are those which reason neither constrains us to perform nor forbids, such as picking up a small twig, holding a writing instrument or scraper, and things similar to these (οὔτε δὲ καθήκοντα οὔτε παρὰ τὸ καθῆκον ὅσα οὔθ' αἱρεῖ λόγος πράττειν οὔτ' ἀπαγορεύει, οἷον κάρφος ἀνελέσθαι, γραφεῖον κρατεῖν ἢ στλεγγίδα καὶ τὰ ὅμοια τούτοις). (DL 7.108–109/ LS59E, Inwood/Gerson [2008] trans.)

Again, there are three clear categories of action: appropriate, inappropriate (mistakes), and neither. Note how the passage says that reason demands the first category and bans the second category. Virtue and vice are the things explicitly said to be chosen and avoided by reason, whereas indifferents are only "selected" (as we saw in the Stobaeus passage above). This supports the interpretation of the three categories of action as those that are required by virtue, forbidden by virtue, and neutral with respect to virtue.

Finally, let's turn to the third source, Cicero. We already saw above that *Fin* III.59 distinguishes perfect appropriate actions from imperfect ones Consider the following:

[58] Now although we say that what is moral (*honestum*) is the only good, it is still consistent to perform an appropriate action (*officio*) despite the fact that we regard *that appropriate action* (*id officium*; Woolf: 'them') as neither good nor evil.[52] This is because reasonableness is found in this area,

---

[52] Woolf translates *officio* as plural, whereas Long and Sedley more accurately render it thus: "it is nevertheless consistent to perform a proper function [their rendering of *kathēkon*], even though we count this neither in good things nor in bad (*nec in bonis ponamus nec in malis*)." Woolf's switch

such that a rational explanation could be given of the action, and so of an action reasonably performed. Indeed, an appropriate action is any action such that a reasonable explanation could be given of its performance. (*Fin.* III.58, Woolf trans., modified)

The account reminds us that "moral" actions are the sole good, which are a class of appropriate actions (I have called them "proper appropriate actions"), but the passage distinguishes these actions from a different sort of appropriate action that "is neither good nor evil"—namely, the intermediate appropriate actions we have seen referred to in Stobaeus and Diogenes. The final sentence reminds us that the generic category of "appropriate action" is simply an action supported by a reasonable explanation.[53] Some of these will end up being "moral" actions, when performed by the Sage, but others will be intermediate, as Cato (the Stoic spokesperson) goes on to say:

[58, cont] **Hence one can see that there is intermediate appropriate action (*officium medium*), falling into the category neither of goods nor their opposites.** Since there may yet be something useful about what is neither a virtue nor a vice, it should not be rejected. Included in this category [of appropriate action] is also a certain kind of action, such that reason demands that one bring about or create one of the intermediates. What is done with reason we call an appropriate action. Hence appropriate action falls under the category of what is neither good nor the opposite. [59] It is evident that even those who are wise act in the sphere of these intermediates (*in istis rebus mediis*), and so judge such action to be appropriate action. And, since their judgment is flawless, appropriate action will belong to the sphere of intermediates (*erit in mediis rebus officium*).

This passage is dense and confusing.[54] Since the wise have "flawless" judgment, and they judge certain actions to be appropriate, although merely intermediate, there will be appropriate action among intermediates (meaning indifferents) and an intermediate class of action. These actions, unlike "proper *kathēkonta*,"

to the plural makes my interpretation particularly difficult to see, for it implies that this is a general claim about all appropriate actions as such, whereas the singular suggests that it is specifying a particular kind of appropriate action, further brought out by the emphasis *id officium*, that is neither good nor bad.

[53] As we discussed above; cf. Stobaeus, 8.
[54] See Long and Sedley's comment, (1987), 366. I will discuss their view in detail below.

are neither good nor bad, but they do have the value (or disvalue) of promoted (or demoted) indifferents, and so they are reasonable to perform (as are all appropriate actions). We would expect, then, as the continuation makes explicit, that the Sage and non-Sages alike perform such actions.

> [59, cont] Now it cannot be doubted that some of the intermediates [i.e., indifferents] should be adopted and others rejected. [...] This shows, since everyone by nature loves themselves, that the foolish no less than the wise will adopt what is in accordance with nature and reject what is contrary. **This is how a certain kind of appropriate action is common to both wise and foolish** (*ita est quoddam commune officium sapientis et insipientis*).

Here Cicero explicitly refers to an intermediate class of appropriate action that may be performed by *both* the foolish *and* the wise. Just as perfect appropriate actions belong only to the wise, so incomplete appropriate actions belong only to the foolish; for a Sage could not perform an incomplete appropriate action, since they are perfect. This leaves *intermediate appropriate actions* as a class of actions that can belong to both.[55] Nevertheless, as we have seen throughout, *all* appropriate actions (complete, incomplete, and intermediate) traffic in intermediates (i.e., indifferents).

8. Objections to Intermediate Appropriate Actions

In the previous two sections we have seen, first, that with the distinction between mistakes and merely imperfect appropriate actions the Stoics classify actions based on what is done and not merely according to the state of the agent that performs them. Second, we have just seen explicit textual evidence from all three of our primary sources for the existence of a distinct class of "intermediate appropriate action." Nevertheless, commentators dismiss intermediate appropriate actions, or, as we shall now see, explain them away, because their existence suggests that there are some appropriate actions

---

[55] Thus, "intermediates" above in "it is here that its involvement in what we call intermediates arises" means "indifferents" and not the class of intermediate actions, which seems plain enough. The term *indifferens* was introduced in III.53 as the translation of ἀδιάφορον. Had Cicero kept using that term through this discussion, rather than the more ambiguous *medium*, sometimes as in *officium medium* (e.g., III.58), referring to an intermediate appropriate action and other times as "intermediate things (*mediis*)" (e.g., III.59), referring to indifferents, the discussion would have been clearer: perhaps the oddness of *indifferens* made him more likely to revert to *medium*.

that would not become "perfect actions" *even when done by the Sage*.[56] As far as I know, all scholars hold as a dogma the idea that *every token action* that is performed by the Sage is a *katorthōma*; indeed, this is precisely what constitutes the Sage's perfection. Let's look in detail at a classic formulation of the objection to intermediate appropriate actions by Long and Sedley in response to the passages from Stobaeus and Cicero quoted above:

> The meaning of "intermediate" can be elicited from Cicero's confusing account in F [*Fin.* III.58–59, quoted above]. He speaks of "proper functions" [i.e., "appropriate actions"] being "neither good nor bad," and of some of them being common to the wise man and the fool. **From this it might seem to follow that there is a whole class of actions which are morally indifferent, intermediate between good and bad, and this is actually asserted in M4** [Stobaeus, 11e, quoted above]. But how is this to be squared with the fundamental Stoic thesis that everything done by the wise man is a right action and everything done by the fool is wrong? The Stoics' exclusive disjunction between these two classes of men appears to leave no room for intermediate actions any more than for intermediate human beings. (Long and Sedley [1987], v. 1, 366; my bold)[57]

Here Long and Sedley refer to the two passages from Cicero and Stobaeus I quoted above. The first sentence in bold is precisely the thesis I am defending; and it is striking how they admit that the thesis is "actually asserted" in the Stobaeus passage. Nevertheless, because of the exclusive disjunction among happy and unhappy human beings, they assume that *everything* done by the fool is wrong. But we have seen that this is not the case: for one miserable person may run to (attempt to) save the drowning person, while the other miserable person may continue to read the *Phaedo*. The first miserable person, despite performing an "imperfect appropriate action" because of their imperfect character, nevertheless *does the right thing* and is not making a mistake nor are they acting "contrary to the appropriate

---

[56] Vogt (2008), ch. 4, 175, n. 36, ignores the category of "intermediate" actions, which she says is "unimportant for her purposes."

[57] In (1987), v. 2, 359, Long and Sedley comment: "This is a difficult passage, largely because Cicero fails to make it explicit that the *wise man's proper functions are always 'perfect'*, and are thus 'intermediate' or shared by fools as well only in an equivocal sense, i.e. when the action is considered independently of the agent's moral character. [...] [the second argument] ignores the fact that *everything done by the wise man is actually a perfect officium*" (my emphases).

action (*para to kathēkon*)." The second person clearly does make a (moral) mistake (*harmatēma*).

As far as the explicitly asserted category of "intermediate appropriate actions" goes, Long and Sedley explain away the textual evidence by reasserting the exclusive disjunction and claiming that "intermediate appropriate actions" refers to actions "in abstraction from their agents" (367).[58] Despite what the texts appear to say, every token action must be a right action when performed by the Sage and so a category of actions that are "intermediate," neither right nor wrong, would be impossible. Thus the Stoics embrace what we might call a "flattening out" view of appropriate actions: there are, only, two types of actions—appropriate and inappropriate—and two types of people—Sages and non-Sages. John Cooper maintains such a position:

> [The Stoic] thought that in doing a virtuous act one is doing it because it is commanded by the universal law and by universal reason applies just as much, and in exactly the same way, to what one does in maintaining an appropriate diet or tending to one's daily hygiene or working hard at one's profession or behaving charmingly at a dinner party, as it does to what, [. . .] we would call *moral* decisions and actions—treating other people fairly and considerately, standing up for moral principle when it is inconvenient [. . .], accepting financial sacrifice or personal hardship in order to serve the public good. The notion of "duty" among Stoics covers a vastly wider range than it does, for example, in Kant: it covers, in fact, crucial aspects of the whole of one's life **and virtually everything one does**, if one is truly virtuous. [. . .] Moreover, because in this theory the more private and personal side of life is lumped together with the morally right and morally wrong, without any fundamental discrimination between them, the latter, though certainly present and accounted for in the theory, do not receive the priority that moralists nowadays typically think they are entitled to. ([1996/1999], 446–447, his emphasis, my bold)[59]

---

[58] See Donini (1999), 730, for a very similar interpretation and agreement that every token action of a non-Sage is an "example of vice." This leave no room for intermediate appropriate actions as a class nor for a distinction between "imperfect appropriate actions" (imperfect because performed by a non-Sage) and "mistakes" (which, of course, are only performed by non-Sages). Dentsoras (2018) by contrast argues against the orthodox view, arguing that it makes *mesa kathēkonta* and *katorthōmata* "two ontologically different kinds of things, the former being a set of action types and the latter a dispositions kind" (6). Although I part company with his description here, I am largely sympathetic with what I take to be the upshot of Dentsoras's objection.

[59] Katja Vogt (2008), 198–200, dismisses that idea that the Stoics see virtue as a value that "trumps" others, such as health, as "anachronistic." It should be already clear from the early chapters of this book, along with Vasiliou (2008), that my attribution to Socrates of a Superseding Practical Principle

For Cooper and most scholars, appropriate actions are simply actions that are to-be-done. In the line I bold in the Cooper passage, we can perhaps already see the idea of ubiquity, which as we know from Chapter 2 is importantly captured by Socrates in the idea of a limiting condition ("it is never right to do wrong"), being exemplified for the Stoics in the idea of comprehensiveness: *every* token action is a duty or contrary to a duty. Thus distinctions that are central to ethical thinking for us and for all the Greek philosophers considered so far—Socrates, Plato, Aristotle, and Epicurus— between the "appropriateness" of drinking a glass of water when thirsty and of saving (or attempting to save) one's polis by standing firm in battle, are "flattened out": they are both simply appropriate actions and, furthermore, they both, without difference, become "perfect actions" when performed by a Sage. The philosophical position would entirely reject the Socratic idea, as I have understood it, that there are actions "when virtue is not at issue" and when commitment to SV operates only as a limiting condition. Nevertheless, of course, this is not a definitive argument that the Stoics did not hold it; scholars consider it simply another peculiarity of the Stoic position, alongside the Sage's feeling no grief at the death of a child.

A second, also indirect argument against the claim that every token action of the Sage is a perfect action is the presence in our passages of *examples* of "intermediate" action types. If *every* token action done by Sage becomes a perfect action, then why list any specific examples? As we have seen, the passages list the following: getting married, going on embassy, conversing (Stobaeus, 8); speaking, asking, answering, walking, going of town (Stobaeus, 11e); picking up a twig, holding a writing instrument or scraper (DL 7.108); in each case the list ends with "and similar things." It can be difficult to see what these examples have in common, but they seem to mark out particular action-types as ordinarily intermediate. If every token action of any type performed by the Sage ends up a perfect action, however, it would make no sense to offer examples of some specific types—it would be entirely arbitrary. On Long and Sedley's explanation the intermediate category considers actions independently of the agent who does them but since every token action is done either by a Sage or a non-Sage, what's the point of providing examples of certain actions and not others? It is striking that examples like "defending one's polis," "saving someone from drowning,"

---

entails a contrary position. I am arguing that the Stoics follow Socrates' lead in adopting the position Vogt describes as anachronistic.

"running away in battle" are not offered; these are examples of action that, in particular circumstances, are plausibly either required or forbidden. The position I am defending, of course, is not one that says "walking" and "speaking" are not action-types some token of which, *in some circumstance*, might be one that is a proper appropriate action, and so one that becomes a perfect action when performed by the Sage. Rather, the position is that on many occasions walking or speaking may well be token intermediate appropriate actions performable by the Sage and non-Sage alike, in accordance with the textual evidence.[60]

9. The Perfection of the Sage

Nevertheless, the considerations adduced so far may seem inconclusive. The driving assumption behind the rejection of a third category of action is that *every* token action performed by a Sage is a perfectly right action (*katorthōma*).[61] This claim seems to be a universal assumption in Stoic scholarship, apparently following from the many descriptions of the Sage as completely perfect and unerring. What is the specific textual evidence? Perhaps the best passage—the sole passage cited by Long and Sedley—is the following: "Zeno and the Stoic philosophers of his persuasion hold that there are two classes of men (δύο γένη τῶν ἀνθρώπων εἶναι), the excellent and the inferior. The excellent kind employs the virtues throughout all of life (διὰ παντὸς τοῦ βίου), but the inferior kind employs the vices. Hence the former always acts rightly in everything which it undertakes, but the latter

---

[60] Long and Sedley (1987), 367, refer to a partial concession to such a view in the case of examples from Diogenes: "The exclusive disjunction between right and wrong actions has sometimes been interpreted to imply that 'picking up a twig' and similarly trivial things are either right or wrong. This would be a silly claim on the Stoics' part [...] If 'picking up a twig' etc. is neither a proper function [*kathēkon*] nor contrary to this, the Stoics are most plausibly interpreted as holding that some 'activities' are too trivial to count as 'actions' and thus as amenable to moral appraisal in any sense. At least it is hard to see how they could regard anything that 'reason neither dictates our doing nor forbids' [ref to DL 7.108] as an action of any ethical significance." We have considered the issue of "behaviors" that are too trivial to count as actions since the beginning of this book. But the examples of "intermediate actions" listed above, especially in Stobaeus' text are not idle semi-conscious behaviors, except perhaps picking up a twig. Rather they are better understood as referring to a class of actions that deserve to be called actions insofar as they are selected on the basis of promoted indifferents, but where virtue is simply not at issue.

[61] Combined with the idea that every token action done by a non-Sage is a mistake (*harmatēma*), which I have argued against above.

makes mistakes (ὅθεν τὸ μὲν ἀεὶ κατορθοῦν ἐν ἅπασιν οἷς προστίθεται, τὸ δὲ ἁμαρτάνειν)" (Stobaeus 11g/LS59N, LS trans.).[62]

Does the Sage's "always act rightly in everything" mean that every token action of the Sage is a right action? The perfection of the Sage need not be interpreted in this way; in fact, there is a better interpretation of what a perfectly virtuous person is like on offer since Socrates. The Sage is the ideal Socratic: they perfectly adhere to the Supremacy of Virtue, a Superseding Practical Principle. One clear way of understanding that someone "always acts rightly" is to understand that that person *never* acts wrongly: *whenever* there is a right or virtuous action to be done, the Sage knows it and does it perfectly. While Socrates's commitment to the Supremacy of Virtue is unfailing, he lacks the knowledge—or at least claims to lack the knowledge—that would enable him to guarantee that he never acts wrongly. Given his commitment to the Supremacy of Virtue, any wrongdoing would only be due to his ignorance; but he still allows that his ignorance could cause him to do wrong—to make a mistake, in Stoic terms.[63] The Sage, part of whose perfection consists in assenting all and only to cognitive impressions, is impervious to such mistakes. Nevertheless, just as Socrates's call for his fellow Athenians to commit to the Supremacy of Virtue did not commit him to believing that absolutely every token action is required or forbidden by virtue, there is no reason to saddle the Stoics with such a view either. As a Superseding Practical Principle, the Supremacy of Virtue tells the Sage (and everyone else) that the virtuous action supersedes any other end one might have in acting, but, crucially, it also includes a limiting condition: that one should never act in a way contrary to virtue. We saw that there is a way for a commitment to virtue to be ubiquitous in the sense that it is always operative as a demand on us via its role as a limiting condition. The advantage of this interpretation is that it quite reasonably allows for token actions that are neither required by nor forbidden by the demands of virtue. There is no reason that the Sage's perfection ought not to be understood in the same way; in fact, there is both significant textual support in the acknowledgment

---

[62] Note the position of "always (*aei*)" within the *men* clause; while the Sage (the excellent person) *always* acts rightly (by, in part, never acting wrongly, as I argue below), non-Sages "make mistakes." As we have seen, they do not, as commentators sometimes assume this passage says, *always* make mistakes; sometimes, even frequently, they may perform appropriate actions, but, because of their inferior characters, they are imperfect appropriate actions. Other times, of course, they do make mistakes and act *para to kathēkon* (Stobaeus 8–8a, quoted above).

[63] See Vasiliou (2008), chs. 1 and 2.

of intermediate appropriate actions, as we have seen, and philosophical and historical support as well.

It would still be true to say, as this passage does, that an excellent person always acts excellently throughout their entire life, and that, likewise, the inferior person must be acting wrongly and badly. But, as we have seen since Plato, it would be an unwarranted and fortunately optional overreading of *panta* to make its scope *absolutely all* actions, including choosing a pair of socks to wear or deciding whether to have coffee or tea. So, the passage above is no reason to reject the existence of a third class of actions, intermediate appropriate ones.

This analysis should facilitate a proper understanding of another important passage: "Chrysippus says: 'he who makes [moral] progress to the highest degree performs all the appropriate actions in all circumstances and omits none' (ὁ δ' ἐπ' ἄκρον, φησί, προκόπτων ἅπαντα πάντως ἀποδίδωσι τὰ καθήκοντα καὶ οὐδὲν παραλείπει)" (LS59I/*SVF* 3.510).

The person close to Sage-hood never misses an appropriate action and omits none. The best way to understand this is to grasp that the appropriate actions referred to are what I have been calling "proper" appropriate actions—that is, those appropriate actions, which are not intermediate, and the omission of which would constitute making a mistake (i.e., acting contrary to right reason). Thus, the person who makes progress "to the highest degree" is one who is a perfect Socratic: he never acts contrary to virtue and always does whatever virtue requires.

Furthermore, understanding intermediate appropriate actions in the way I have urged shows that the Stoics offer guidance about how to live and make "choices" (or, more technically, "selections") when virtue is not at issue. The classes of promoted and demoted indifferents, possessing value and disvalue respectively, are a guide to how to act when one is subject to the commitment to SV as a limiting condition. This makes sense too, as we have seen, of how the indifferents *remain* indifferent even for mainstream Stoics, despite the division into promoted and demoted: any putative promoted indifferent must be sacrificed if to pursue it would be to act contrary to virtue. In some circumstances a token instance of walking may be required (or forbidden) by virtue; other times it may be merely intermediate. Nothing in the Stoic account precludes the existence of the latter as well as the former.[64]

---

[64] See, again, LS59A, Plutarch, *Comm.* 1069e: "[Chrysippus] says: 'What am I to begin from, and what am I to take as the foundation of appropriate action and the matter of virtue if I pass

Finally, even if the mental state of the Sage is such that every token action is simply to-be-done and so not conceptualized at all at the level of types, still *we* and the Stoic philosophers write about these actions as constituting two different types.[65] We can be quite extreme particularists at the level of token-action determination, even though there are two different sorts of deliberation that can be engaged in: what is the virtuous action here and now and also, among actions that are not contrary to virtue, which action genuinely follows nature and pursues *axia*.

To summarize, then. Among appropriate actions, there are "proper" appropriate actions and intermediate appropriate actions. The latter are performed alike by Sages and non-Sages and aim at promoting value and avoiding disvalue. The former, when performed by the Sage, become perfect appropriate actions (and so, right actions, *katorthōmata*). When they are performed by non-Sages, however, they are merely imperfect appropriate actions (but not mistakes). Moreover, Sages will never fail to perform a proper appropriate action and of course will never act contrary to appropriate action, and so the Sage will never make a mistake; the rest of us will fail in both of these ways and, as just mentioned, even our performance of proper appropriate actions will remain imperfect.

Even when a Sage performs an intermediate appropriate action, it does not become a right or virtuous action. To be sure, it is not an action that is *contrary to* virtue either; it is simply an action where virtue is not at issue one way or the other. As I said above, I need not deny that there will still be a difference epistemically and dispositionally between the Sage's performance of an intermediate appropriate action and our own, insofar as, among other things, the Sage will *know* that the action is of this sort, while we will at best have a true opinion about it. Moreover, the Sage will never confuse an intermediate appropriate action with a proper one, while we ordinary people may.

---

over nature and what accords with nature?'" I cited this passage earlier without comment, but I read the "and" in "the foundation of appropriate action and the matter of virtue" as connecting two types: mere appropriate actions (intermediate appropriate actions) and virtuous actions, which would constitute a mistake to omit. Nature and indifferents provide the foundation for both classes of action—that is, *all* appropriate action in the most generic sense. See below.

[65] This addresses a worry that Stoics are metaphysically nominalists and so, ultimately, would reject the classification of actions into types. I owe this objection to George Boys-Stones.

10. The Stoics on Suicide

As a coda to the argument, there are a couple of interesting passages on suicide, which lend further support to the account of intermediate actions argued for in this chapter. Two issues will concern us. The more local and immediate one considers whether the act of committing suicide is being understood as an action required by virtue (a proper appropriate action) or an intermediate appropriate action. Of course, to fail to perform the former is to act contrary to virtue and to make a mistake. The larger issue is how this decision relates to eudaimonia, and what it says about the role of eudaimonia as a practical principle for the Stoics.

It will be useful to contrast my interpretation with that of Jacob Klein. According to Klein, indifferents have a role in deliberation not as part of what justifies why a certain action is appropriate, but, instead, indifferents provide defeasible evidence of whether an action is in conformity to nature.[66] Thus, he has a way of avoiding attributing to the Stoics any axiological dualism, according to which there are two disjoint spheres of value:[67] one, what is good and bad, occupied solely by virtue and vice, and another category that has some "value" but is not to be counted as good or bad, namely certain indifferents. While Klein's view is unique on the role of indifferents, he adheres to the idea that the Stoics are rational eudaimonists, meaning that the normative justification of all truly rational action is eudaimonia.[68] In our language, eudaimonia serves as a Comprehensive Practical Principle. Moreover, he holds the standard view that *all* appropriate actions become virtuous actions when performed by the Sage. Thus, there are no actions that are appropriate, yet not relevant to virtue; that is, there are no intermediate appropriate actions.

Suicide will provide an important test case. There are two main sources: Cicero's *De Finibus* and remarks by Plutarch, quoted by Klein.[69]

> [1] Chrysippus, they say, thinks that remaining alive or taking leave of life is measured neither by goods nor by evils but by the intermediates in accordance with nature, which is why it sometimes becomes appropriate

---

[66] Klein (2015).
[67] See Irwin (1986), (2007), ch. 13; Cooper (1989/1999), 532, both of whom attribute axiological dualism to the Stoics.
[68] See also Klein (2012).
[69] Klein (2015), 269, also cites Stobaeus 8a, but that passage is not clearly about suicide.

(καθῆκον) for those who are happy to take leave of life and for those who are bad to remain. (Plut. *Stoic Repugn.* 1042d, Cherniss, as modified by Klein)

[2] It is the appropriate action to live when most of what one has in according with nature. When the opposite is the case, or is envisaged to be so, then the appropriate action is to depart from life. **This shows that it is sometimes the appropriate action for the wise person to depart from life though happy and the fool to remain in it though miserable.** . . . Thus the whole rationale for either remaining in or departing from life is to be measured by reference to those intermediates I mentioned above. **One who is endowed with virtue need not be detained in life, nor need those without virtue seek death. Often the appropriate action for a wise person will be to depart from life when utterly happy, if this can be done in a timely way.** (Cicero, *Fin.* III.60–61, Woolf trans.)

First, it is important to realize that the passage from Cicero follows immediately after the passages we discussed (*Fin.* III.58–59) above, delineating the category of intermediate appropriate action. Furthermore, Klein does not quote the sentences in bold, but they are crucial, not least for appreciating the similarity between the descriptions in Plutarch and Cicero. Both sources make explicit that the Sage, under certain circumstances, will commit suicide, *despite being happy*. This must mean that situation being considered is *not* one in which virtue requires the Sage to commit suicide, since in that case performing that action would be essential to maintaining his happiness. It is impossible to understand the Sage as determining what virtue requires and not see such an action as essential to their happiness. Rather, the reference to suicide despite being happy suggests that we are now in the realm of intermediate appropriate actions: selections with a view to promoting value and avoiding disvalue.[70]

Klein's contrasting interpretation is as follows: "Accordingly, to say that a particular outcome is promoted is not to say that an agent thereby has a normative practical reason to select it. It is rather to say that an agent has a defeasible reason to *believe* that selecting it is what conformity to nature requires. In selecting what is promoted, the Stoic agent is doing her epistemic best, as it were to conform to the single rational pattern laid down by nature."[71]

---

[70] As we would expect, since suicide is brought up in Cicero, as I mentioned, on the heels of the discussion of intermediate appropriate actions.

[71] Klein (2015), 270.

Klein applies his position to the Stoic remarks on suicide:

> In circumstances of extreme deprivation, faced everywhere with dispromoted outcomes, suicide may be appropriate *and obligatory* for a rational agent. This is not because such outcomes present a threat to her happiness, however, but because they indicate that suicide conforms in this circumstance to nature's plan, which the sage must follow in order to preserve the conformity to nature that characterizes her activities while she remains alive. The appropriateness of suicide is dictated, as it were, by external circumstances, but it is justified on other grounds" (269–270, my emphasis).

Klein understands indifferents as providing epistemic reasons for thinking that a certain action is in conformity with Nature's plan and so is *kathēkon*. He claims that in cases where disprompted indifferents sufficiently dominate, suicide is "obligatory" and, earlier in the same article, that awareness of these disprompted indifferents helps the Sage contemplating suicide to arrive "at knowledge of what virtue requires" (254). He is thus reading the Stoic passages on suicide as part of an epistemological determination of what the virtuous action *is*; but if this is correct, how could such a determination be divorced from one's happiness, since being virtuous and acting perfectly virtuously just is what happiness is for the Stoics? I am not of course denying that in some circumstances suicide might be what virtue requires, but such circumstances are not philosophically problematic—the Sage will always do what virtue requires—or, therefore, particularly noteworthy. Rather the discussion of the permissibility and appropriateness of suicide concerns a situation where suicide is *not* required ("despite being happy"), which is apposite in a context where Cicero has just described intermediate appropriate actions.

The resolution is to reject the two standard assumptions: (1) that there are no actions for the Stoics where virtue is not at issue and (2) that the Stoics are rational eudaimonists, with eudaimonia operating as a Comprehensive Practical Principle. We can now further appreciate the importance of the argument that mainstream Stoics reject the former and allow for intermediate appropriate actions. By doing this, they also reject the idea that eudaimonia must function as a Comprehensive Practical Principle, providing the justification for all rational actions whatsoever; that is, they reject the essential element of rational eudaimonism as Klein and others understand it. The example of suicide supports the case that the Stoics' eudaimonism does not make eudaimonia a Comprehensive Practical Principle and, as a corollary, that the Stoics allow that there are certain appropriate actions, which even the Sage will engage in, when virtue is not at issue: of these, the most vivid, and paradoxical sounding, is suicide.

Moreover, there is good evidence that this is specifically Chryisppus's view, which is to be precisely expected, if Chrysippus uses the appropriate suicide of the Sage as an example—a very provocative one—of the Sage engaging in a most extreme intermediate appropriate action. The decision is made based upon the balance of promoted and demoted indifferents. It cannot be a matter of determining what token action constitutes the virtuous action; the value of indifferents must be real, but secondary. This would be a coherent rejection of Aristo's position, which, I argued earlier, may well have made *every* action, as we would say, a moral issue. Thus, on my view, mainstream Stoicism rejects the idea that there are no intermediate actions, and, further, that all of our rational actions are rational because they constitute or lead to our eudaimonia. These remarks on suicide show dramatically that sometimes the most drastic of actions might be taken, although virtue and so also happiness have nothing to do with it.

Careful consideration of our best evidence for early Stoicism shows that they did not conceive of eudaimonia as a Comprehensive Practical Principle. Rather, they countenanced rational, non-acratic, deliberate actions where virtue was not at issue, maintaining a position that we have seen in Socrates, Plato, Aristotle, and Epicurus. Like Socrates, Plato, and Aristotle, the Stoics of course hold that virtue is essential to happiness; unlike them, they hold that virtue is clearly sufficient for happiness and the sole component of a happy life. While Socrates says nothing about how to choose among alternatives when none of them is contrary to virtue, the Stoics with their account of promoted and demoted indifferents provide an account of how to select among indifferents even when that selection is not one that will affect one's virtue and so will not affect one's happiness one way or the other. So, I have argued that by this point in the historical story—somewhere in the late third century—we have yet to encounter any major philosopher or school that advocates conceiving of happiness as a Comprehensive Practical Principle of the sort endorsed by the most prominent ancient scholars of the last half century. In keeping with this, happiness does not explain the rationality of all of our actions; there are reasons to act in certain ways that fall outside the scope of happiness.

Epilogue

Reassessing Eudaimonism

1. Overview

This book has attempted to assess the claim that Greek ethical theory is eudaimonist by critically examining three specific roles that eudaimonia has been understood to play in various theories. The first is as a practical principle, as an end for the sake of which we do and ought to act. The second role, labeled the Eudaimonist Hope, holds that the right or virtuous action has no independent content of its own, but is determined by reference to eudaimonia (the highest good): right action is whatever action leads to or constitutes eudaimonia. The idea is that whereas the nature of virtue is problematic and contested, we might instead be able to determine what truly benefits a human being (namely, happiness) and then simply define virtue as whatever achieves or constitutes that end. As we saw, this is most clearly exemplified in the Hedonist Argument in the *Protagoras*: given that pleasure is the good, right action would be whatever action yielded the most pleasure and could be determined through the exercise of technical expertise in the measurement of pleasures and pains.[1] If one holds the Eudaimonist Hope, then one believes that eudaimonia is the ground of virtue (by supplying its actual content), justifies actions and states of character as virtuous (by reference to the good it leads to or constitutes), and motivates the pursuit of virtue (by means of the natural human desire for the good).

The third role is expressed in the idea that eudaimonia provides some motivation for the pursuit of and commitment to virtue, even if it does not supply its content. Appeal to happiness is made explicitly in Plato and Aristotle, but also in the Epicureans and Stoics, as part of the motivation for being virtuous and acting virtuously—at least for certain types of well-brought-up agents. For these philosophers, eudaimonia may plausibly be thought to be part of an

---

[1] In Chapter 2 I argued against scholars who believe that Socrates in fact holds the Eudaimonist Hope throughout the Socratic dialogues.

answer to some version of the "why be moral?" question. In this book, however, I have not focused on moral psychology. I do not think that appeal to eudaimonia as a justification or motivation for attachment to the Supremacy of Virtue is something that will appeal to just any rational agent, but, as Aristotle says, to a certain subset of the "well brought up" who have already been, to some extent at least, properly habituated. For such an agent, I agree that appealing to eudaimonia might deepen and extend their attachment to being virtuous, even if I do not think it provides the basis for an argument that would be persuasive to a committed moral skeptic.[2] If a reader thinks this is sufficient to warrant labeling a theory "eudaimonist," I do not dispute it. I would, however, still insist that the genuinely virtuous agent is committed to virtue and performs virtuous actions for their own sakes and certainly not for the sake of eudaimonia, understood as a further end of the action one hopes to bring about.[3] So, while I agree that appeal to eudaimonia may be intended to provide some motivation to commit to virtue for certain Greek philosophers, I do not think that this by itself makes a good case that the ethical theory of the Greeks is "eudaimonist" where that constitutes a significantly alternative way of doing ethical theory. For, as I argued in Chapter 1, many defenders of virtue and morality have *something* to say to those who ask why they should be virtuous and moral—in other words, have something to say about how it might benefit them or at least some best version of themselves.

The primary critical target of this book across all the chapters has been eudaimonia conceived of as what I have called a Comprehensive Practical Principle. As we have seen, a conception of eudaimonia must function at least as a Prudential Practical Principle; since it is, *ex hypothesi*, a conception of the best life for a human being, every human being has reason to pursue it. That said, however, there is nothing distinctive about this in the Greek context: this is the case for whatever plausible conception of eudaimonia or well-being is proposed.[4] Furthermore, as I emphasized in the Introduction and Chapter 1, having a conception of eudaimonia and committing to it as a Prudential Practical Principle is compatible with any number of ethical or

---

[2] See Vasiliou (1996) and (2007a).

[3] See Whiting (2002) on similar issues about eudaimonism in the interpretation of Aristotle on virtuous action; also Vasiliou (2011a).

[4] Of course, one might think that there is no objective conception of eudaimonia to be had, perhaps because eudaimonia is so different for different individuals that nothing substantive can be said about it that applies for (almost) all human beings. This is perhaps Kant's view, which was influential in the nineteenth and twentieth centuries. See the papers in Engstrom and Whiting (1996) and Auferheide and Bader (2015) and Merritt (2025) for further discussion.

moral philosophies: from deontology and utilitarianism to intuitionism and virtue ethics. Most versions of these ethical philosophies, however, would readily agree that in some circumstances one might have to set pursuit of one's happiness aside because of a moral or ethical obligation—however it is determined (epistemologically and meta-ethically) what that obligation in fact is. Thus, merely holding that eudaimonia operates as a Prudential Practical Principle clearly allows for the possibility that pursuit of my happiness may conflict with my ethical obligations.[5]

As should by now be clear, the almost universal understanding of the practical role of eudaimonia in the eudaimonist framework, and so in the study of Greek ethics, is as a Comprehensive Practical Principle. The lion's share of the overall argument of this book has been to deny that this is a correct interpretation of eudaimonia in the Socratic dialogues, Plato, Aristotle, Epicurus, or the early Stoics. None of these figures understands eudaimonia (or whatever they prefer to call the "highest good") as an end that all of one's non-acratic deliberate actions aim at, as Vlastos and almost all other scholars of ancient philosophy hold. I have argued here (and previously in Vasiliou [2008]) that for Socrates and Plato, the ethical focus is primarily on virtue, with eudaimonia playing a secondary, motivational role in its appearance as the effect of virtuous action on one's soul. Furthermore, virtue for Socrates operates as a Superseding Practical Principle: an aim that trumps any other one might have in acting. Crucially, however, this leaves open that many deliberate, non-acratic actions are ones that one may perform where virtue is not at issue. Even in these cases, however, Socrates's adherence to the Supremacy of Virtue applies to absolutely all of one's actions in its ubiquitous role as a limiting condition; this role is captured in Socrates's well-known formulations such as "it is never right to do wrong" and "it is worse to do wrong than to suffer it." I argued further that when one examines the practical role of eudaimonia in Plato it is most plausibly understood simply as a Prudential Practical Principle. Socrates and Plato certainly believe that being virtuous and acting virtuously are necessary for happiness, but there is little explicit evidence that they think it is also sufficient; or so I argue in Chapters 2 and 3. Further, I have maintained that the mere fact that a philosopher believes that one (or one's best self) is better off behaving virtuously or morally, and so, in that respect happier, ought not to be considered sufficient

---

[5] See White (2002) for a rare ally in my push-back against the assumption that (almost) all the Greeks share the eudaimonist framework.

for a theory to be eudaimonist. One final point to note is that the Socratic and Platonic accounts say very little about what to do or pursue when virtue, either moral or intellectual, does not dictate or forbid some course of action.

When we come to Aristotle, I argue that he distinguishes between the activity (*energeia*) of happiness (eudaimonia) and being a happy person or having a happy life. He holds that virtuous activity and the activity that constitutes eudaimonia are the same; there is no textual evidence that suggests that he holds the implausible view that every deliberate action we engage in is either itself an instance of virtuous activity or a means to such activity. Rather, he adheres, as does Plato and the Stoics, to the Socratic Supremacy of Virtue and holds that it operates as a Superseding Practical Principle. Contrary to traditional interpretations, I have rejected the idea that Aristotle intends eudaimonia to function as a Comprehensive Practical Principle. In the body of the *Nicomachean Ethics*, the activity (*energeia*) that constitutes eudaimonia is morally virtuous action, which is a kind of *praxis*, namely *eupraxia*; in X.7–8, we learn that there is a species of *energeia* that is not action (*praxis*), let alone a "making" (*poiēsis*), but is of a distinct kind, contemplation (*theōria*). While Aristotle consistently views eudaimonia as an activity, only the claim that eudaimonia is morally virtuous activity is relevant to *praxis*, including, I argued, the action that stems from the decision (itself ideally governed by practical wisdom) to engage in *theōria*.[6] So, for Aristotle the Supremacy of Virtue remains a Superseding Practical Principle, just as it had with Socrates and Plato, despite the fact that there is a superior type of *energeia*, namely, contemplation. While our highest practical aim in life is acting virtuously, Aristotle is *also* interested in the long-standing question of what makes the best life for a human being: thus, the *Nicomachean Ethics* inquires not only into what eudaimonia is, but also what a *eudaimōn* life is, and these are not the same thing. A happy life must include the best (or second best) activity, but it needs other things as well: a complete time and a suitable amount of external goods. But having a happy life (and having the things one needs for a happy life) never becomes a practical goal that competes with acting virtuously, because *eudaimonia*, not *being happy*, remains the superseding practical aim.[7] Knowledge of what makes a happy

---

[6] This explains, as I argued in Chapter 5, Aristotle's complete lack of worry about any conflict between a supreme commitment to virtuous activity and the claim that contemplation is the best kind of activity.

[7] And so there is no need to try to find hierarchical principles (as there is on inclusivist readings) that tell us how to weigh the value of just action versus money or pleasure.

life (including the knowledge at the end of the *Nicomachean Ethics* that contemplation is in fact the best activity) is important as a Prudential Practical Principle. That is, when it is not contrary to virtue to do so (i.e., contrary to our superseding practical aim), then a rational person ought to pursue a life that is most happy, and this life would be a life of contemplation.[8]

As Aristotle himself repeatedly says, the activity constituting eudaimonia can be more or less *impeded*. What is inclusive—namely, what is a set containing all (or enough) of the relevant goods—is a *happy life*, which consists in engaging in eudaimonia (of the primary and secondary kinds), in a complete life, with a suitable amount of external goods. His concept of the happy person, however, is of one who engages in the activity that constitutes eudaimonia, in a complete life, with a suitable amount of external goods—that is, without being impeded. Once we appreciate that eudaimonia as virtuous activity is the highest aim of *praxis*, and that it operates as a Superseding Practical Principle, there is no concern about how or whether, say, gaining some external good via an action that would be contrary to virtue would somehow be beneficial. Thus, in an extreme case where, say, a courageous action requires the sacrifice of one's young life, one would still be engaging in eudaimonia but without the prospect of a happy life, since one's life would not be complete.

In Chapters 6 and 7 I argued that the highest goods for the early Stoics and Epicureans, virtue and katastematic pleasure, respectively, function in their practical role as Superseding Practical Principles as well. In the "space of permissions"[9] allowed by this principle functioning as a limiting condition, the Epicureans and Stoics, unlike Socrates, Plato, and Aristotle, offer guidance about how to make choices and lead one's life. For the Epicureans, once katastematic pleasure has been achieved, one ought to pursue kinetic pleasure and avoid pain to the extent, and only to the extent, that it does not disturb one's blessed state. For the Stoics, intermediate appropriate actions pursue the secondary value of promoted indifferents and avoid the disvalue of demoted indifferents, in whatever circumstances the superseding commitment to virtue allows. The fact that for both the Epicureans and the Stoics there are such rational actions that are not aiming at or relevant to one's happiness (or blessedness) shows that they also do not hold that the highest good functions as a Comprehensive Practical Principle.

---

[8] I set aside Aristotle's views about which human beings have the requisite abilities to do this.
[9] As Meyer (2011) labels this idea.

2. Coda: Cicero and the Eudaimonist Framework

My study of eudaimonia and its relationship to virtue and virtuous action stops sometime in the late third century BCE. In Cicero's *De Finibus*, however, we find the full-fledged eudaimonist framework at work in the classification and critical discussion of various ethical theories. I hypothesize that the theoretical structure for Greek ethics presented by Cicero, inherited in part from Carneades (and other Academic skeptics), is one that continues to be read back into the foundational periods of Greek ethics from the fifth to the third centuries. If this is correct, then on the issue of eudaimonism there is something actually historically backward in much of contemporary scholarship's interpretation of Greek ethical philosophy: it begins essentially with Cicero's perspective, moves to the Stoics, Epicureans, and Aristotle, and then seeks its elemental roots back in Plato and Socrates. I am not claiming that this reading is intentional. A related project for another occasion would examine in detail the influence of Cicero's work (and the *De Finibus* in particular) on the reception of Greek philosophy from the modern period into Anglo-American philosophy in the twentieth century. While Vlastos's ascription of the eudaimonist framework to all Greek ethical theory beginning with Socrates has been a target, I certainly do not think that Vlastos himself arrived at his conclusions by reading Cicero. Rather, the idea that all Greek ethical theory is distinctively eudaimonist—however that was exactly articulated—is a background assumption. One would need to trace the roots of this assumption carefully back from the early twentieth century to the early modern period to see whether and how the reception of the *De Finibus* may have had an undue influence on the development of such a dogmatic view about how Greek ethical philosophy operates.

The issue of historical reception aside, it is widely recognized that Cicero employs what is called the *Carneadea divisio*, named after Carneades, which in the hands of Cicero, at least, purports to classify all actual and possible ethical philosophies (see, e.g., *Fin* V.15). The structure of the *divisio* itself is not entirely rigid and, as many have noticed, various ethical theories pop out of the pigeon-holes in which they are placed. Nevertheless, the fundamental structure is one that places all ethical theory from the time of Socrates to Cicero as operating within something very like the "eudaimonist framework" in terms of the roles it sees eudaimonia playing within a theory and the relationship of virtue to it.

Cicero's account makes demands on the adequacy of any ethical theory, which results in "full-blown" eudaimonism, highlighting the three central roles we have seen eudaimonia being asked to play in most scholarship on Socrates, Plato, and Aristotle, as well as the Epicureans and Stoics. An ethical theory must have a conception of what happiness is and that conception must play the following roles on Cicero's account:[10] (1) it must operate as a Comprehensive Practical Principle, functioning as the end for the sake of which we ought to do everything we do;[11] (2) it must operate as a standard of right action (*Fin* IV.46–47, 68–69; V.15–19); so right or virtuous actions, or "appropriate actions" in Stoic terminology (*ta kathēkonta*; *officia* in Cicero), are to be determined, metaphysically and epistemologically, by reference to eudaimonia; and the failure to provide a clear standard is frequently deemed a failure of an ethical theory as such; (3) the conception of eudaimonia functions as the ground or justification for acting rightly because the conception of eudaimonia itself is grounded in human nature; this is, in part, the function of the so-called cradle arguments (e.g., *Fin* V.19).

Given these demands, Cicero then critiques competing ethical theories in terms of how well, meaning how perspicuously and consistently, their conceptions of eudaimonia are able to play each of these three roles. While this may be an accurate assessment of second- and first-century thinking about ethical theories and their structures, I would hypothesize that the collective assemblage of these demands originates in this same period. In any case, as I argued in Chapters 6 and 7, they do not fit with our best evidence for Epicurus and the early Stoics—let alone with Plato and Aristotle.

According to Cicero, the *summum bonum* should properly serve to determine the *content* of virtuous action not only metaphysically, insofar as the ground for something's being the content of virtue is based in the *summum bonum*, but also epistemologically, insofar as the agent determines what their appropriate action or duty is by reference to it. This is markedly distinct from

---

[10] When I say "Cicero's account," it is shorthand for the account we find in Cicero; I am not claiming that the account is his invention or that he endorses it as true.

[11] This interpretation of "highest good," I have argued, is not the correct understanding of any of the preceding Greek figures. The earlier Greek philosophers hold that the highest good must be something desirable and choiceworthy for its own sake and not also for the sake of something further; but they do not make the further claim that there is only one such good, even if they believe that there is one, *best* such good. So, as we have seen throughout, the highest good around which we organize our lives tells us what the best life is and of what it consists. But it does not operate as a Comprehensive Practical Principle, even in the case where the account of a happy life, if not happiness itself, is in some sense an inclusive or comprehensive one; see above, and especially Chapter 5 on Aristotle's distinction between eudaimonia and a happy life.

216 VARIETIES OF HAPPINESS

Socrates, Plato, and Aristotle. What I briefly call attention to here, however, is how this limits what acceptable candidates for the *summum bonum* must be like, which may be captured by examining three assumptions that underlie the division in the first place (*Fin* V.15–16).[12]

The first is that inquiry into the *summum bonum* will yield some sort of knowledge or expertise about it. So, practical reason will be an "art of living" (*sic vivendi ars est prudentia*, V.16). Moreover, all branches of knowledge have an object, something external to them that the knowledge in question is *about*, as the art of medicine is about health. So, the art of living, embodied in practical wisdom, must also have some object.

The second background assumption is that this object must be something adapted to human nature, attractive in itself, and capable of arousing our desire (V.17). Cicero notes that controversy rages around what the first and most basic object of desire for human beings actually is. The assumption here is that whatever this basic desire is, it will be the source and foundation of the supreme end. Brad Inwood, who attributes the insight to Gisela Striker, dubs this assumption "the alignment condition."[13] As Julia Annas has pointed out, this second assumption is quite controversial and conflicts with what one might prima facie think are important elements of ancient ethical theories.[14] In particular, it seems to conflict with views in Plato and Aristotle that identify the highest good as consisting in theoretical contemplation (and, relatedly, in some sort of relationship to the divine) and also views, perhaps like Plato's, Aristotle's, and the Stoics's, that hold that moral development and habituation yield new ends, and a new ultimate end, such as morally virtuous action, for adult human beings. In Chapter 6, we saw that Epicurus' conception of katastematic pleasure is a hard won product of intense study, not the natural and immediately obvious kinetic pleasure of, say, drinking when thirsty. Thus, even if one were to agree that the causal origin of such an end was supplied by a natural end attributable to a human being "from the cradle," one might well reject that the natural end was the ground or justification of the mature end.[15] Moreover, we should note that

---

[12] See Annas (2001), xxiii–xxiv, and Annas (2007).
[13] Inwood (2014), 118; cf. Striker (1996).
[14] Annas (2001), xxv–xxvi.
[15] Moreover, in the primary ethical works of Plato and Aristotle there is no robust consideration at all of what the ends of human beings are from the time they are infants. Aristotle's argument in *NE* I.7 that the function of a human being is rational activity and that an excellent human being is one who actively engages in rational activity excellently does not appeal in any way to what is some "original" urge or desire in human beings for this. Rather, he is concerned with adult (male) human beings. In addition, as we have seen, he seems to think that the highest good is engaging in rational

the preceding is a claim about the *content* of the highest good. Any proper account must be based in these fundamental natural desires or drives and therefore justification for a particular account of eudaimonia must appeal to these same desires. Such a position about the *content* of eudaimonia, however, does not by itself dictate what sort of *role* eudaimonia will play when it comes to virtuous action; that will come with the third assumption.

The third assumption is the one that is most explicit in the introduction of the division in the first place: the *summum bonum* will supply the standard of right action (V.19).[16] Given the fact that this requirement is repeated and that it is used against theories to dismiss them as inadequate, it seems to be particularly highlighted, despite being arguably the least emphasized when it comes especially to the ethics of Plato and Aristotle.[17]

The ramifications of these assumptions for ethical philosophy in the second and first centuries are too complex for me to explore further here. My hypothesis is only that if one wishes to find the eudaimonist framework and to understand its emergence, this would be the period to study. My aim in this Coda is simply to note that the eudaimonist framework is robustly present in Cicero, as it has not been in figures from the fourth and third centuries BCE. What the eudaimonist framework does to or for ethical theory at that point, however, is complicated. Perhaps, it results, as Brad Inwood has argued, in a flattening out of ethical theories.[18] This is plausible insofar as it is correct that

---

activity, whether practical or theoretical, for its own sake. Further, Inwood (1985), 218–223, argues that there is no evidence for connecting ultimate goals with neo-natal impulses in the early Stoics, particularly not in Chrysippus. He argues that this emerges later with Carneades, and Cicero's account of the *divisio*. Inwood usefully insists, 221, "Texts which can be traced to the *Carneadea divisio* as their source must not be used as evidence for the old Stoa." See too Inwood (2014), 48–49, for the fundamental change in philosophy as it was it brought into the Roman world by Cicero in the first century.

[16] Contrast how explicitly this view is presented here, and taken up by Annas and others, with how firmly it is rejected by Broadie (2005) as not "the ancient way," as discussed in Chapter 1.

[17] As we have seen Plato refers to knowledge of the Form of the Good (or the Forms more generally) and Aristotle to the *kalon* as the standards that determine how we ought to act. See Striker's remark (1988/1996), 175–176: "If one wanted to extract a thesis about the justification of moral decisions from Plato's theory, one would presumably have to say that right decisions are made by the rulers on the basis of their knowledge of the Form of the good—which has remained a mystery ever since Plato wrote the *Republic*."

[18] See Inwood (2014), 63–64: "For one effect of the [Carneadean] division, a dialectical tool for ordering and sifting what are supposed to be all possible theories of the *telos*, deployed with an eye to showing that all of them faced insuperable problems, was to flatten out the conceptual landscape. And when debates are structured by grand synoptic frameworks they are bound to miss out or deemphasize distinctive features of particular theories." Inwood sees the effect of this flattening tendency in the downplaying of the importance of cosmology to Stoic ethics in *De Finibus* and also in the complete omission of the idea of activity (so important to Aristotle's own account, as we have seen) as an even possible understanding of the *telos* in the *divisio*.

the *divisio* emerges as part of a skeptical project of casting doubt on positive theories. On the other hand, perhaps the eudaimonist framework, emerging at this historical point, generates new and interesting philosophical questions that contemporaneous ethical theories are now forced to clarify and address, thereby leading to the development of theories that are, at least in certain respects, more detailed and subtle than those that preceded.[19] Only careful work on this later ethical theorizing can address such details. I would hope, however, that this book supports such an effort to the extent that it disabuses us of the idea that Greek ethical theory has *always*, since its Socratic infancy, been operating within such a framework.

[19] I thank Phillip Mitsis for discussion of these possibilities.

Bibliography

Ackrill, John L. 1980. "Aristotle on Eudaimonia." In *Essays on Aristotle's Ethics*, edited by A. O. Rorty, 15–33. Berkeley: University of California Press.
Adkins, Arthur. 1960. *Merit and Responsibility: A Study in Greek Values*. Oxford: Oxford University Press.
Ahbel-Rappe, Sara. 2010. "Cross-examining Happiness: Reason and Community in Plato's Socratic Dialogues." In *Ancient Models of Mind*, edited by Andrea Nightingale and David Sedley: 27–44. Cambridge: Cambridge University Press.
Algra, Keimpe. 1997. "Chrysippus, Carneades, and Cicero: the Ethical *Divisiones* in Cicero's *Lucullus*." In *Assent and Argument*, edited by Brad Inwood and Jaap Mansfeld, 107–139. Leiden: Brill.
Algra, Keimpe, Jonathan Barnes, Jaap Mansfeld, and Malcolm Schofield, eds. 1999. *The Cambridge History of Hellenistic Philosophy*. Cambridge: Cambridge University Press.
Annas, Julia. 1993. *The Morality of Happiness*. Oxford: Oxford University Press.
Annas, Julia. 1995. "Prudence and Morality in Ancient and Modern Ethics." *Ethics* 105: 241–257.
Annas, Julia. 1999. *Platonic Ethics: Old and New*. Ithaca, NY: Cornell University Press.
Annas, Julia. 2001. "Introduction." In *Cicero On Moral Ends*, edited by Julia Annas and translated by Raphael Woolf, ix–xxvii. Cambridge: Cambridge University Press.
Annas, Julia, ed. 2001. *Cicero On Moral Ends*. Translated by Raphael Woolf. Cambridge: Cambridge University Press.
Annas, Julia. 2006. "Virtue Ethics." In *The Oxford Handbook of Ethical Theory*, edited by David Copp, 515–536. Oxford University Press.
Annas, Julia. 2007. "Carneades' Classification of Ethical Theories." In Ioppolo, Anna-Maria and Sedley, David (eds.). 2007. *Pyrrhonists, Patricians, and Platonizers: Hellenistic Philosophy in the Period 155–86 BC*. Naples: Bibliopolis, 187–224.
Annas, Julia. 2008. "Virtue Ethics and the Charge of Egoism." In Paul Bloomfield (2008), 205–221.
Annas, Julia. 2011. *Intelligent Virtue*. Oxford: Oxford University Press.
Annas, Julia, and Gábor Betegh, eds. 2016. *Cicero's De Finibus: Philosophical Approaches*. Cambridge: Cambridge University Press.
Atkins, Jed, and Thomas Bénatouïl, eds. 2022. *The Cambridge Companion to Cicero's Philosophy*. Cambridge: Cambridge University Press.
Aufderheide, Joachim, and Ralf M. Bader, eds. 2015. *The Highest Good in Aristotle and Kant*. Oxford: Oxford University Press.
Badhwar, Neera. 2014. *Well-Being*. Oxford: Oxford University Press.
Barney, Rachel. 2003. "A Puzzle in Stoic Ethics." In *Oxford Studies in Ancient Philosophy* 24: 303–340.
Barney, Rachel. 2011. "Callicles and Thrasymachus." In *Stanford Encyclopedia of Philosophy*, edited by Edward Zalta et al. http://plato.stanford.edu/archives/win2011/entries/callicles-thrasymachus/.
Beaton, Ryan Stuart and Whiting, Jennifer. 2013. "Eudaimonism." In *The International Encyclopedia of Ethics*, edited by Hugh LaFollette: 1759–1766. Oxford: Blackwell.
Becker, Lawrence. 1999. *A New Stoicism*. Princeton: Princeton University Press.
Bett, Richard. 1997. *Sextus Against the Ethicists*. Oxford: Oxford University Press.

Bloomfield, Paul, ed. 2008. *Morality and Self-Interest*. Oxford: Oxford University Press.
Bobonich, Christopher. 2002. *Plato's Utopia Recast*. Oxford: Oxford University Press.
Bobonich, Christopher. 2010. "Socrates and Eudaimonia." In Donald Morrison (2010), 293–332.
Bobonich, Christopher, ed. 2017. *The Cambridge Companion to Ancient Ethics*. Cambridge: Cambridge University Press.
Boys-Stones, George. 1996. "The ἐπελευστικὴ δύναμις in Aristo's Psychology of Action." *Phronesis* 41, no. 1: 75–94.
Brennan, Tad. 1996. "Reasonable Impressions in Stoicism." *Phronesis* 41, no. 3: 318–334.
Brennan, Tad. 2003. "Stoic Moral Psychology." In Brad Inwood, ed., (2003), 257–294.
Brennan, Tad. 2005. *The Stoic Life*. Oxford: Oxford University Press.
Brennan, Tad. 2014. "The *Kathēkon*: A Report on Some Recent Work at Cornell." In *Le Devoir:origins stoïciennes, postérité, réévaluations*, edited by Andre Laks and M. Narcy, 41–70. Philosophie Antique 14. Villeneuve d'Ascq.
Brennan, Tad. Unpublished. "The *Elpistikoi*: A little-known School of Greek Philosophers."
Brickhouse, Thomas and Nicholas Smith. 1994. *Plato's Socrates*. Oxford: Oxford University Press.
Brickhouse, Thomas and Nicholas Smith. 2000. *The Philosophy of Socrates*. Boulder: Westview Press.
Brittain, Charles. 2006. *Cicero On Academic Scepticism*. Indianapolis: Hackett.
Brittain, Charles. 2016. "Cicero's Sceptical Methods: the example of the *De Finibus*." In Julia Annas and Gabor Betegh (2016), 12–40.
Broadie, Sarah. 1991. *Ethics With Aristotle*. Oxford.
Broadie, Sarah. 2005. "On the Idea of the *summum bonum*." In *Virtue, Norms, and Objectivity: Issues in Ancient and Modern Ethics*, edited by C. Gill, 41–58. Oxford: Oxford University Press.
Broadie, Sarah. 2017. "What Should We Mean by 'the Highest Good.'" In *Aristotle and Beyond*, I, edited by Sarah Broadie, 153–165. Oxford: Oxford University Press.
Broadie, Sarah, and Christopher Rowe. 2002. *Aristotle: Nicomachean Ethics*. Oxford: Oxford University Press.
Brown, Eric. 2005. "Wishing for Fortune, Choosing Activity: Aristotle on External Goods and Happiness." In *Proceedings of the Boston Area Colloquium in Ancient Philosophy* 21, edited by J. J. Cleary and G. Gurtler, 57–81. Leiden: Brill.
Brunschwig, Jaques, and Martha Nussbaum, eds. 1993. *Passions and Perceptions*. Cambridge: Cambridge University Press.
Charles, David. 1999. "Aristotle on Well-Being and Intellectual Contemplation." *Proceedings of the Aristotelian Society Supplementary Volume* 73, no. 1: 205–223.
Charles, David. 2014. "*Eudaimonia*, *Theōria*, and the Choiceworthiness of Practical Wisdom." In Pierre Destrée and Marco Zingano (2014), 113–134.
Charles, David. 2015. "Aristotle on the Highest Good: A New Approach." In Joachim Aufderheide and Ralf Bader (2015), 60–82.
Charles, David. 2017. "Aristotle on Virtue and Happiness." In Bobonich (2017), 105–123.
Cooper, John. 1985. "Aristotle on the Good of Fortune." *Philosophical Review* 94: 173–196. Reprinted in Cooper, John. 1999. *Reason and Emotion*. Princeton: Princeton University Press, 292–311 (page refs to latter).
Cooper, John. 1989. "Greek Philosophers on Euthanasia and Suicide." In *Suicide and Euthanasia*, edited by Baruch A. Brody, 9–38. Kluwer Academic Publishers. Reprinted in Cooper, John. 1999. *Reason and Emotion*. Princeton: Princeton University Press, 515–541 (page refs to latter).
Cooper, John. 1996. "Eudaimonism, the Appeal to Nature, and 'Moral Duty' in Stoicism." In *Aristotle, Kant and the Stoics*, edited by Stephen Engstrom and Jennifer Whiting, 261–284. Cambridge: Cambridge University Press. Reprinted in Cooper, John. 1999. *Reason and Emotion*. Princeton: Princeton University Press, 427–448 (page refs to latter).
Cooper, John. 1999. *Reason and Emotion*. Princeton: Princeton University Press.
Crisp, R. 2000. *Aristotle: Nicomachean Ethics*. Cambridge: Cambridge University Press.

Darwall, Stephen. 2011. "The Development of Ethics." *British Journal for the History of Philosophy* 19, no. 1: 131–147.
Dentsoras, Dimitrios. 2018. "Intermediate and Perfect Appropriate Actions in Stoicism." *Proceedings of the XXIII World Congress of Philosophy* 2, no. 3: 5–10.
Denyer, Nicholas. 2008. *Plato: Protagoras*. Cambridge: Cambridge University Press.
De Filippo, Joseph and Mitsis, Phillip. 1994. "Socrates and Stoic Natural Law." In Paul Vander Waerdt (1994), 252–271.
Destrée, Pierre, and Marco Zingano, eds. 2014. *Theoria: Studies on the Status and Meaning of Contemplation in Aristotle's Ethics*. Louvain-La-Neuve: Peeters.
Donini, Pierluigi. 1999. "Stoic Ethics." In Keimpe Algra, Jonathan Barnes, Jaap Mansfeld, Malcolm Schofield (eds.) (1999), 705–738.
Doyle, James. 2018. *No Morality, No Self*. Boston: Harvard University Press.
Engstrom, Stephen, and Jennifer Whiting, eds. 1996. *Aristotle, Kant, and the Stoics*. Cambridge: Cambridge University Press.
Foot, Phillipa. 2001. *Natural Goodness*. Oxford: Oxford University Press.
Frede, Michael. 1994. "The Stoic Conception of Reason." In *Hellenistic Philosophy*, edited by K. J. Boudouris, 2:50–61. Athens: International Center for Greek Philosophy and Culture.
Frede, Michael. 1996. "Introduction." In *Rationality in Greek Thought*, edited by Michael Frede and Gisela Striker, 1–28. Oxford: Oxford University Press.
Frede, Michael. 1999. "On the Stoic Conception of the Good." In Katerina Ierodiakonou (1999), 71–94.
Gill, Christopher, ed. 2005. *Virtue, Norms, and Objectivity: Issues in Ancient and Modern Ethics*. Oxford: Oxford University Press.
Gosling, Justin C.B. and Taylor, Christopher C.W. 1982. *The Greeks on Pleasure*. Oxford: Oxford University Press.
Graver, Margaret. 2016. "Honor and the Honorable: Cato's discourse in *De Finibus* 3." In Julia Annas and Gabor Betgh (2016): 118–146.
Heinaman, Robert. 1988. "Eudaimonia and Self-Sufficiency in the *Nicomachean Ethics*." In *Phronesis* 33: 31–53.
Heinaman, Robert. 2002. "The Improvability of Eudaimonia in Aristotle's *Nicomachean Ethics*." *Oxford Studies in Ancient Philosophy* 23: 99–145.
Heinaman, Robert, ed. 2003. *Plato and Aristotle's Ethics*. Hampshire, UK and Burlington, VT: Ashgate.
Heinaman, Robert. 2007. "Eudaimonia as an Activity in *Nicomachean Ethics* 1.8–12." In *Oxford Studies in Ancient Philosophy* 33: 221–253.
Herman, Barbara. 1993. *The Practice of Moral Judgment*. Boston: Harvard University Press.
Hursthouse, Rosalind. 1999. *On Virtue Ethics*. Oxford: Oxford University Press.
Ierodiakonou, Katerina. 1999. *Topics in Stoic Philosophy*. Oxford: Oxford University Press.
Inwood, Brad. 1985. *Ethics and Human Action in Early Stoicism*. Oxford: Oxford University Press.
Inwood, Brad. 1986. "Goal and Target in Stoicism." *Journal of Philosophy* 83: 547–556.
Inwood, Brad. 1999a. "Stoic Ethics." In Keimpe Algra, Jonathan Barnes, Jaap Mansfeld, Malcom Schofield (eds.) (1999), 675–705.
Inwood, Brad. 1999b. "Rules and Reasoning in Stoic Ethics." In Katerina Ierodiakonou (1999): 95–127, reprinted in Brad Inwood (2005), 95–131.
Inwood, Brad, ed. 2003. *Cambridge Companion to the Stoics*. Cambridge: Cambridge University Press.
Inwood, Brad. 2005. *Reading Seneca: Stoic Philosophy at Rome*. Oxford: Oxford University Press.
Inwood, Brad. 2014. *Ethics After Aristotle*. Boston: Harvard.
Inwood, Brad, and Lloyd Gerson. 1998. *Hellenistic Philosophy*, 2nd ed. Indianapolis: Hackett.
Inwood, Brad, and Lloyd Gerson. 2008. *A Stoic Reader*. Indianapolis: Hackett.
Ioppolo, Anna-Maria. 2012. "Chrysippus and the Action Theory of Aristo of Chios." In Rachana Kamtekar (ed.), *Oxford Studies in Ancient Philosophy*, Supplementary volume 12, *Virtue and Happiness: Essays in Honor of Julia Annas*: 197–222.

Ioppolo, Anna-Maria, and David Sedley, eds. 2007. *Pyrrhonists, Patricians, and Platonizers: Hellenistic Philosophy in the Period 155–86 BC*. Naples: Bibliopolis.

Irwin, Terence H. 1985. "Permanent Happiness: Aristotle and Solon." *Oxford Studies in Ancient Philosophy* 3: 89–124.

Irwin, Terence H. 1986. "Stoic and Aristotelian Conceptions of Happiness." In Malcom Schofield and Gisela Striker (eds.) (1986), 205–244.

Irwin, Terence H. 1988. *Aristotle's First Principles*. Oxford: Oxford University Press.

Irwin, Terence H. 1991. "The Structure of Aristotelian Happiness." *Ethics* 101, no. 2: 382–391.

Irwin, Terence H. 1995. *Plato's Ethics*. Oxford: Oxford University Press.

Irwin, Terence H. 1995. "Prudence and Morality in Greek Ethics." *Ethics* 105: 284–295.

Irwin, Terence H. 1999. *Aristotle: Nicomachean Ethics*. 2nd ed. Indianapolis: Hackett.

Irwin, Terence H. 2003. "Glaucon's Challenge: Does Aristotle Change his Mind?" In Robert Heinaman (2003), 87–108.

Irwin, Terence H. 2006. "Aristotle's Use of Prudential Concepts." In Graham Macdonald and Cynthia Macdonald (2006), 180–197.

Irwin, Terence H. 2007. *The Development of Ethics*, Volume 1: *From Socrates to the Reformation*. Oxford: Oxford University Press.

Irwin, Terence H. 2008. *The Development of Ethics*, Volume 2: *From Suarez to Rousseau*. Oxford: Oxford University Press.

Irwin, Terence H. 2009. *The Development of Ethics*, Volume 3: *From Kant to Rawls*. Oxford: Oxford University Press.

Irwin, Terence H. 2012a. "Conceptions of Happiness in the *Nicomachean Ethics*." In Christopher Shields (2012), 495–528.

Irwin, Terence H. 2012b. "Antiochus, Aristotle, and the Stoics on Degrees of Happiness" in David Sedley (2012), 151–172.

Jones, Russell E. 2013. "Wisdom and Happiness in *Euthydemus* 278–282." In *Philosopher's Imprint* 13: 1–21.

Kamtekar, Rachana. 2004. "What's the Good of Agreeing? *Homonoia* in Platonic Politics". In *Oxford Studies in Ancient Philosophy* 26: 131–170.

Kamtekar, Rachana. 2017. *Plato's Moral Psychology*. Oxford: Oxford University Press.

Karamanolis, George. 2006. *Plato and Aristotle in Agreement?* Oxford: Oxford University Press.

Klein, Jacob. 2012. "Stoic Eudaimonism and the Natural Law Tradition." In *Reason, Religion, and Natural Law from Plato to Spinoza*, edited by Jonathan Jacobs, 57–80. Oxford: Oxford University Press.

Klein, Jacob. 2015. "Making Sense of Stoic Indifferents." *Oxford Studies in Ancient Philosophy* 49: 227–281.

Kraut, Richard. 1989. *Aristotle on the Human Good*. Princeton: Princeton University Press.

Kraut, Richard. 1993. "In Defense of the Grand End." *Ethics* 103, no. 2: 361–374.

Lærke, Mogens, Justin E. H. Smith, and Eric Schliesser, eds. 2013. *Philosophy and its History: Aims and Methods in the Study of Early Modern Philosophy*. Oxford: Oxford University Press.

Langton, Rae. 2007. "Objective and Unconditioned Value." *Philosophical Review* 116, no. 2: 157–185.

Lear, Gabriel Richardson. 2004. *Happy Lives and the Highest Good: An Essay on Aristotle's Nicomachean Ethics*. Princeton: Princeton University Press.

Lear, Gabriel Richardson. 2009. "Happiness and the Structure of Ends." In *A Companion to Aristotle*, edited by Georgios Anagnostopoulos: 385–403. London: Blackwell.

Lesses, Glen. 1989. "Virtue and the Goods of Fortune." *Oxford Studies in Ancient Philosophy* 7: 95–127.

Lesses, Glen. 2002. "Happiness, Completeness, and Indifference to Death in Epicurean Ethical Theory." *Apeiron* 35, no. 4: 57–68.

Lévy, Carlos. 1992. *Cicero Academicus: Recherches sur les Académiques et sur la philosophie cicéronienne*. Rome: École française de Rome.

Long, Anthony A., and David Sedley. 1987. *The Hellenistic Philosophers*, volumes 1–2. Cambridge: Cambridge University Press.

Louden, Robert B. 2015. "'The End of All Human Action'/'The Final Object of All my Conduct': Aristotle and Kant on the Highest Good." In Aufderheide and Bader (2015), 112–128.

Macdonald, Graham, and Cynthia Macdonald, eds. 2006. *McDowell and His Critics*. London: Blackwell.

Mansfeld, Jaap. 1999. "Sources." In *Cambridge History of Hellenistic Philosophy*, edited by Algra Barnes et al.: 3–30.

McDowell, John. 1979. "Virtue and Reason." *The Monist* 62: 331–350.

McDowell, John. 1980/1998b. "The Role of Eudaimonia in Aristotle's Ethics." In Rorty (1980), 359–376; reprinted in McDowell (1998b), 3–22; pagination from the latter.

McDowell, John. 1995/2009. "Eudaimonism and Realism in Aristotle's Ethics." In *Aristotle and Moral Realism*, edited by Robert Heinaman, 201–218. London: UCL; reprinted in McDowell (2009), 23–40; pagination from the latter.

McDowell, John. 1996a/2009. "Deliberation and Moral Development in Aristotle's Ethics." In Engstrom and Whiting (1996), 19–35; reprinted in McDowell (2009), 41–58; pagination from the latter.

McDowell, John. 1996b/2009. "Incontinence and Practical Wisdom in Aristotle." In Lovibond and Williams (1996), 95–112; reprinted in McDowell (2009), 59–76; pagination from the latter.

McDowell, John. 1996c. *Mind and World*, with a new Introduction. Boston: Harvard.

McDowell, John. 1998a/1998b. "Some Issues in Aristotle's Moral Psychology." In Stephen Everson (1998), 107–128; reprinted in John McDowell (1998b), 23–49; pagination from the latter.

McDowell, John. 1998b. *Mind, Value, and Reality*. Cambridge: Harvard University Press.

McDowell, John. 2006. "Response to T. H. Irwin." In Graham Macdonald and Cynthia Macdonald (2006), 198–202.

McDowell, John. 2009. *The Engaged Intellect*. Cambridge, MA: Harvard University Press.

Merritt, Melissa McBay. 2017. "Practical Reason and Respect for Persons". In *Kantian Review* 22, no. 1: 53–79.

Merritt, Melissa McBay (ed.). 2025. *Kant and the Stoics*. Cambridge: Cambridge University Press.

Meyer, Susan Sauvé. 2011. "Living for the Sake of an Ultimate End." In Jon Miller (2011), 47–65.

Meyer, Susan Sauvé. 2016. "Aristotle and Moral Motivation." In Iakovos Vasiliou (2016), 44–64.

Miller, Fred. 1976. "Epicurus on the Art of Dying." *The Southern Journal of Philosophy* 14, no. 2: 169–177.

Miller, Jon, ed. 2011. *Aristotle's* Nicomachean Ethics: *A Critical Guide*. Cambridge: Cambridge University Press.

Mitsis, Phillip. 1986. "Moral Rules and the Aims of Stoic Ethics." *Journal of Philosophy* 83: 556–558.

Mitsis, Phillip. 1988. *Epicurus' Ethical Theory*. Ithaca: Cornell.

Mitsis, Phillip. 1993. "Seneca on Reason, Rules, and Moral Development." In Jacque Brunschwig and Martha Nussbaum (eds.) (1993): 285–312.

Mitsis, Phillip. 1994. "Natural Law and Natural Right in Post-Aristotelian Philosophy: The Stoics and Their Critics." In Wolfgang Hasse and Hildegard Temporini (eds.) *Aufstieg und Niedergang der römischen Welt*, Part II, 36.7: 4812–4850. Berlin: De Gruyter.

Mitsis, Phillip. 2003. "The Stoics and Aquinas on Virtue and Natural Law." In *The Studia Philonica Annual* 15: 35–53.

Mitsis, Phillip, ed. 2020. *The Oxford Handbook of Epicurus and Epicureanism*. Oxford: Oxford University Press.

Mitsis, Phillip. 2024a. "Epicurus on Living Blessedly." In *The Oxford Handbook of Hellenistic Philosophy*, edited by Jacob Klein and Nathan Powers: 163–183. Oxford: Oxford University Press.

Mitsis, Phillip. 2024b. "On Revisiting 'Epicurus on the Art of Dying.'" In *Principles and Praxis in Ancient Greek Philosophy: Festschrift for Fred J. Miller Jr.*, edited by David Keyt and Christopher Shields: 399–417. New York: Springer.

Morrison, Donald. 2003. "Happiness, Rationality, and Egoism." In *Rationality and Happiness*, edited by Jiyuan Yu and Jorge Gracia, 17–34. Rochester: University of Rochester Press.

Morrison, Donald. 2010. *Cambridge Companion to Socrates*. Cambridge: Cambridge University Press.

Moss, Jessica. 2014. "Hedonism and the Divided Soul in Plato's *Protagoras*." *Archiv für Geschichte der Philosophie* 96: 285–319.

Natali, Carlo. 2001. *The Wisdom of Aristotle* (trans. by G. Parks). Albany: SUNY Press.

Nikolsky, Boris. 2001. "Epicurus on Pleasure." In *Phronesis* 46: 440–465.

Nussbaum, Martha. 1986. *The Fragility of Goodness*. Cambridge.

Nussbaum, Martha. 1994. *The Therapy of Desire: Theory and Practice in Hellenistic Ethics*. Princeton: Princeton University Press.

O'Keefe, Timothy. 2022. "The Cyrenaics on Pleasure, Happiness, and Future-Concern." In *Phronesis* 47.4: 395–416.

Parry, Richard, and Harald Thorsrud. 2021. "Ancient Ethical Theory." In *The Stanford Encyclopedia of Philosophy*, edited by Edward Zalta et al.

Penner, T. 2010. "Socratic Ethics and the Socratic Psychology of Action." In Donald Morrison (2010), 260–292.

Penner, Terence, and Christopher Rowe. 2005. *Plato's Lysis*. Cambridge: Cambridge University Press.

Polansky, Ronald. 2014. *The Cambridge Companion to Aristotle's* Nicomachean Ethics. Cambridge: Cambridge University Press.

Pomeroy, Arthur J. (ed.). 1999. *Arius Didymus Epitome of Stoic Ethics*. Atlanta: Society of Biblical Literature.

Price, Anthony W. 2011. *Virtue and Reason in Plato and Aristotle*. Oxford: Oxford University Press.

Prichard, H. A. 1968 [1912]. "Does Moral Philosophy Rest on a Mistake?" In H. A. Prichard, *Moral Obligation and Duty and Interest*, 1–17. Oxford: Oxford University Press. Originally in *Mind* 21 (1912), 21–37.

Reeve, Charles D. C. 1992. *Practices of Reason*. Oxford: Oxford University Press.

Reeve, Charles D. C. 2012. *Action, Contemplation, and Happiness*. Boston: Harvard University Press.

Reeve, Charles D. C. 2014. *Aristotle: Nicomachean Ethics*. Hackett.

Reshotko, Naomi. 2006. *Socratic Virtue: Making the Best of the Neither-Good-Nor-Bad*. Cambridge: Cambridge University Press.

Reshotko, Naomi. 2011. "Socratic Eudaimonism." In *The Bloomsbury Companion to Socrates*, edited by John Bussanich and Nicholas D. Smith: 156–184. London: Bloomsbury.

Richardson, Henry. 1992. "Degrees of Finality and the Highest Good in Aristotle." *Journal of the History of Philosophy* 30: 327–351.

Roche, Timothy. 2014. "Happiness and the External Goods." in Polansky (2014), 34–63.

Rorty, A. O., ed. 1980. *Essays on Aristotle's Ethics*. Berkeley: University of California Press.

Rorty, Richard. 1984. "The Historiography of Philosophy: Four Genres." In Richard Rorty, Jerome Schneewind, Quentin Skinner (1984), 49–75.

Rorty, Richard, Jerome Schneewind, and Quentin Skinner eds. 1984. *Philosophy in History: Essays in the Historiography of Philosophy*. Cambridge: Cambridge University.

Rossi, Mauro, and Christine Tappolet. 2016. "Virtue, Happiness, and Well-Being." *The Monist* 99: 112–127.

Rudebusch, George. 1999. *Socrates, Pleasure, and Value*. Oxford: Oxford University Press.

Russell, Daniel. 2005. *Plato on Pleasure and the Good Life*. Oxford: Oxford University Press.

Russell, Daniel, ed. 2012. *The Cambridge Companion to Virtue Ethics*. Cambridge: Cambridge University Press.

Scott, Dominic J. 1999. "Primary and Secondary Eudaimonia." *Proceedings of the Aristotelian Society Supplementary Volume* 73: 225–242.

Schofield, Malcolm, and Gisela Striker, eds. 1986. *The Norms of Nature*. Cambridge: Cambridge University Press.

Sedley, David. 1999. "The Stoic-Platonist Debate on *kathēkonta*." In *Topics in Stoic Philosophy*, K. Ierodiakonou (ed.), 128–152. Oxford: Oxford University Press.

Sedley, David, ed. 2012. *The Philosophy of Antiochus*. Cambridge: Cambridge University Press.

Sedley, David. 2017. "Epicurean versus Cyrenaic Happiness." In *Selfhood and the Soul: Essays on Thought and Literature in Honor of Christopher Gill*, edited by Richard Seaford, John Wilkins, and Matthew Wright, 89–106. Oxford: Oxford University Press.

Shaw, J. Clerk. 2015. *Plato's Anti-hedonism and the* Protagoras. Cambridge: Cambridge University Press.

Sheffield, Frisbee. 2006. *Plato's Symposium: The Ethics of Desire*. Oxford: Oxford University Press.

Sheffield, Frisbee. 2012. "The *Symposium* and Platonic Ethics: Plato, Vlastos, and a Misguided Debate." *Phronesis* 57: 117–141.

Shields, Christopher, ed. 2012. *The Oxford Handbook of Aristotle*. Oxford: Oxford University Press.

Shogry, Simon. 2021. "The Stoic Appeal to Expertise: Platonic Echoes in the Reply to Indistinguishability." *Apeiron* 54, no. 2: 129–159.

Skorupski, John. 2012. "Aristotelianism and Modernity: Terence Irwin on the Development of Ethics." *European Journal of Philosophy* 20, no. 2: 312–337.

Smyth, Herbert Weir. 1984. *Greek Grammar*. Revised by Gordon Messing. Harvard.

Sorell, Tom, and G. A. J. Rogers, eds. 2005. *Analytic Philosophy and History of Philosophy*. Oxford: Oxford University Press.

Striker, Gisela. 1991/1996. "Following Nature." *Oxford Studies in Ancient Philosophy* 9: 1–73, reprinted in Gislea Striker (1996), 221–280.

Striker, Gisela. 1996 [1993]. "Epicurean Hedonism." In *Passions and Perceptions*, edited by Jacques Brunschwig and Martha Nussbaum, 3–17, Cambridge: Cambridge University Press; reprinted in Striker (1996): 196–208 (Page refs. to latter).

Striker, Gisela. 1996. *Essays in Hellenistic Epistemology and Ethics*. Cambridge: Cambridge University Press.

Swanton, Christine. 2003. *Virtue Ethics: A Pluralist View*. Oxford: Oxford University Press.

Taylor, Christopher. 1991. *Plato: Protagoras*. 2nd ed. Oxford: Oxford University Press.

Tsouna-McKirahan, Voula. 2002. "Is There an Exception to Greek Eudaemonism?" In *Le Style de la Pensée*, Monique Canto-Sperber and Pierre Pellegrin (eds.), 464–489. Paris: Les Belles Lettres.

Tsouna, Voula. 2020a. "Hedonism." In Phillip Mitsis (ed.) 2020, 141–188.

Tsouna, Voula. 2020b. "Aristippus of Cyrene." In *Early Greek Ethics*, David Wolfsdorf (ed.), 380–411. Oxford University Press.

Tsouni, Georgia. 2019. *Antiochus and Peripatetic Ethics*. Cambridge: Cambridge University Press.

Uleman, Jennifer. 2010. *An Introduction to Kant's Moral Philosophy*. Cambridge: Cambridge University Press.

Uleman, Jennifer. 2016. "Kant and Moral Motivation: The Value of Free Rational Willing." In Iakovos Vasiliou (2016), 202–226.

Vander Waerdt, Paul, ed. 1994. *The Socratic Movement*. Ithaca: Cornell.

Vander Waerdt, Paul. 1994a. "Philosophical Influence on Roman Jurisprudence? The Case of Stoicism and Natural Law." In Wolfgang Hasse and Hildegard Temporini (eds.) *Aufstieg und Niedergang der römischen Welt*, Part II, 36.7: 4851–4900. Berlin: De Gruyter.

Vander Waerdt, Paul. 1994b. "Zeno's *Republic* and the Origins of Natural Law." In Paul Vander Waerdt (1994), 272–308.

Vasiliou, Iakovos. 1996. "The Role of Good Upbringing in Aristotle's Ethics." *Philosophy and Phenomenological Research* 56, no. 4: 771–797.
Vasiliou, Iakovos. 2002. "Disputing Socratic Principles: Character and Argument in the 'Polus Episode' of the *Gorgias*." *Archiv für Geschichte der Philosophie* 84, no. 3: 245–272.
Vasiliou, Iakovos. 2007a. "Virtue and Argument in Aristotle's Ethics." In *Moral Psychology*, edited by Sergio Tenenbaum, 37–78. Amsterdam/New York: Rodopi.
Vasiliou, Iakovos. 2007b. "Review of Gabriel Richardson Lear's *Happy Lives and the Highest Good*." *Journal of Philosophy* 104, no. 5: 263–268.
Vasiliou, Iakovos. 2008. *Aiming at Virtue in Plato*. Cambridge: Cambridge University Press.
Vasiliou, Iakovos. 2011a. "Aristotle, Agents, and Actions." In *Aristotle's Nicomachean Ethics: A Critical Guide*, edited by Jon Miller, 170–190. Cambridge: Cambridge University Press.
Vasiliou, Iakovos. 2011b. "From the *Phaedo* to the *Republic*: Plato's Tripartite Soul and the Possibility of Non-Philosophical Virtue." In *Plato and the Divided Self*, edited by Rachel Barney, Tad Brennan, and Charles Brittain, 9–32. Cambridge: Cambridge University Press.
Vasiliou, Iakovos. 2015. "Plato, Forms, and Moral Motivation." *Oxford Studies in Ancient Philosophy* 49: 37–70.
Vasiliou, Iakovos, ed. 2016. *Moral Motivation: A History*. Oxford: Oxford University Press.
Vasiliou, Iakovos. 2019. "Ancient Philosophy and Disjunctivism: The Case of the Stoics." In *New Issues in Epistemological Disjunctivism*, edited by Casey Doyle, Joseph Milburn and Duncan Pritchard, 61–88. New York: Routledge.
Vasiliou, Iakovos. 2021. "Psychological Eudaimonism and the Natural Desire for the Good: Comments on Rachana Kamtekar's *Plato's Moral Psychology*." *Philosophy and Phenomenological Research* 103: 234–239.
Vigani, Denise 2019. "Virtuous Construal: In Defense of Silencing." *Journal of the American Philosophical Association* 5, no. 2: 229–245.
Vigani, Denise. 2021. "Beyond Silencing: Virtue, Subjective Construal, and Reasoning Practically." *Australasian Journal of Philosophy* 99, no. 4: 748–760.
Visnjic, Jack. 2021. *The Invention of Duty: Stoicism as Deontology*. Leiden: Brill.
Vlastos, Gregory. 1991. *Socrates: Ironist and Moral Philosopher*. Ithaca: Cornell University Press.
Vogt, Katja. 2008. *Law, Reason, and the Cosmic City*. Oxford: Oxford University Press.
Vogt, Katja. 2017. "The Virtues and Happiness in Stoic Ethics." In *Cambridge Companion to Ancient Ethics*, edited by Christopher Bobonich, 183–199. Cambridge: Cambridge University Press.
von Arnim, Johannes. 1903–1924. *Stoicorum Veterum Fragmenta*, vols. 1–4. Leibzig: Teubner.
Walker, Matthew. 2018. *Aristotle on the Uses of Contemplation*. Cambridge: Cambridge University Press.
White, Nicholas. 1995. "Conflicting Parts of Happiness in Aristotle's Ethics." *Ethics* 105: 258–283.
White, Nicholas. 1999. "Harmonizing Plato." *Philosophy and Phenomenological Research* 59, no. 2: 497–512.
White, Nicholas. 2002. *Individual and Conflict in Greek Ethics*. Oxford: Oxford University Press.
White, Stephen. 1990. "Is Aristotelian Happiness a Good Life or the Best Life?" In *Oxford Studies in Ancient Philosophy* 8: 103–143.
White, Stephen. 1992. *Sovereign Virtue: Aristotle on the Relation between Happiness and Prosperity*. Stanford: Stanford University Press.
Whiting, Jennifer. 2002. "Eudaimonia, External Results, and Choosing Virtuous Actions for Themselves." *Philosophy and Phenomenological Research* 65: 270–290.
Whiting, Jennifer. 2023. *Living Together: Essays on Aristotle's Ethics*. New York: Oxford University Press.

Wiggins, David. 1995. "Eudaimonism and Realism in Aristotle's Ethics: A Reply to John McDowell." In *Aristotle and Moral Realism*, Robert Heinaman. London: UCL Press.
Williams, Bernard. 1985. *Ethics and the Limits of Philosophy*. Cambridge: Harvard University Press.
Wolfsdorf, David. 2013. *Pleasure in Ancient Greek Philosophy*. Cambridge: Cambridge University Press.
Wood, Allen. 2008. *Kantian Ethics*. Cambridge: Cambridge University Press.
Woolf, Raphael. 2004. "What Kind of Hedonist was Epicurus?". *Phronesis* 49: 303–322.
Zeyl, Donald. 1980. "Socrates and Hedonism: *Protagoras* 351b–358d." In *Phronesis* 25: 250–269.

Index Locorum

For the benefit of digital users, indexed terms that span two pages (e.g., 52–53) may, on occasion, appear on only one of those pages.

Aristotle
  Magna Moralia (MM)
    1208a28, 125–26
    1212b18–20, 118–19
    1219a38–39, 125–26

  Nicomachean Ethics (NE)
    I.1, 106–7
    I.1–2, 107–8
    I.1–I.7, 121–22
    I.2, 20–21, 72
    I.4, 20–21, 121–22
    I.4–5, 9–11
    I.5, 116–17, 138
    I.7, 9–11, 72, 107–8, 109–10, 122–23, 216–17
    I.8, 123–25
    I.8–12, 125–26
    I.9, 126
    I.10, 115–16, 122–23
    I.13, 101, 121, 122–23
    II.1–4, 20–21, 36–37
    II.4, 165–66
    II.6, 115–16
    VII.13, 116–17, 121, 125–26
    IX.9, 121, 129, 131
    X.3, 131–32
    X.4, 131–32
    X.6–8, 121, 138–39
    X.7, 119
    X.7–8, 15, 96, 101, 106–7, 113–14, 119, 131–32, 134–37, 138, 212–13
    X.8, 133, 138

    1094a1–3, 108
    1095a16, 107
    1095a18, 121–22
    1095a19, 118–19
    1095a20, 121–22
    1095b4–14, 20–21
    1095b15, 121–22
    1095b31–1096a2, 116–17
    1096a1–2, 124–25
    1096a2, 121–22

    1097a18–24, 107–8
    1097a34, 121–22
    1097b, 9–11
    1097b4, 121–22
    1097b6, 121–22
    1097b6–21, 115
    1097b15, 108–9
    1097b16, 121–22
    1097b17, 98
    1097b20, 121–22
    1097b20–21, 107–8
    1097b22, 121–22
    1098a16–18, 105–6
    1098a18, 113, 123, 131–32
    1098a18–20, 113–14, 123
    1098a18–20, 113–14
    1098a20–21, 123
    1098b15–16, 123–24
    1098b23–1102a17, 121
    1098b31–1099a7, 105–6
    1099a29–31, 105–6
    1099a31–33, 124–25
    1099a31–b8, 115
    1099b2–8, 123–24
    1099b32–1100a9, 126
    1100a5, 113
    1100a5–9, 115–16
    1100b8ff, 127
    1100b8–11, 124–25
    1100b12 ff, 128
    1100b30–1101a6, 115–16, 128
    1100b33–35, 127
    1101a1–5, 127
    1101a6–13, 127–28
    1101a14–17, 118–19, 122–24
    1101a16, 113
    1102a2–3, 107
    1102a5–6, 122–23
    1102a17–18, 122–23
    1153a10, 119
    1153b10ff, 131–32
    1153b16–19, 125–26
    1153b19–21, 116–17
    1153b19–25, 124–25

Aristotle (*cont.*)
    1169b5, 129–30
    1169b10, 129
    1169b10–16, 129
    1169b16–22, 129
    1169b19, 129–30
    1169b22–27, 129
    1169b25, 129–30
    1169b28–30: 105–6, 129–30
    1169b29, 129–30
    1169b30, 129–30
    1169b30–32, 130
    1169b33–1170a4, 130
    1170a4, 130
    1170a5–8, 118–19
    1170b2, 118–19
    1170b17, 129–30
    1170b18, 129–30
    1170b18–19, 131
    1173a5–13, 100
    1173a29–1173b7, 131–32
    1173a32–b7, 131–32
    1173b26, 100
    1174a28, 131–32
    1174b5–6, 131–32
    1177a10, 123–24, 132
    1177a12, 123–24
    1177a17, 132–33
    1177a17–18, 132
    1177a19–20, 132
    1177a21, 132
    1177a22–27, 132
    1177a27–1177b1, 132
    1177b3–4, 138
    1177b17–19, 138
    1177b22–23, 132–33
    1177b24–5, 132
    1177b24–26, 132
    1177b25, 113
    1177b26–27, 132–33
    1178a8, 132–33
    1178a21–22, 133
    1178b7, 132–33
    1178b8–9, 133
    1178b20–21, 138
    1178b24–28, 119
    1178b26, 113
    1178b32, 133
    1178b33–1179a32, 133
    1179a1–2, 133
    1179a2–3, 133
    1179a9, 133
    1179a10, 133
    1179a14, 133
    1179a31, 133
    1179a32, 133
    1179a33–35, 140–41

    Politics (Pol.)
        1328a37–38, 121–22
        1328b35–36, 125–26
        1329a22–23, 125–26
        1332a9, 121–22

    Rhetoric (Rh.)
        1360b15–30, 121–22

Athenaeus
    Deipnosophists
        12, 546f, 165–66

Cicero
    De Finibus Bonorum et Malorum (Fin.)
        I, 145–46
        I.33, 145–46
        I.49, 148–49
        II.43, 181
        III.22, 182
        III.48, 187–88
        III.53, 197–98
        III.58, 195–96, 197–98
        III.58–59, 196, 198, 206
        III.59, 189, 193, 195, 196–98
        III.60–61, 206
        IV, 171
        IV.46–47, 173–74, 215
        IV.47, 181
        IV.68–69, 173–74, 179–80, 181, 215
        V.15, 214
        V.15–16, 215–16
        V.15–19, 215
        V.16, 216
        V.17, 216–17
        V.19, 215, 217

Diogenes Laertius (DL)
    Lives of the Philosophers
        7.87–89, 185–86
        7.88, 183–84
        7.104, 170–71
        7.104–5, 183–84
        7.107, 183–85
        7.108, 200–2
        7.108–9, 195
        7.160, 180
        10.136, 146

INDEX LOCORUM

Epicurus
Letter to Menoeceus (Men.)
122, 151–52
123–24, 147
124, 147
125, 164
127, 154–55
128, 143, 154–55
129, 157–58
130, 162
130–31, 152–53
131, 143, 152–53, 159–60
131–32, 159–60
132, 165
135, 147

Principle Doctrines (KD)
1, 147
2, 147
3, 143, 148–50, 151, 152–53
10, 148–49, 150
11, 150
15, 164–65
16, 164–65
17, 164–65
18, 148–49, 151–53, 160–61
19, 152–53, 160–61
19–21, 148–49
20, 152–53, 160–61
25, 154–55
26, 154–55, 164–65
29, 154–55, 164–65
30, 154–55, 164–65
33–35, 166

Sententiae Vaticanae
59, 154–55

Homer
Odyssey
11, 18–19

Immanuel Kant
Groundwork of the Metaphysics of Morals
4:394, 182–83
4:431, 11–12

Plato
Apology
28b, 47–48
32a–d, 70–71
32d, 179
38a5–6, 96

40c, 148–49

Crito
47e, 77
48b, 46–47
54b, 46–47

Euthydemus
278d1–2, 55–56
278e, 48–49
278e3–5, 56
278e3–6, 64
278e3–279c9, 20–21
278e–282d, 50–51, 55–56
279a3, 56
279d–280b, 56
280b1, 56
280e–281e, 56
280e3, 56
281a1–4, 57
281a6–b1, 57
282a1–c1, 59
288d9–e2, 60
291b6–7, 60

Gorgias
467–68, 48–49
469a–b, 73–74
469b–c, 73–74
477b8–c2, 73–74
477c2–4, 73–74
478d–e, 73–74
479a–b, 73–74
494b–495, 64–65
494e–495a, 78
499b, 78
509b–c, 73–74
500c, 76
523a–527a, 76–77

Lysis
219c6, 72
219d1, 72
219d6–220a1, 73
219–20, 48–49, 55, 72, 93–94

Meno
77e–78b, 48–49
78a4–5, 60–61, 64
78b9–d1, 60–61
78c3–79a2, 60–61
80b, 61–62
87d–89a, 50–51, 61–62

232 INDEX LOCORUM

Plato (*cont.*)
    88e5–6, 61–62
    89a3–4, 61–62
    96e3–4, 62
    97a3–4, 62–63

  Philebus
    11d4–6, 81–82
    20bff., 81–82
    20d, 81–82
    22c, 92
    60a–e, 81–82
    65a, 81–82

  Protagoras
    351b3–358c, 63–64
    351b3–4, 64
    351b4–7, 64
    351c1, 64
    351d7–e1, 65
    352b–e, 65
    353b, 64–65
    353c–355b, 64–65
    353e6–354a1, 66–67
    354b5–c2, 66–67
    354d1–3, 66–67
    354d7–e2, 66–67
    354e8–355a5, 66–67
    356c8–d3, 68–69
    356d3, 70–71
    356d4, 68–69
    356e2, 70–71
    356e5–6, 70–71
    356e8–357a1, 70–71
    357a–b, 69
    357b6–7, 70–71
    359a, 64–65
    361c2–6, 66–67

  Republic
    347b–d, 89–90
    361d2–3, 82–83
    367c5–c4, 83
    419a–420a, 85
    419a ff., 88–89
    419a9, 85–86
    420a7, 85–86
    420b, 86
    420b5, 85–86
    421c3–5, 86
    443e–444a, 83–84
    465b–466c, 87–88
    466b, 88–89
    466b–c, 88–89
    519c, 89–90
    519c4–6, 96
    520a–d, 89–90
    540b–c, 87–88
    540b2, 90–91
    612b–614a, 90–91

  Symposium
    202c–d, 93
    202c4, 91
    202c6–202d7, 92
    204b, 92
    204d–e, 72
    204d5–205a8, 93
    204e–205a, 64–65
    205a, 20–21
    206a11–12, 94
    206e, 94–95
    208e ff., 94
    208e4, 94
    209e5–210a2, 95
    210a1–5, 94–95
    210a2, 94–95
    210e5–6, 95
    211c2, 95
    211d–212b, 95–96

Plutarch
  De Communibus Notitiis (Comm.)
    1063a–b, 187–88
    1069e, 203

  De Stoicorum Repugnatis (Stoic. Repug.)
    1042d, 205–6

Sextus Empiricus
  Against the Ethicists
    11.64–67, 175–76
    11.66, 177
    11.67, 178–79

Stobaeus
  Epitome of Stoic Ethics
    8, 183–85, 189, 192–93, 196–97, 200–1
    8–8a, 202–3
    8a, 190–91, 205–6
    8a, 193
    11a, 189
    11e, 194, 198, 200–1
    11g, 201–2

General Index

For the benefit of digital users, indexed terms that span two pages (e.g., 52–53) may, on occasion, appear on only one of those pages.

Academic Skeptics, 13–14, 171, 214
Achilles, 18–19
Ackrill, John, 99n.2, 119n.4
actions
   appropriate (*see* appropriate action)
   autonomous vs. heteronomous, 42–45
   and character (*see under* character)
   just, 27–28, 41–42, 57–58, 71, 74–79, 84, 86, 138
   moral, 6, 6n.15, 18–19, 25–27, 42–43, 45, 84
   virtuous (*see* virtuous action)
   when virtue is not at issue, 12–13, 33, 109–11, 112n.41, 171–75, 185–86, 188, 191–92, 193–94, 200, 202n.62, 203–4, 207–8, 211–12
   See also Supremacy of Virtue; Superseding Practical Principle
activity. *See* energeia
Adeimantus, 82–84, 85–86, 89–91
Adkins, Arthur, 1–2n.3, 18n.1
Agathon, 93n.15
aiming/determining distinction. *See under* deliberation; virtuous action
akrasia, 65, 68–69
   denial of, 65, 66n.48, 68–69
   See also incontinence
Alcibiades, 66–67
Annas, Julia, 10n.22, 14, 18n.1, 19–20n.6, 21–27, 29, 32, 47–48, 49n.12, 164, 176n.14, 216–17
Apology, 47–48, 58, 63n.37, 70–71, 148n.13
appropriate action (*kathēkon*), 178n.21, 183–88, 213, 215–16
   contrary to (mistake, *harmatēma*), 186–91, 193–95, 197–99, 201–4
   intermediate, 15–16, 187–88, 191n.48, 192–201, 202–8, 213
   perfect or right (*katorthōma*), 185–91, 192–94, 197–99, 201–3, 204
   See also duty; virtuous action
Aquinas, 37–39

aretē. See virtue
Aristo, 173–81, 208
Aristotle, 1, 2n.5, 4n.12, 7n.17, 7–8, 9–11, 14, 15, 16, 20n.7, 20n.9, 26–28, 35–37, 39–40, 43n.51, 49–50, 54, 63–64, 71–72, 88n.9, 93, 95n.18, 96–97, 142–44, 149n.14, 150n.16, 162, 165–67, 168, 169n.2, 171–72, 208, 209–18
ataraxia, 143, 146, 149–50, 153–54, 155–61, 164, 166–67, 169–70
autonomy
   rational, 42–45, 74–75, 84

Badhwar, Neera, 19n.3, 27–28n.24
Barney, Rachel, 78n.66, 172n.5, 174n.11
basilikē technē, 60, 62–63
Bett, Richard, 178n.20
Bobonich, Christopher, 28n.26, 51–54, 57n.31, 59–60, 71n.59, 79
Brennan, Tad, 2n.5, 184n.35, 187n.42, 191n.46
Brickhouse, Thomas and Smith, Nicholas, 4n.11, 48n.7, 50n.17, 51–52, 59–60
Broadie, Sarah, 14, 30–34, 38, 87–88, 97, 106n.26, 110n.37, 114n.47, 119n.3, 122n.14, 123n.17, 127n.24, 217n.16
Brown, Eric, 119n.3, 122n.14
Butler, Joseph, 38–39

Callicles, 27–28, 36–37, 64–65, 76–79, 83
Carneadean Division (*Carneadea divisio*), 2, 214, 216–17n.15, 217n.18
Carneades, 13–14, 214, 216–17n.15
Categorical Imperative, 6, 42–43, 44–45
"chain of desire," 72–73
character, 1, 81, 89, 188
   and actions, 45, 63, 79–80, 188, 189–90, 198–99, 202n.62
   states of, 27–29, 52–53, 209
   virtues of, 101n.10
   See also soul

GENERAL INDEX

Charles, David, 99n.3, 101n.9, 103–4, 119n.5, 120–21, 134n.32, 136n.35, 139n.40
Charmides, 58
Cicero, 9–11, 13–14, 50n.14, 142, 144–47, 148n.12, 154, 157, 160n.28, 161n.31, 168, 169–70, 171, 173–75, 179n.22, 181, 185n.37, 192, 195–99, 206, 207, 214–18
  and eudaimonist framework (*see under* eudaimonist framework)
Cleinias, 55–56, 57–58, 60, 61–63
Comprehensive Practical Principle (CPP)
  account of, 9–13
  eudaimonia as, 14–15, 23–25, 29, 31–32, 38, 51–52, 59–60, 63, 73, 74–75, 81, 84, 86–88, 90–91, 93–94, 97, 98–99, 101–3, 108–12, 113n.45, 114n.47, 119, 120–21n.9, 134–37, 142, 143–44, 155n.23, 168–70, 171–72, 186n.41, 205, 207–8, 210–13, 215
  contemplation, 15, 26n.22, 64n.41, 85–90, 96, 101n.10, 103–4, 106–7, 119, 121–22, 134–40, 142, 147, 168, 212–13, 216–17. *See also theōria*
Cooper, John, 122n.16, 128n.27, 187n.42, 199–200, 205n.67
Crito 34–35, 46, 48–49, 58, 63, 74–75, 77, 81, 83–84, 174–75n.12
Cyrenaics, 2n.5, 6n.14, 146–47

Darwall, Stephen, 7n.17
death, 171
  and deliberation, 47–48, 114, 116–17, 174–75n.12
  fear of (*see under* Epicurus)
  as indifferent, 169, 171, 173–74, 177–78, 180–81, 186, 200
deliberation
  aiming and determining, 34, 46–48, 116–17, 139–40, 169, 173–74, 204
  about the good and the right, 33–34, 38, 40, 138–39
  happiness as a guide for, 89, 100, 104, 114
  about self-interest and virtue, 19–20, 39–40
  Socratic, 46–48, 116n.51, 140, 174–75n.12
  when virtue is not at issue (*see under* action)
  See also under practical reasoning
Dentsoras, Dimitrios, 191n.48, 194n.51, 199n.58
Denyer, Nicholas, 65n.46
De Quincey, Thomas, 1–2n.3
Diogenes Laertius, 146–47, 149, 175, 183–84, 192, 194–96, 202n.62
Diotima, 91–96
Doctrine of the Mean, 115–16

Donini, Pierluigi, 199n.58
Doyle, James, 6n.15
duty, 31–32, 86, 89–90
  and appropriate action, 186–87, 199–201, 215–16
  and Kant, 41–45
  motive of, 11–12n.25, 44–45
  and self-interest, 1, 19–20
  as Superseding Practical Principle, 44–45
  as translation of *kathēkon*, 185n.37
  See also appropriate action; virtuous action

egoism, 18–19, 37–40, 41, 42–43
Elpistikoi, 2n.5
endoxa, 121, 140–41
energeia, 96, 105–7, 122n.15, 124–25, 131–32, 136–38, 168, 212–13
Epicurean Sage, 151, 156–57, 162–63
Epicurus, 2n.5, 8, 9–11, 15, 16, 64n.41, 169–70, 172–73, 200, 209–10, 211–12, 213, 215, 216–17
  and fear of death, 15, 144–46, 147–53, 154, 156–57, 158–60, 162–66
Eros (the divinity), 91–92
ethical theory, 1, 4–6, 22–24, 25, 27. *See also* eudaimonism; eudaimonist framework
eudaimonia
  as activity (*see energeia*)
  vs. being happy/happy life (*see eudaimōn/eudaimonia* Distinction)
  as comprehensive, 12–13, 19–20, 23–25, 99n.1, 119n.4, 215n.11
  comprehensivist/inclusivist vs. exclusivist/monistic interpretation of, 15, 99–110, 111–13, 119n.4, 134–35, 168, 212n.7
  and external goods (*see under* goods)
  as giving content to virtue (*see* Eudaimonist Hope)
  as motivating commitment to virtue, 7–9, 34–37, 41–45, 82–84, 209–10
  "paradigm-case account" of, 99n.3, 103–5, 120–21, 134n.32, 136n.35
  as possession, 105–6, 129–30
  as practical principle, 23–27, 29, 31, 38, 55, 63, 74–78, 81–82, 86–88, 91, 98–112, 114, 116–17, 119, 134, 135–40, 142, 144, 155–56, 162, 168, 205, 209
  as psychological state, 19–20
  as requiring a "complete life", 99–100, 106–7, 112–17, 121–28
  See also Comprehensive Practical Principle; Prudential Practical Principle; Superseding Practical Principle

eudaimōn/eudaimonia Distinction (EED), 15, 118–34, 140–41, 212–13
eudaimonism
  as ethical theory (*see under* eudaimonist framework)
  necessary and sufficient conditions for, 4–6, 22–23, 26, 29, 41–43, 72–73, 147n.9, 209–11
  psychological vs. rational, 12n.27, 51–52, 68n.52, 71n.59
  See also eudaimonist framework
eudaimonist framework
  and ancient ethical theory, 5–6, 13–14, 17, 20–21, 22–23, 37, 43, 82, 209–10, 214–15, 217–18
  and Cicero, 13–14, 214–18
  See also eudaimonism
Eudaimonist Hope, 28–29, 32, 112, 134–35, 209
  account of, 7–8
  and Epicurus, 15, 144, 164–67
  and Socrates, 14, 50–55, 58, 59–60, 67, 70–71, 75–76, 79, 142
Euthydemus, 48–49, 50–51, 55–60, 63, 67, 69–70, 71, 81, 84, 92n.14

fine, 35–36, 59–60, 61, 92, 112n.42, 135–37, 139–40, 142, 165–66, 168
  as limiting condition, 61, 139–40, 168
  See also kalon; noble
Foot, Phillipa, 118, 141n.45
Forms (Platonic), 8, 41, 43, 44–45, 54, 55, 75–76, 81, 84, 95–97
Frede, Michael, 186n.40
friendship, 129–31
Function Argument (Aristotle), 7–8, 101n.9, 108–9, 121, 122–23

Glaucon, 82–83, 84, 89–90
goods
  external, 15, 46–48, 49n.12, 59–60, 84n.6, 86–87, 89, 91, 99–101, 105–7, 112–17, 118–27, 129–31, 133, 134, 136–38, 140–41, 168, 170, 179, 180–81, 212–13
  three classes of, 34–35
  See also indifferents
Gorgias, 14, 27–28, 34n.38, 34–35, 48, 55, 58n.33, 59n.34, 63, 69n.53, 73–80, 81, 83–84

happiness
  contemporary view of, 18–27, 29
  See also eudaimonia
hedonic calculus. *See under* pleasure

hedonism, 14, 15, 30–34, 63–71, 79, 143–44, 146–47, 164, 166–67
Heinaman, Robert, 99n.1, 99n.2, 100n.6, 101n.9, 106n.24, 106n.26, 107n.28
Herman, Barbara, 11–12n.25, 182n.31
Hesiod, 88–89
highest good. *See summum bonum*
Homer, 94–95
Hursthouse, Rosalind, 27–28n.24, 29, 33, 115n.48

immortality, 94–95
incontinence, 65–69. *See also akrasia*
indifferents (Stoic), 112n.41, 161–62, 168–81, 182, 183–86, 188, 191, 192–97, 201n.60, 203, 205, 207–8, 213
Inwood, Brad, 174n.10, 176n.14, 178n.19, 181n.26, 183n.32, 216–18
Inwood, Brad and Gerson, Lloyd, 149–50n.15, 192n.50
Irwin, Terence, 4n.12, 7n.17, 10n.22, 14, 18n.1, 37–40, 41, 43n.52, 48–49, 50n.13, 84n.6, 100n.5, 102n.11, 109n.34, 112n.42, 118n.1, 119n.4, 126–27, 128n.26, 169

Jones, Russell, 57

kalon, 7–8, 20n.9, 35–37, 43n.51, 45, 59–60, 64–65, 68, 96n.19, 104, 111–12, 128, 134–35, 136–40, 165–66, 217n.17
  as limiting condition, 64–65, 111–12, 139–40
  See also fine; noble
Kamtekar, Rachana, 68n.52, 69n.54, 87n.8
Kant, Immanuel, 11–12n.25, 33n.35, 36n.41, 37, 41–45, 84, 182–83, 185n.37, 199, 210n.4
Karamanolis, George, 122n.14
katastematic pleasure. *See under* pleasure; Superseding Practical Principle
kathēkon. *See* appropriate action
kinetic pleasure. *See under* pleasure
Klein, Jacob, 168n.1, 169, 191n.49, 205–8
Kraut, Richard, 100n.5, 102n.13, 123n.17

Langton, Rae, 43n.50
Lear, Gabriel Richardson, 100n.5, 102–4, 107n.30, 111n.38, 136n.35
Lesses, Glen, 149n.14, 168n.1
limiting condition, 11–12, 64–65, 110–12, 171–72, 188, 191, 200, 202–3, 211–12, 213
  kalon as (*see under* kalon)
  katastematic state of pleasure as, 154, 155–56, 157–59, 172–73
  See also under Supremacy of Virtue

GENERAL INDEX

Long, Anthony and Sedley, David, 148n.12, 149–50n.15, 160–61, 184–85, 195n.52, 197–201
Louden, Robert, 134n.33
Lysis, 48, 72–73, 81

McDowell, John, 8n.19, 15, 98–99, 105–17, 119n.3, 128n.27, 135–36, 140–41
Meno, 48–49, 50–51, 55, 58n.33, 59–63, 64–66, 67, 69–70, 71, 84, 92n.14, 93–94
Merritt, Melissa, 43n.50
Meyer, Susan Sauvé, 104n.18, 111–12, 139–40, 213n.9
Mill, John Stuart, 30, 33n.35
Miller, Fred, 150n.16
Mitsis, Phillip, 148n.12, 149n.14, 154n.22, 160n.29, 162n.32, 174n.10, 178n.19, 182–83, 184n.36, 191n.47
Moss, Jessica, 66n.49, 71n.58
motivation, for commitment to virtue. *See under* eudaimonia

Natali, Carlo, 136n.36
Nicomachean Ethics (NE), 15, 16, 36–37, 72, 98–99, 106n.27, 118, 121–22, 143, 212–13
Nietzsche, Friedrich, 20–21, 23–24
Nikolsky, Boris, 146n.7, 147n.8, 148n.12
noble, 20n.9, 59–60, 64–65, 88–89, 92, 103, 124–25, 129, 165–66
  as limiting condition, 59–60, 64–65
  See also fine, *kalon*
nous, 81–82, 98, 132–33
Nussbaum, Martha, 168n.1

obligation. *See* duty
Odysseus, 18–19
opinion (*doxa*), 62–63, 188, 204

pain,
  freedom from (*see ataraxia*)
  mental and physical, 15, 145–46, 149–50, 151, 155–56, 157, 158–59, 162–63
Parry, Richard and Thorsrud, Harald, 27–28n.24
Penner, Terence, 48n.8, 50n.15
Penner, Terence and Rowe, Christopher, 50n.15, 72n.60
Philebus, 81–82, 143
phronēsis
  101n.10, 104, 136–37, 165
  165. *See also* practical wisdom

phronimos, 43n.51, 139–40
Plato, 2n.4, 4–5, 8, 9–12, 14–15, 20n.7, 20n.9, 21–22, 26, 27–28, 34–37, 41–45, 98–99, 102–3, 111–12, 116–17, 142–44, 165–66, 168, 171–72, 191, 200, 208, 209–10, 211–13, 215–17
pleasure, 129–33
  as freedom from pain, 143–44, 146–47, 149–50, 156–57, 160–61, 163, 165–66
  and hedonic calculus, 52n.20, 67, 68–71, 145–47, 149, 153–54, 157–59, 160, 166–67, 209
  katastematic, 15, 145–50, 152–54, 156–67, 172–73, 213, 216–17 (*see also under* Superseding Practical Principle)
  kinetic, 15, 143n.2, 145–49, 151–54, 156n.24, 157–65, 213, 216–17
  See also hedonism
Politics, 118, 121–22, 125n.20
Polus, 34n.38, 36–37, 73–76
practical principle
  account of, 7, 9–13
  eudaimonia as (*see under* eudaimonia)
  See also Comprehensive Practical Principle; Prudential Practical Principle; Superseding Practical Principle
practical reasoning
  about good vs. right, 25 (*see also* Eudaimonist Hope)
  See also deliberation; *phronēsis*; practical wisdom
practical wisdom, 104, 136–37, 212–13, 216. *See also phronēsis*
Priam, 115n.49, 126–28
Price, Anthony, 57n.29, 72n.61, 73n.62
Prichard, H.A., 20n.7
Protagoras, 64–68
Protagoras, 14, 15, 52n.20, 55, 63–71, 79, 142, 143–46, 209
Prudential Practical Principle (PPP)
  account of, 9, 12–13
  eudaimonia as, 14–15, 29, 32–33, 51–52, 87–88, 97, 114n.47, 138–39, 168, 171–72, 210–13
  summum bonum as, 32–33, 87–88, 97, 114n.47

Reeve, Charles, D.C., 120–21, 126n.22
Republic, 14–15, 27–28, 34–35, 36–37, 41–42, 44, 58n.33, 62n.36, 63, 66–67, 68, 70–71, 74–75, 79–80, 82–91, 96

GENERAL INDEX 237

Reshotko, Naomi, 112n.42
Richardson, Henry, 102n.13, 103n.15, 107n.30
Roche, Timothy, 119n.4, 120n.7, 122n.16
Russell, Daniel, 56n.26, 56n.27, 73n.63

Sage
   Epicurean, 151, 156–57, 160n.29, 162–63
   Stoic, 15–16, 151n.18, 170–71, 182–83, 184n.35, 185–208
Schopenhauer, Arthur, 37
Scott, Dominic, 103n.16, 133n.31, 136n.35
Sedley, David, 147n.8, 149n.14, 176n.14. *See also* Long and Sedley
self-interest, 19–20, 37, 39–40, 45, 58. *See also under* deliberation
Shaw, J. Clerk, 65n.47
Sheffield, Frisbee, 94n.17, 96n.20
Sidgwick, Henry, 1, 39
Skorupski, John, 40n.47
Socrates (Platonic character), 2–4, 11–12, 13–14, 18–19, 20–21, 27–29, 34–35, 36n.40, 36–37, 45, 98, 110–12, 116–17, 140, 142, 148n.13, 155–56, 171–73, 174–75n.12, 179, 180–81, 188, 200, 199–200n.51, 202–3, 208, 211–13, 214–16
Solon, 94–95
soul, 34–37, 41–42, 45, 55, 58n.33, 61–63, 70–71, 73–80, 81–84, 94, 123–24, 143, 146, 154n.22, 155–56, 158–60, 211–12
   as independent locus of harm/benefit, 34–35, 36–37, 73–74
   See also character
Stoics, 2n.5, 8, 9–11, 15–16, 22–23, 27–28, 35n.39, 45, 117n.52, 142, 151n.18, 161–62, 163, 209–10, 211–17
Striker, Gisela, 144n.3, 175, 177–80, 181n.26, 216–17, 217n.17
Suarez, Francisco, 38–39
suicide
   Stoics on, 205–8
summum bonum, 30–34, 38, 87–88, 97, 114n.47, 215–17. *See also* Comprehensive Practical Principle; eudaimonia; Prudential Practical Principle; Superseding Practical Principle
Superseding Practical Principle (SPP)
   account of, 11–13
   eudaimonia as, 14–15, 26, 29, 59–60, 84, 86–88, 90–91, 93–94, 97, 98, 102–3, 107, 110–11, 113–14, 119, 120, 135–41, 168, 171–72, 212–13

   katastematic pleasure as, 154–56, 164
   living blessedly as, 154–56, 162
   summum bonum as, 38
   Supremacy of Virtue as, 14, 15–16, 31–32, 33, 44–45, 46, 48, 55, 58–60, 63, 71, 74–75, 77–78, 84, 98, 110–11, 135–36, 138–41, 142, 155–56, 168, 171–72, 188, 201n.61, 202–3, 211–13
   See also Supremacy of Virtue
Supremacy of Virtue (SV), 14–16, 31–32, 33, 41–42, 44–45, 209–10
   account of, 11–13
   adherence of Stoic Sage to, 15–16, 177, 188, 191, 202–3
   and Aristotle, 135–36, 138–39, 140–41, 168, 171–72, 212–13
   commitment to as necessary for happiness, 74–78, 79–80, 83–84
   and Epicurus, 155–56
   as limiting condition, 11–12, 46–47, 54, 64–65, 74–75, 171–72, 200, 203
   and Socrates, 46–48, 49–50, 55, 58, 59–60, 63, 64–65, 71, 74, 78–80, 83, 97, 98, 110–12, 140–41, 168, 171–72, 211–12
   and Stoics, 171–72, 177, 188, 191, 200, 203
   as Superseding Practical Principle (*see under* Superseding Practical Principle)
   ubiquity of (*see under* ubiquity)
   See also limiting condition; Superseding Practical Principle
Symposium, 14–15, 72, 81–82, 91–97

theōria, 88n.9, 99–100, 101, 112n.41, 120–21n.9, 134–41. *See also* contemplation
Thrasymachus, 27–28, 36–37, 48n.6
tranquility. *See* ataraxia
Tsouna, Voula, 147n.9

ubiquity, 46–47, 139, 172n.7, 200
   account of, 11
   and Superseding Practical Principle, 11–12, 78, 155n.23, 212–13
   and Supremacy of Virtue, 11–12, 46–48, 112n.41, 191, 212–13
Uleman, Jennifer, 43n.49, 183n.31
Understanding. *See* nous
utilitarianism, 6, 23–24, 27, 210–11

Vander Waerdt, Paul, 183n.32
Vigani, Denise, 109n.35

virtue
    determining content of (*see* Eudaimonist Hope)
    as wisdom (*see under* wisdom)
    See also character; Supremacy of Virtue; virtuous action
virtuous action, 18–21, 34–37, 45, 53–63, 82–83, 103–4, 114–17, 121–22, 128, 165–67, 168, 178–81, 182–83, 187–88, 194, 202–4, 205–8, 209–10, 211–13, 215, 216–17
    vs. contemplation, 134–39
    effect on the soul of, 34–37, 76–77, 79–80, 83–84, 211–12
    and eudaimonia, 6–8, 26–29
    and hedonism, 67, 69–70
    identifying/determining, 31–32, 34, 46–48, 71, 76–77, 79, 84, 116–17, 173–75, 191, 204, 206–8, 209, 215–16, 217n.17
    as superseding, 20–21, 29, 44–45, 46, 119, 202–3 (*see also* Superseding Practical Principle)
    See also Supremacy of Virtue
Visnjic, Jack, 183n.33, 184n.36

Vlastos, Gregory, 2–4, 9–11, 12–14, 25n.19, 31, 32, 36–37, 38, 49n.12, 51–52, 102n.14, 102–3, 109–10, 111–12, 211–12, 214
Vogt, Katja, 184n.36, 187n.42, 198n.56, 199n.59

Walker, Matthew, 137n.37
White, Nicholas, 2n.7, 48–50, 211n.5
Whiting, Jennifer, 8n.19, 19n.2, 210n.3
Wiggins, David, 141n.45
Williams, Bernard, 6n.15, 7n.17
wisdom
    as best life, 81–82, 97
    as independent good, 56–57
    practical (*see phronēsis*, practical wisdom)
    theoretical, 101n.10
    as virtue, 50–51, 55–64, 67, 69–71, 175–76, 185–86
    See also theōria, contemplation
Wolfsdorf, David, 145n.5
Wood, Allen, 43n.50, 182n.31
Woolf, Raphael, 13n.28, 148n.12, 157n.26, 195n.52